GOD, SELF, AND EVIL:

A Miracle Theodicy

GOD, SELF, AND EVIL:

A Miracle Theodicy

By
Robert J. Hellmann

ENLIGHTENMENT PUBLICATIONS
Norfolk, VA

Published by Enlightenment Publications
3762 Karlin Avenue, Norfolk, Virginia 23502

Library of Congress Control Number: 2002093158

ISBN 0-9716196-0-3

Portions from *A Course in Miracles*® copyright 1975, 1992, 1999, reprinted by permission of the Foundation for *A Course in Miracles*® - 1275 Tennanah Lake Road - Roscoe, NY 12776-5905

The ideas represented herein are the personal interpretation and understanding of the author and are not necessarily endorsed by the copyright holder of *A Course in Miracles*.®

Printed in the United States of America

To Janet,

My loving and devoted wife.

TABLE OF CONTENTS

**PART THREE
MISCREATION:
EVIL AND THE SELF YOU MADE**

**PART FOUR
FORGIVENESS:
THE WAY TO GOD**

INTRODUCTION

What am I? What caused me to be? Do I live forever, or does my life end? What can bring me love and happiness? What is the way and means to peace and joy?

The orphanage at which I was raised from age 3 to 14 was run by German Catholic nuns. The nuns provided us with room and board, a normal education, and a regular time and place to work and to play. But they also taught us what they learned in becoming Catholic nuns. They were diligent in teaching all children left in their care about God and Jesus, about heaven, hell and purgatory, and of course, they taught us about sin and confession.

I learned that I was created by God and that I had an immortal soul. If I died with no sin on my soul - like right after going to confession - I would go to Heaven and be perfectly happy with God for all eternity.

On the other hand, if I died with even one mortal sin on my soul, I would go to hell. Not only would I never see

God, but I would suffer pain and torment in the fires of hell for all eternity!

In between heaven and hell was purgatory. That was for those who died with only venial sins on their soul. They would suffer for a certain amount of time, but sooner or later they too would enter Heaven once their soul was purified from all sin. While living here on earth if one had recited prayers of "indulgence" he would have his time in purgatory reduced by the amount of days he accumulated in reciting all those prayers during his lifetime. "Limbo" was a place reserved for babies who died without being baptized.

The nuns made sure we understood the difference between mortal and venial sin. After all, "what does it profit a man to gain the whole world and suffer the loss of his soul" - or suffer the torment and pain of hell for all eternity?

We children were well versed in our Catholic Christian religion, and were given many opportunities to participate in religious practices and rituals. We attended mass not only on Sunday, but every school day at 6 a.m. We also recited memorized prayers out loud together when we arose at 5 a.m. each morning. We prayed before and after each meal, and at noon every school day we recited the "Angeles". And we recited our prayers right before going to bed at night. Furthermore, we participated in the special services during the church seasons of the year. The Lenten calendar was particularly filled with these "services"; the stations of the cross is just one of many examples of these services. "Benediction" is another.

Basically, I took it all in stride, as most of the children did. I became not only a good catholic, but I was a good student and a good athlete as well, having been voted most valuable player of the year on our knothole baseball team. Everything seemed so normal and natural. The orphanage was efficiently run; everyone was well fed, well trained, and fairly treated, all within a relatively rational structure. However, despite all the positive aspects of "Saint Joe's", by the eighth grade I was "ready to leave this place."

After graduating from Saint Joseph's Orphanage, I was sent by Catholic Charities to high school at Father Flanagan's Boys' Home, *Boys Town*, located at the time 10 miles west of the city of Omaha, Nebraska. With regard to religion, school and athletics, things were nearly the same, except we did not have to pray and attend mass quite as often. In 1960, my junior year of high school, I was selected by the *Omaha World Herald* as an all-star baseball catcher, and in my senior year I was awarded by *Boystown* a "scholar-athlete" trophy for achieving the highest academic average for the 4 years of any member of the varsity baseball team. And I was voted the most representative member of the senior class, by the junior class of that year.

After Boys Town, I attended undergraduate school at Creighton University, Omaha, Nebraska. Creighton is a Jesuit university and at that time every student, regardless of his major, was required to take 5 courses in philosophy (Thomism) and 4 courses in (Catholic) Theology.

Things started to change with regard to my religious thinking. I began questioning the things I had learned so well at the orphanage. By age 21 I was agnostic. I was not sure there was a God, a heaven or hell, or a "life after death". There was neither proof, nor even any good evidence of the reality of these things.

As far as *proof* was concerned there seemed to be more proof *against* the existence of God than for it! In addition, to me "religion" seemed merely to be a myth made up by the weak and non-thinking - or those seeking control over them. On the practical level I lived as if there were no God or "afterlife", and no longer attended church.

At college I was not rebelling against religious ideas merely for the sake of rebelling against what I was taught as a youngster. I have never been seriously considered a rebel. I simply perceived myself as a philosophy student seriously seeking the truth. And, as a serious and enthusiastic philosophy student, I found David Hume's (1711-76) powerful argument against belief in God valid and sufficiently sound to justify my unbelief - regardless of what psychological or social reasons, conscious or unconscious, for which I refused to accept there was a God and an afterlife, and that it was important to know "God's Will for me."

I soon learned in the course of my studies that Hume's argument is an ancient one. It was first formulated by the famous Greek philosopher Epicurus (341-270 B.C.). The argument has long since been called "the argument from evil". It is an argument that reasons from the existence of evil in the world, to the conclusion that there *cannot be* an all-knowing, all-loving, and all-powerful God.

Briefly and informally stated, the argument runs like this: Being perfect, God must be at least perfectly loving and perfectly powerful. However, if God is perfectly loving He does not will that there be evil. In addition, if God is perfectly powerful His Will is done. Therefore, we must conclude that there is no evil. There *cannot* be evil. Thus, if God is real, there is no evil.

But there is evil! Evil exists. I see it. I experience it. So does every human being whom I ask about it. Therefore, since there is evil, there cannot be a Being Who is both perfectly loving and perfectly powerful. And any being who is not perfectly loving and perfectly powerful does not deserve the name "God". Therefore, there is no God.

The argument from evil gave intellectual support to my unbelief for more than 13 years; years which included, among other things: a tour in Vietnam as an infantryman (a "grunt" as we were called) with the U.S. Army, graduate school at the University of Cincinnati (where I attained a masters degree in Philosophy), moderate success as an encyclopedia salesman and sales manager, marriage, a new home, and fatherhood (the birth of a daughter on July 1, 1978).

However, at age 34, on October 26, 1977, between 1 and 2 p.m., I was "born again". I accepted Jesus Christ as my lord and savior. I was "saved". And I was gloriously surprised and happy! In fact, I was ecstatic for nearly a year.

Radical changes took place in my life. I became, as Paul says, a "new creature". My values and goals, my thinking and feeling, my perception, activities and state of mind - all were radically changed. I looked upon life and death differently; I looked on myself, God, and others differently. After reading the entire Bible in four months (I had never read the entire Bible before that time), attending church and Bible study classes, reading many books on spirituality, and associating with an entirely new group of friends – due to joining *New Jerusalem*, a Catholic charismatic community founded by the Franciscan priest, Richard Rohr - I was solidly set on a spiritual path.

Oh, yes, questions still arose, many difficult to answer with certainty, but my faith in a loving God, and my hope of an eternal life of happiness with Him, never seriously wavered.

As the months and years passed, I faced some deep and tough questions related to my spiritual path and my belief in an all-loving and all-powerful God. Specific questions arose regarding what scholars were saying about the Jewish and Christian scriptures, and about the teachings of other world religions. Questions arose regarding what scientists were saying about the nature and origin of the physical universe and about human nature. More questions arose about God, Jesus, the afterlife, resurrection and reincarnation, ESP and other "psychic powers". And perhaps most importantly, questions arose about whether there could ever be peace in this world, about whether and how we humans, Christian or not, can live a life of love; whether and how we could learn to forgive ourselves and others, to live in peace and joy, and be truly happy in this world.

But as the questions arose, I would almost immediately find just the right book, or lecture, or conference, or some person who provided an answer that satisfied me, at least at the time.

By the time this book is published, 25 years will have passed since my born again experience. My faith in a loving God, and an eternal life of perfect happiness, has grown stronger, and my sense of inner peace more consistent and persistent. And this is true despite the fact that from an external observer's point of view it might seem I passed through many "hard times". And despite the fact too, that my concept of God, and my overall theology has changed radically since my born again experience, as this book will soon make clear.

Within 5 years of my born again experience I found a satisfactory refutation of the argument from evil. But I did not find it where one might expect to find it. One might expect to find it in *theodicy* literature, the books and articles written by philosophers of religion who specifically deal with trying to give answer to the argument from evil.

What is Theodicy?

"Theodicy" is a technical term. It comes from two Greek words: *theos*, meaning "God", and *dike*, meaning "justice". Theodicy, then, is normally understood as being an attempt to rationally or logically defend the concept of God as perfectly just and loving even though there is evil in the world He supposedly created. More specifically, theodicy concerns itself with *refuting the argument from evil*. Philosophers who lecture and write books on theodicy, in which they attempt to refute the argument from evil, are called *theodicists*. It is fair to say that some philosophers are specialists in this area of the philosophy of religion. There is abundant literature in the subject area of theodicy, and the number of books and articles written on the problem of evil in the last few decades has increased dramatically, as evidenced by Barry Whitney's book listed in the bibliography.

Since I will be using the terms quite frequently in this book I wish to make a few more general remarks about theodicy and theodicists.

As just mentioned theodicy is an attempt to solve the problem of evil, or to refute the argument from evil, whether the argument is stated as above, or in some other way. There are a number of ways of setting forth the argument from evil *as an argument*. But regardless of how the argument is presented, it amounts to a "proof" that there is no God. The argument always involves the idea that the evil in the world -- the attack and violence, the pain, suffering and death propagated and experienced by humans -- is proof (or at least strong evidence) against the existence of a perfectly knowing, perfectly loving, and perfectly powerful God. For if such a God were real it logically follows there could be no evil.

It could perhaps be argued that everyone is a theodicist at some level, even though he or she may not be a professional philosopher or theologian who lectures and writes on the problem of evil. Everyone, even though he or she may believe in God, regardless of the reason for this belief, is faced with this problem. Perhaps in moments of reflection or in conversation, we find ourselves wondering how God, who supposedly is all-knowing, all-loving, and all-powerful, would allow some of the horrendous evil we see in this world -- both personal and collective. We wonder, for example, why God allowed the holocaust to occur, why an "all-loving Father" would allow millions of Jewish people, who supposedly are his "chosen ones", to be systematically murdered due to the orders of one man - a man who supposedly is also one of God's creations as well. We wonder why God does not prevent mass murders like the millions of Cambodians who were massacred at the instigation of Pol Pot, who also is supposedly one of His children. Why would an "almighty God", supposed "creator of the heavens and the earth", and supposed creator of "man" as well, and One Who has the power to prevent these evils, allow them to happen if He is also an "all-loving Father"? Why would such a "Perfectly Loving and Perfectly Powerful Being" allow millions of African mothers and children to suffer the pain of starvation and finally die due to lack of food and nutrition? Could not God prevent this from happening to His children? And would He not want to prevent it if He could? Then why doesn't He? Such questions comprise "the problem of evil." These are some of the questions with which theodicists deal.

On a more personal level there are many people who have questions like: how could God have allowed my daughter to be raped? or my son to be murdered? - or my spouse, my mother, or my friend? How could he have allowed 20 or so of his supposed children to fly airplanes into the twin towers of the World Trade Center and kill thousands of their brothers and sisters who also are loved by Him?

Human violence and suffering seem to surround us all. Personal attacks, war, and mass murders; poverty and disease, ignorance and greed, loss and grief; pain, sickness, suffering and inevitable death - these are the evils that make us question: Is there a God? Really? And if there is, how do we conceive His love, power, and knowledge as *perfect*?

Some people do not believe God exists or that life continues after the body stops functioning. And so they do not experience the intellectual conflict that the problem of evil poses for those who do believe. But there are many "believers" who find themselves questioning just how loving and just how powerful God really is, given the evil in the world. There seems to be some limits on His love and power. Those who question God's existence or His perfection, may think that if there is a God, He, She, or It must not be aware of what is going on in this world! He is either asleep, uninterested, or doesn't care -- or is unaware for some other reason. Some critics might think that God, if there is one, must be downright cruel and may even enjoy watching all the insane and evil things that happen in this world.

Finally there are those who are convinced that God is real, and that He does care and wants us to be happy. He doesn't want us to suffer. But the fact is that He simply doesn't have the power to prevent evil by Himself. He needs our cooperation. Humans can oppose His will with their power of choice. Humans can choose to attack one another, and cause one another suffering, and there is little or nothing God can do by Himself to prevent it, even though He doesn't want it to happen. He may be powerful, but He is not "all" powerful; He doesn't have all the power, human beings have some too.

I already mentioned that I have found a solution to the problem of evil. I sincerely believe I have. This solution, unlike many other attempts to solve the problem, does not rely on an appeal to the limitations of the human mind, or to "the mysterious ways of God with men". On the contrary, I am convinced that the argument from evil can be refuted without appeals to "mystery". God does not hide

Himself. He wants to be known. And ultimately we all will know Him - again.

Offering a solution to the problem of evil, or a refutation of the argument from evil, however, as many theodicists throughout the centuries have experienced, is not an easy task. A satisfactory solution cannot be offered in a few words, or even a few pages of words. For as soon as a refutation is offered, innumerable questions and objections immediately arise.

And that is why I am writing this book, to share with you, in a systematic way, the happy solution I have found. After I present the solution, I will attempt to answer the most significant questions which arise from this solution; questions which must be answered before the solution can be fully understood and accepted by any thinking person.

Furthermore, I want to show how this solution can be applied to our daily life by pointing to the single choice we all need to make to guarantee peace of mind, and escape from all fear, pain and suffering; a choice that allows us to experience the love and joy and happiness that is our natural inheritance as children of God.

A Constructive Approach

The approach of many contemporary theodicists is to begin their theodicy by presenting the thoughts of other theodicists who have gone before them. In taking this approach these authors summarize other theodicies and then point out the strength and weakness of the arguments and counter-arguments they contain. They use the ideas of other theodicists with which they agree, and reject those with which they disagree. All of this serves to clear the way for the contemporary author to finally offer his "more satisfactory solution" to the problem of evil.

This approach has its benefits. Such books can be very informative and interesting. For one thing the reader is offered one insight after another as he follows the thinking of great minds at work in their attempt to solve this problem. And many great minds, indeed, have made the attempt. We need but mention thinkers like Augustine and Aquinas, Spinoza, Luther, Calvin, Leibniz (the one who coined the term "theodicy"), Barth, Berkeley, and Brightman, just to name some whose thought was discussed in a book entitled, *God, Power, and Evil*, written by David Griffin, a well known contemporary theodicist.

Such books also give the reader a sense of just how difficult it is to solve this problem! One begins to see clearly the inconsistency involved in various concepts of God and God's relation to this world in which His supposed creatures sin, suffer and die. One begins to sense the logical force of the argument from evil, and to experience how very difficult it has been throughout centuries of philosophical and religious thought to refute the argument in a way that leaves a reasonable person convinced and fully satisfied. Furthermore, such books point to very specific difficulties involved in favoring one general kind of solution rather than another, thus pre-warning any potential theodicist of the pitfalls he may encounter in taking one direction rather than another in his attempt at a refutation.

Generally, however, these books contain many "technical" or specialized terms. As a result, only a few people, other than professional philosophers and theologians, are willing to spend the time and effort necessary to understand and gain the benefits such a book offers. Personally I have been willing to spend this time, and I have benefited greatly. In the Bibliography I have listed some books that contributed to my understanding of the difficulties and pitfalls involved in trying to solve this ancient problem. It will soon become clear, however, why I find all previously offered solutions neither rationally convincing nor personally acceptable.

This book takes a somewhat different approach than most contemporary books on theodicy. Although it does not ignore other theodicies, it uses very little space for discussing their intricacies. Nor is much space used in pointing out what this author would consider their mistakes, whether the error be one of inconsistency in the reasoning process, a false assumption or premise, a mistaken analysis of the human condition, or an error in evaluating the human experience of evil and of good.

Thus, although there are points of agreement as well as disagreement with other theodicies (mostly the latter), this book is not particularly concerned with explicitly pointing to these agreements and disagreements. They will be clear enough to those familiar with other theodicies. Every now and then, however, views different than the one presented here are mentioned primarily as a means of providing a contrast, if such would help the reader to better understand the point under discussion.

My intention, then, is to offer a solution to the problem of evil that is radically different from that offered by any other fully developed theodicy, whether it be Classical Theodicy, Person-Making Theodicy, or Process Theodicy (see chapter 2).

After the solution is offered in Part One of this book (chapter 3), I raise three questions which naturally arise from such a radically different solution. None of these questions arise in other theodicies simply because their "solution" to the problem is entirely different being based on entirely different premises. These three questions must be satisfactorily answered before the solution offered in

Chapter 3 can be fully understood and accepted by any intelligent and reasonable person.

This book, then, is primarily a constructive project. It offers a radically new theodicy, a radically new approach to refuting the argument from evil.

But not only that. In the last part of the book (Part Four) I set forth the *practical implications* of this theodicy for our daily life. This is done by pointing to the one choice we must make if we would escape from all evil, and find the true peace and joy, love and happiness, we all want and seek, but seem unable to find.

Miracle Theodicy

I label the theodicy presented here "Miracle Theodicy" mainly because it is based on the spiritual teachings of *A Course In Miracles*. Miracle Theodicy, then, is simply a theodicy which offers a solution to the problem of evil based on the concepts and principles found in *A Course In Miracles*.

For those who are not familiar with this Course, some brief remarks are in order. *A Course In Miracles* is a set of books originally published in three volumes: *Text, Workbook for Students,* and *Manual for Teachers.* The Course was first published in 1976, by the Foundation for Inner Peace which is still the publisher. It is available in many book stores in one volume containing all three: Text, Workbook, and Manual, totaling more than 1200 pages. There are now more than one and one-half million copies in print. Over 2000 study groups have emerged throughout the world in which students gather in private homes to study this spiritual masterpiece together, as an added element to their individual study and application of the Course's teachings.

A brief summary of the Course's teachings is found in Appendix A. In the Bibliography I have included several books which tell the story of how the Course was written and the impact it has had in the world during the first 20 years since its publication. I have also included a list of books that present the Course's ideas from one perspective or another.

In Appendix B is an explanation of the referencing system used in this book to refer to passages quoted from the Course.

To my awareness this is the first book whose specific purpose is to present and discuss the teachings of *A Course in Miracles* explicitly in terms of *how these teachings provide a solution to the logical problem of evil.*

This book has a long history, not only in terms of my personal concern with finding a solution to the problem of evil, but also in terms of its actual writing. It started as a paper I wrote in graduate school in 1985 and expanded into a masters thesis in 1987. As far as I know this was the first masters thesis explicitly based on *A Course in Miracles* ever accepted and approved by a Graduate Department of Theology at an accredited university. Later that year, after the thesis had been accepted and approved, and I had received my degree, I sent a copy to Dr. Kenneth Wapnick, a well known student and teacher of the Course, who in turn shared it with a friend who is a philosopher and a Jesuit priest.

I had mentioned to Ken at the time that some day I wanted to expand the thesis into a book. We had several exchanges by letter and audio cassette in 1988 wherein Ken made comments on the thesis and suggested things that would need to be done if the thesis were to become a book.

As the years passed during which I did various things to make a living -- including teaching graduate level courses as an adjunct instructor at a local university on topics directly or indirectly related to the problem of evil, and giving lectures on the Course's teachings -- my thoughts on the issue gradually became clearer and clearer until the book took its present form.

I hope the results of my happy labors will be helpful to all thinking people who seek the joy that comes from having faith in a God Whose knowledge, power, and love are perfect, and Whose Will for us is an eternal life of perfect happiness with Him.

The author also intends this book to be helpful to those who also want to believe and feel that such faith makes sense in light of reason. For too long, reason's legitimate demand for consistency has been seen as an enemy to faith in God. This book attempts to show that reason and logic, far from being an enemy, actually provide strong support to faith in a perfectly loving and powerful God. It also makes clear how one can sustain this faith even though he is well aware that nearly every human being, at one time or another, experiences sickness, pain and suffering; lack, loss and grief; uncertainty, loneliness, and fear of injury and death.

It is my hope that this book will direct you to your own Inner Teacher and Guide, Comforter and Friend. For He is a Companion with Whom you can walk this world, certain of your purpose, free from fear, and with a mind at peace and a heart so filled with joy that your one desire is but to share your light with everyone you meet.

ACKNOWLEDGEMENTS

I thank the following authors whose books and other publications have been helpful to my understanding of the particular Course teachings which play a central role in this book: Kenneth Wapnick, Ph.D.; Robert Perry; and Alan

Watson. My thanks are also due to the following faculty members of Xavier University, Cincinnati, OH, who shared my confidence that this project was worthwhile: Catherine Keller, Ph.D., the instructor of the class for which I wrote the original paper, and through whom I was introduced to the works of David Griffin and other Process theologians; Paul Knitter, Ph.D.; William Madges Ph.D.; and Joseph Bracken S.J., Ph.D., the three members of my thesis committee. Although, at the time, they may not have agreed with everything I said, they were, nonetheless, gracious and open-minded enough not to discourage me from seeing that the ideas in the thesis could be developed and used for constructing a new and more fully developed theodicy.

My gratitude extends also to all the students who attended my lectures and classes on *A Course in Miracles* during the years 1991 to the present. They know who they are. Their questions and comments moved me to greater clarity in presenting the Course's teachings. In this regard I want to especially thank Judy Craig, Patrick Brown, Cindy Flick, Suzi Crawford, Alan Steel, Mark and Chris Mazzeo, and the late Blanche Mazzeo. Thanks also to those members of the study group which met every Thursday from 1990-1999 to discuss the Course's teachings and our practical application of its ideas and principles. In this regard I want to mention Mike Childress, Don and Dora Lou Southern, Anita Peterson, and the late Kay Jones. My gratitude also extends to Tom Baker, a local fellow teacher of *A Course in Miracles* with whom I have had many enlightening conversations.

Finally deep gratitude is offered to my wife, Janet. Her reading and commenting on each chapter as it was completed led to many improvements in the presentation. Without her support, encouragement, and patience this book would still be just something I hope to do some day.

PART ONE

A SOLUTION TO
THE PROBLEM OF EVIL

PART ONE

A SOLUTION TO THE PROBLEM OF EVIL

Introduction to Part One

Part One is organized as follows: Chapter 1 introduces the distinction between the *practical* or *experiential* problem of evil and the *theoretical* or *logical* problem of evil. The solution to the practical problem will be set forth mainly in Part Four, after we have offered a solution to the theoretical problem.

The remainder of Chapter 1, then, is devoted to making clear what exactly the *logical problem* is. Basically the problem is that belief in God seems not to be rationally or logically justified. The argument from evil (AFE) shows that it is impossible that God and evil both be real. In other words, if God is real there is no evil. If evil is real there is no God. Thus a crucial belief that serves as a premise in the argument against the existence of God is: *evil is real*.

Chapter 2 briefly discusses several approaches theodicists have used in their attempt to refute the AFE.

These approaches are represented by Classical Theodicy, Person-Making Theodicy, and Process Theodicy. Each Theodicy is briefly discussed in terms of the particular premise it denies in order to escape the conclusion of the AFE..

Chapter 3 contains the basic argument of this book. It is the core of Miracle Theodicy, for here we present, straight out without much debate, our solution to the logical problem of evil.

Miracle Theodicy denies a different premise than denied by any of the other three theodicies we discuss in chapter 2. After I show how Miracle Theodicy offers a logical and successful escape from the conclusion of the argument from evil, I then state three general questions that naturally arise from this new and radical way of refuting the argument. These questions must be answered in order for the solution to be fully understood and accepted. It is the task of Part Two, Three, and Four, respectively, to answer each of these three questions. I will reserve the statement of these questions for after we have refuted the AFE, for only then will they be truly meaningful.

1

THE PROBLEM

The problem of evil is perhaps the most
powerful objection ever raised against belief
in God, and it cannot be dismissed lightly.
David Stewart,
Exploring The Philosophy of Religion

THE PRACTICAL PROBLEM

There are two general aspects of "the problem of
evil". The one is theoretical, the other practical. The practical
problem of evil is quite simply: *we humans suffer*. Solving
that problem involves eliminating suffering, so that we are
happy instead.

As humans we do indeed suffer loss and grief, pain
and sickness and death - and the fear of all these things. And
fear is not happiness. We humans very often perceive
ourselves as attacked, physically or verbally. And out of fear
and anger we counter-attack to defend ourselves. Not a day

or hour or minute goes by where some human has not attacked another somewhere in the world.

The daily news tells us of domestic quarrels and violence, child abuse, rape and murder, assault and battery, theft and burglary, drug abuse and shootings. In the United States there are numerous people whose name appears on the list of those waiting trial for one crime or another. We humans seem to be in continual conflict with one another. We are constantly at war in one form or another. It would seem that "peace on earth" is mere fantasy. When has there ever been peace on earth?

The list of ways we humans suffer, and the things that cause our suffering, seems to be endless. As we have said, the mass media gives us many examples of the attack and suffering humans experience. Human suffering is far from a rare occurrence. In fact, the ignorance and poverty, violence and greed we hear about may sometimes overwhelm us, and make us wonder whether it is even possible to be truly happy in this world.

But we hardly need the mass media to tell us that humans attack one another and suffer pain, loss and death. We need but look at our own individual lives. We can, if we want, note the times we perceived ourselves as attacked; cheated, mistreated and betrayed; unappreciated, misunderstood, needy and lonely; angered, outraged, depressed and sad; anxious, worried, sick and diseased; and grieved over loss. And finally how often we have been afraid of injury and death for ourselves and our children.

Our perceptions of attack, and our experiences of suffering in all its forms, are what theodicists refer to when they use the term "evil". This attack and suffering is what they point to when that say "there is evil in the world, or "evil exists", or "evil is real."

Attack (sometimes called "sin" when the attack is thought to be on God, or God's Will) and suffering are evil.

When we are attacked and suffer we are not happy. Evil and happiness are opposites. This is why *A Course in Miracles* says, "What is not happiness is evil" (L66,6:3). Unhappiness, and what brings unhappiness or misery, is "evil". Happiness and what brings happiness is "good".

The term *attack* is the most general term the Course uses for what brings suffering. Attack produces fear or pain or injury, or even death. Another term often used by the Course for describing the source of suffering is *loss or lack.* We sometimes experience a sense of loss, deprivation or lack. We don't have what we think we want, or we once had it and lost it - perhaps a loved one, or a job, or money, or a healthy body. Even this sense of lack or loss can be seen as a form of attack producing suffering. When I perceive myself as lacking something I want, or having lost something I had and wanted to keep, this too is a kind of attack on myself. When we use the general term *"evil"*, then, we are referring to attack, suffering, and death in whatever form they may take.

The human experience of evil, of attack and suffering, can be called the practical problem of evil. No one is really happy when he sees himself attacked and losing by attack. When we don't have what we want, and have what we don't want, we are unhappy. We want to be happy. We want peace. We would like to be free of conflict, pain and suffering. And we would like to be free of death too! We want a life of happiness, abundance, peace and joy. And a happy life that does not end. Can we be truly happy knowing that our life will end?

The practical problem of evil then is that we seldom experience the happiness, the peace and joy, the love and abundant life we would expect if God our Father were a perfect being. Unhappiness, then, is the practical or experiential aspect of the overall problem of evil. It is because we suffer that we raise the question whether there is a perfectly loving and powerful God at all.

Is there a solution to the problem of our suffering? Can we attain the happiness all of us want? I have often hoped so. And the promise of *A Course in Miracles* is that we can, - and will. It is guaranteed!

Love and happiness are your natural inheritance. The Course offers a sure escape from pain and suffering of any kind, a certain way to true and constant happiness. And constant happiness is the only real happiness there is. A happiness that comes and goes, shifts and changes is meaningless; at best but an illusion of happiness.

It is fair to say that solving the practical problem of evil is the aim of *A Course in Miracles*. For it aims at "removing the blocks to the awareness of love's presence" (T-IN,1:7). And where love is, there happiness must be ("God, being Love, is also Happiness" L103).

The purpose of the Course is to train your mind so you experience and share the love and happiness which is yours and everyone's because of what we really are. Once we have learned what the Course would teach us, we have a mind at peace, and through forgiving eyes we look upon a world "free from fear" and "filled with blessing and with happiness" (29.6,6:2).

The Course's Workbook sets forth a series of lessons aimed at training our mind to be at peace and to experience a joy we cannot help but share with everyone we meet. When we are so trained we "give the miracles we have received" (L159). This means we give the love we have received, for a miracle is an expression of love. In this world this includes giving the forgiveness we have received. For forgiveness is an earthly form of love.

It is, however, only in doing the exercises in the Workbook that we can achieve the Course's goal for us. We can view these exercises as the Course's practical solution to the experiential problem of evil. Its training leads us to the happiness and peace and joy we all want and seek, for it provides a way out of the conflict and fear and pain and suffering we now so often experience.

But the exercises will not be meaningful or fully effective until there is first some understanding of the theoretical framework within which the exercises are meaningful. As the Course puts it, "A theoretical foundation such as the text provides is necessary as a framework to make the exercises in this workbook meaningful" (W-IN,1:1) In other words, in order to solve the practical problem of evil, we need first to understand the Course's solution to the theoretical problem. We need to understand what I am calling "Miracle Theodicy". Miracle Theodicy consists of those teachings in *A Course in Miracles* which directly relate to its solution to the theoretical problem of evil.

The solution to the practical problem is tied up with the solution to the theoretical one in the sense that we cannot really attain true and constant happiness unless we have some understanding of why it is really possible, in fact, inevitable. In other words, if we understand how the Course solves the logical problem of evil we may be more willing to accept and use the means it offers for solving the practical one. If we do not believe that constant happiness is even possible, it is unlikely we will be willing to do the practice and application that will lead to it.

THE LOGICAL PROBLEM

The practical and theoretical problem of evil are more closely related than the impression one receives from most of the literature which deals only with the theoretical problem. Most theodicy books say little or nothing about the relation between the solution it offers to the theoretical problem, on the one hand, and the practical implication of this solution, on the other. In other words, if we ask what does this solution tell me about how I should change the way I respond to the persons, situations and events of my daily life - what kind of response will guarantee my happiness? - we find that most theodicies offer us little or no answer. And, if some answer is offered, it is usually something like "follow God's Will for you" or "love God and love your neighbor as yourself".

Perhaps many would say they are willing to do this. But nearly as many find themselves failing at most every turn. They may find themselves asking what is God's Will for me? How do I know God's Will for me in this situation or relationship? What *is* love - really? Or, as the Pharisees asked Jesus, who is my neighbor? Am I to love everyone, or only specific individuals? And what exactly does loving God and loving my neighbor as myself really mean in relation to all the happenings throughout the day? What does it really mean on a *practical level*? What is it supposed to mean for me from the time I arise in the morning till the time I retire to bed at night? And even, perhaps, in my dreams?

The fact that we do not find much practical advice in theodicy literature is, however, somewhat understandable, and forgivable. The theoretical problem of evil encompasses nearly every issue with which philosophers of religion deal. Attempting to solve the theoretical problem alone involves countless arguments and counterarguments on a variety of issues. And thus dealing solely with the theoretical aspect of the problem results in many a lengthy book, which would have been even longer if the author had not tempered his or her tendency to make "one more important point".

I have purposely kept this book from being too lengthy. Even so, there is enough said to make the Course's solution to the theoretical problem of evil clearly understandable. The answer to any question left unanswered can be found in the Course itself, or will have to be dealt with in my responses to readers of this book.

Moreover, I have drawn out enough practical implications of this solution to make clear exactly what the choice for happiness really is, how we can learn to make this choice in response to every person, situation, and event in our daily lives, and why making it guarantees peace and joy, and a sense of being truly loving and truly loved.

Dealing with the theoretical problem of evil is similar to dealing with any other theoretical problem. We are concerned with *explanations*. And thus we are concerned as to whether the statements we make in giving explanations are coherent and are consistent with one another. We want to avoid contradictions. This is not easy to do in the field of theodicy. In giving his critique, many a critic of a particular theodicy has pointed to the contradictions therein.

The theoretical problem of evil involves a claim that there is a contradiction in believing that *both* "God is real" *and* "evil is real". More specifically, there seems to be an inconsistency in claiming *both* there exists a God Who is perfectly knowing, powerful, and loving *and* that this same God allows His creations to suffer. In other words, if God created creations who suffer then God is not perfectly loving. And if we want to claim that God *is* perfectly loving even though He created creations who can and do suffer, then we must admit that He cannot be perfectly knowing *and* perfectly powerful as well.

Thus the theoretical problem is often called "the logical problem of evil" because the problem is one of *logical inconsistency*. Contradictions are a problem for a sane and reasonable mind. It cannot believe a *contradiction* is true. We are irrational, unreasonable, or illogical when we believe a contradiction is true because we violate the most fundamental law of reason, of logic, of mind, of right thinking.

What is this law which governs reason? It is *the law of non-contradiction*. It basically says "no contradictions allowed". The law of non-contradiction says that if one statement is true then any statement which contradicts it must be false. And visa versa: if one statement is false then any statement which contradicts it must be true. In other words, a statement and its opposite cannot both be true.

The logical problem of evil amounts to saying that the statement 1) "Evil is real" contradicts the statement 2) "God is real". Thus by the law of non-contradiction if (1) is true then (2) must be false. And vice versa: if (2) is true then (1) must be false. In other words, reason would tell us that if evil is real there is no God. If God is real there is no evil.

The Law of Non-Contradiction

It is worthwhile to say a little more about this fundamental law of reason and how it applies to the logical problem of evil. This law is the guiding principle of rational thinking and it always takes the front seat -- especially when we deal with theoretical issues, and specifically the theoretical issue of the relationship between our concept of God and our concept of evil. Are each such that the two are compatible? The *law of non-contradiction* is often stated as follows:

> *A thing cannot both be and not be*
> *at the same time and in the same respect.*

This law can be stated in various ways. For example when the law is applied to propositions it is stated as follows:

*A proposition cannot be both true and false
at the same time and in the same sense (or
with the same meaning).*

This law functions in the simplest of conversations. Suppose I say "George Washington is president of the United States". You might say, "No, George Washington is not president of the United States." So now we have a contradiction. The statement, "George Washington *is* president of the United States" is contradicted by the statement, "George Washington *is not* president of the United States". If one statement is true the other must be false. Both statements cannot be true at the same time and in the same sense.

I might say, - perhaps trying to avoid conflict with you, but still believing Mr. Washington is president - "well, perhaps we both are right."

"What do you mean?", you might say. And I would say, "Well, perhaps George Washington both *is* and *is not* president of the United States".

Would you feel satisfied with that response? Probably not. More likely you would realize my response is senseless and irrational - and that perhaps I was insane. You might begin wondering what kind of person you are talking with.

Why would you consider me irrational? Well, because I am violating a fundamental law of rational thinking. I am violating the law of non-contradiction. According to this law the proposition "George Washington is president of the United States" cannot be both true and false at the same time and in the same sense. Either George Washington *is* president of the United States or George Washington *is not* president of the United States, but not both.

If, however, in 1790, I say, "George Washington is president of the United States", the statement is true. If I make the same statement in 2001, it is false. So this statement is true at one time, and false at another time. So in that sense it can be both true and false. But the proposition cannot be both true and not true *at the same time*.

The problem of evil involves the claim that we are violating the law of non-contradiction when we state "Evil is real *and* God is real". How so? Because when we say "evil is real" we are, by implication, saying, "God is not real". When we say "evil is" we are saying "God is not". When we say, "evil exists" we are saying "God does not exist".

The claim, then, is that *God and evil cannot coexist.* Like light and darkness, God and evil are opposites; where one is the other cannot be. Where one is present the other must be absent. The problem, then, is that when we say "God is real *and* evil is real" we are stating a contradiction, namely:

God is real and God is not real.

(or God is and God is not, or God exists and God does not exist, or there is a God and there is no God.)

This can be put in terms of evil as well; when we say, "Evil is real and God is real" we are stating a contradiction, namely:

Evil is real and evil is not real.

(or evil is and evil is not, or evil exists and evil does not exist, or there is evil and there is no evil)

All these conjunctions are contradictions. Each one is a violation of the fundamental law of rational thinking. The law of non-contradiction tells us that God cannot both *be* and *not be* at the same time and in the same respect. The proposition "God is real" cannot be both true and false at the same time and in the same sense.

Anyone who violates the law of non-contradiction is making a fundamental mistake in thinking; he is holding two ideas which contradict one another. His mind is thus conflicted, and a conflicted mind is not at peace because conflict is the opposite of peace.

Some of the propositions involved in the logical problem of evil have a special character because we are speaking of God. When we say "God is" we are saying God *always* is! If it is *God* we are talking about we are talking about something which by definition does not go out of existence. Thus it cannot be that "God is" at one time and "God is not" at another time. "God is real" is a proposition whose truth status never changes; it is not a statement like the one about the president of the United States, where the truth status can change with time, and the statement can be true at one time and false at another. God by definition is eternal. He cannot die. He has no beginning and no end. It is not the case that at one time "God exists", and at another time "God does not exist". In other words, if the statement "God is real" is true, then it is always true, regardless of time. If the statement "God is real" is true, then the statement "God is not real" is always false, regardless of time.

This brief discussion on the law of non-contradiction makes it clear why some thinkers believe that it is a *contradiction* to say "God is real and evil is real". It is the same as saying "God is real and God is not real"; or again, to put the contradiction in terms of evil instead of God, it is the same as saying "evil is real and evil is not real."

Let us turn now to the long-famous argument that many great thinkers have employed to support the position that if evil is real there is no God, and if God is real there is no evil.

A Deductive Argument

The logical problem of evil is usually stated in the form of a deductive argument. Philosophers of religion generally call this argument the "argument from evil" (AFE). It is a logical argument which reasons from the human experience and perception of evil to the conclusion that there is no God.

There is a very simple version of the AFE with which all theodicists are familiar. It has a long history dating back to the first Greek philosophers. It has been used throughout the history of philosophy and Christian Theology and is still used by some contemporary theodicists. It runs as follows:

If God is all-powerful He *could* prevent evil.
If God is all-loving He *would* prevent evil.
But evil exists.
Therefore, there is no God.

This argument is typically used by atheists to prove there is no God. At least there is no God as conceived by traditional theism; which includes the religions of Judaism, Christianity, Islam, and others. The a-theist argues that the theist's conception of God leads to contradictions. It forces one to accept the truth of statements which are obviously false, or which, when combined together, contradict one another.

Examples of such *combinations of statements* are: God created the world including human beings, and God knows everything that each and every human desires, thinks, feels, does, and will do in the future, and yet human beings are free to choose what they want to do, and this does not change what God knows, He always knows what every human being does in his lifetime before it is finished – even before it began! Another example: God is all-powerful, His will is done and cannot be opposed, so nothing happens that is not God's Will, yet humans have freedom of choice whereby they can disobey God's Will. A third example: God loves human beings, and wills they be happy and do not suffer, and God's Will is done and cannot be opposed. Yet humans beings suffer. And finally, a fourth example of contradictory statements made by theists: God's knowledge is timeless and changeless, and yet God knows of everything that happens in a world of time and change. God, for example, at one time knows that George Washington is president of the United States and at another time, like 2002, knows that George Washington is not president of the United States, but that George Bush is.

The atheist believes that the AFE is a valid argument against the existence of God. A valid argument is one whereby if the premises are true, the conclusion *must* be true; it cannot be false. Or to put it another way, if you accept the premises you must accept the conclusion – given that you are a *rational and sane person*, one who is willing to follow the rules of logic and correct thinking.

The conclusion of this simple statement of the AFE is that there is no all-powerful and all-loving God. The atheist accepts this conclusion because he accepts the premises. He wants to be rational and intellectually honest. He respects reason and logic. He, rightly, does not want to violate the law of non-contradiction. This argument seems to show that the atheist's position is firmly based on the proper use of reason and logic, given the universal human experience of evil.

This simple statement of the argument from evil is, indeed, *simple*. At first glance it may also be very disturbing - at least to one who not only wants to believe in an almighty and loving God, but who also considers himself a rational person.

In recent years those philosophers and theologians who find themselves disturbed by the logical force of this argument also find this simple version of the AFE *too* simple, and too *ambiguous*.

Many theodicists today construct their own version of the AFE. There are many reasons for this. First, they already know how they intend to refute the argument. Thus they state the premises in such a way that their refutation can most easily be accomplished and understood. This is fair enough. Many versions of the AFE are stated clearly enough so that the movement of thought is easy to follow. Secondly, they want to be more precise about what each premise actually implies so they can be certain which premise they want to refute, and how they can refute it, in order to escape the conclusion of the argument.

The form of the argument I present below is based on a version constructed by the contemporary theodicist, Jane Mary Trau, in her book, *The Co-existence of God and Evil.* I have made some changes in her phrasing, but the basic movement of thought and logical force of the argument still remain.

The argument, of course, is one which reasons from the reality of evil in the world to the conclusion that God is either not omniscient, not omnipotent, or not omnibenevolent.

There is much debate about what each of these three attributes of God mean or imply. We will discuss this more in later chapters. But to start with we can say that God is "omniscient" (all-knowing, or perfectly knowing) means that God "knows everything that is knowable."

God is "omnipotent" (all-powerful, or perfectly powerful) means God "can do what He wants to do". In other words, if God is omnipotent God's Will is done; nothing can really oppose God's Will. If God wants to do so, He can prevent all evil from occurring.

God is "omnibenevolent" (all-loving, or perfectly loving - literally, "wills everyone well") means God "wills only good" or God "wills only happiness" for His creatures. Stated in negative terms, God is omnibenevolent means that God does not will evil (or does not want there to be evil) or God does not will that His creatures suffer (or does not want His creatures to suffer).

The argument from evil (AFE), then, runs as follows:

1. God is omniscient, omnipotent, and omnibenevolent.
2. The evil in the world is real.
3. Either, God does not know about the evil in the world, in which case God is not omniscient,
4. or God knows about it, but cannot prevent the occurrence of evil in the world, in which case God is not omnipotent,
5. or God knows about it, can prevent it, but wants there to be evil in the world, in which case God is not omnibenevolent.
6. Therefore God is either not omniscient, not omnipotent, or not omnibenevolent.

COMMENTS ON THE ARGUMENT FROM EVIL

There are several points worth noting about this version of the argument from evil. First, this is a valid argument. In other words, if you accept the premises you must accept the conclusion. The premises cannot be true and the conclusion false.

Second, this version of the AFE clearly displays the *contradiction* which makes the problem of evil a *logical problem*; a problem of *inconsistency*. This version of the argument puts the contradiction in plain view by stating, on the one hand, that *God is* omniscient and omnipotent and omnibenevolent (Premise 1), and, on the other hand, *God is not* omniscient *and* omnipotent *and* omnibenevolent (the conclusion). The contradiction is clearly displayed when (1) and (6) are placed together:

(1) God is omniscient, omnipotent, and omnibenevolent

(6) God is either not omniscient, not omnipotent, or not omnibenevolent

Third, there is a good reason why philosophers of religion say that God must have *all three attributes* stated in premise 1. The reason is that, by definition, God is a *perfect* reality or a perfect being.

A *perfect* being would have every one of these attributes. A perfect being would be perfectly knowing, perfectly powerful, and perfectly loving. A being which does not posses each and every one of these attributes would not be a *perfect* being.

So the problem is that if we accept premises 2 through 5 of this argument we must accept its conclusion that God lacks at least one of these three attributes. And if we say this, we are saying that God is not a *perfect* being.

This is a crucial point. Most philosophers claim, and the Course would agree, that if we say that God is not a *perfect* being we are saying *there is no God*. We are actually denying that God exists if we say that God is not perfect. For to be perfect is *what it means* to be "God". A being Who is not perfect is not "God". Thus if no perfect being exists then no God exists. This argument proves that no perfect being exists. And thus it proves that no God exists. And that is why the argument from evil is said to be "the most powerful objection ever raised against belief in God."

Theodicy is an attempt to refute this argument. Since the AFE is a deductive argument the only way to refute it is to show that at least one of its premises is untrue or false. A theodicist attempts to do this by presenting at least one good reason why one premise or another can be reasonable rejected and not accepted.

Let us put this another way. It is important to realize that the task of theodicy is not a positive task, but a negative one. The task of theodicy is not to give arguments *for* the existence of God, but to refute an argument *against* the existence of God. In other words, theodicy attempts to show that if a person claims that he believes in God, he can with faith, supported by reason, claim that the God he believes in *is* truly *God*, and that, in holding this belief, he can still account for the human experience of evil in light of the fact that there is a God -- a Being Who is *perfectly knowing, perfectly loving, and perfectly powerful.*

Those who accept the argument from evil say otherwise. They say if you believe in God, you cannot affirm the reality of evil *and* consistently affirm that the God you believe in is perfect. They further state, if you believe in a god that is not perfect, then the god you believe in is not truly God, but something else. For to be *God is* to be a perfect being. If the God you believe in is not perfect, then your God is not really God.

Therefore, those who accept the conclusion of the AFE, do so because they believe the premises are true, or at least sound, and the conclusion of the argument logically follows from the premises. To the atheist, then, the argument is an *irrefutable proof* that there is no God. For it proves *there is no perfect being*. In other words, the AFE proves that a being with perfect knowledge, power, and love does not exist because it is impossible such a being exist, given that the evil in the world is real.. Only if a contradiction is true can it be that God exists. But a contradiction cannot be true, therefore it cannot be that there is a God, a perfect being.

Thus, if a person believes in "God", he must be illogical, irrational, and insane. Either that, or he believes that the evil in the world is not real, and is thus an illusion in some sense. And, if He believes the evil in the world is unreal then the atheist would most likely still consider him somewhat insane, although he would have to admit that the believer would at least be *consistent* in his belief, even though he may be denying that his experience and his perception is experience and perception of reality.

But to the atheist, the "believer", who does believe that *the evil in the world is real*, as the atheist believes, must be terribly deceived, because the God he believes in is not really God at all. He may have faith in something or someone, but whatever it or he/she is, it is *not* God. It *cannot* be God. It cannot be a *perfect being* that he has faith in.

The Premise on Evil

So it seems that the AFE constitutes a serious problem for a person who claims *both* that he is reasonable *and* that he believes in God. The argument from evil shows that no rational person can believe that God is real and also believe that evil is real. In other words, the argument forces us to face the following dilemma:

(1) If evil is real, there is no God

(2) If evil is not real then I am deceived. For evil seems real to me.

We are indeed trapped by a dilemma. We cannot escape between the two horns. For there is no space between them. And so, to escape being gored by the bull we must strongly and confidently grab one of its horns and bring him down to the dust. We must choose either (1) the evil is real or (2) the evil is not real. There is no in between.

If we accept (1) and say that the evil in the world is real, then we must deny that God exists. But many of us do not want to do that. We want to believe in God, and many of us do believe in God or in Something or Someone we call "God". But while believing in God we do not want to be considered irrational, illogical, or insane, either by our selves or by others. Yet the argument from evil clearly shows that we are irrational if we believe *both* the evil we see in the world is real *and* there is a God Whose knowledge, power, and love are perfect.

On the other hand, if we accept (2) and say that the evil in the world is not real then we are denying what seems true based on our own perception and experience. But we do not want to do that either. We want to trust our perception and experience in this world. We don't want to believe that we are deceived when we perceive and experience evil. We too often perceive attack and suffering. It is very difficult not to believe what we see with our own eyes, hear with our own ears, and sense and suffer with our own body.

Premise 2 of the AFE, which states that the evil, the attack and suffering, in the world is real, seems obviously true. Our perception tells us so. We perceive evidence of the truth of this statement everyday. The statement that the evil in the world is not real seems obviously false. It is contrary to our personal perception and experience. Most, if not all, human beings believe that the attack and death they perceive, and the fear, loss, pain and suffering they experience, are quite real.

Most humans, then, would affirm premise 2 of the AFE. We base our assertion on own personal experience of attack and suffering, as well as our perception that others experience attack and suffering -- and often tell us about it -- thus confirming our own experience of evil. Most of us would not deny premise 2 by saying that humans are merely deceived when they perceive attack and suffering in the world. We do not want to deny what our experience and perception tells us is true. What else can we rely on if not our own perception and experience, and those of others who confirm it? We perceive evil. We believe there is evil. Evil is real to us. We are sometimes attacked. We sometimes attack. We sometimes suffer. We sometimes cause suffering. At times we are very unhappy indeed, as are family members and friends. And what is not happiness is evil.

So how do we escape this dilemma? Is there an escape? It seems not. For we must choose between 1) evil is real or 2) evil is unreal. These are the only alternatives between which we can choose. There are no others. The evil in the world either *is* or *is not* real. Reason would tell us we must choose one or the other.

So which do we choose? If we choose to believe that God exists we must admit that evil is unreal, and thus admit we are deceived in our perception of evil as real. If, on the other hand, we choose to believe that our experience and perception of evil is experience and perception of *reality*, then reason would tell us there is no God Whose love, power, and knowledge are perfect.

We can see, then, that the argument from evil, by the sheer force of logic and reason, compels us to make a decision that either God is real or evil is real. It cannot be that *both* are real. If we claim that both God and evil are real we proclaim that a contradiction is true, and proclaim our own insanity in doing so. And if we do that we have excluded ourselves from all rational discussion. What right do we have to enter any rational discussion if we are not willing to abide by the most fundamental law of reason? What rational person should we expect to listen to us?

An even more significant consequence of holding both God and evil as real is that our own mind is conflicted. A mind that holds a contradiction must be conflicted. Not sure of itself, it experiences doubt, sometimes believing God is real, sometimes not; sometimes believing evil is real, sometimes not. Such a mind is not at peace, nor wholly safe, joyful and happy.

Theodicy is an attempt to resolve this dilemma and put an end to the irrationality, contradiction, conflict, and doubt. For Theodicy is an attempt to refute the argument which seems to convincingly prove that there is no God Whose knowledge, power, and love are perfect.

The Premises on God's Attributes

When we seriously consider the possibility of escaping from the conclusion of the AFE, we are led to carefully examine its premises. In doing so we notice that it not only contains a premise about the reality of evil but that it contains premises which are based on *specific conceptions of God's attributes as a perfect being.*

In other words, we notice that premises 3, 4, and 5 - the ones concerning God's omniscience, omnipotence, and omnibenevolence, respectively - are based on *definitions.* They are not based on scientific observations or experiments, nor on scientifically established theories or laws, nor common observations made by human beings in their daily lives. Nor are these premises based on a direct experience of God, at least not one which can be verified publicly.

Suppose, for example, someone claims he had a "mystical" experience; he experienced direct union with God and with all things. Suppose further, this person claims that from this experience he is convinced there is a God Who really is all-knowing, all-powerful, and all-loving. He proclaims, "I have reached God directly and I *know* there is a God Who is truly God, a perfect being Whose love, power, and knowledge are perfect."

There are a variety of ways we may sincerely respond to this person's report. We may, for example, rejoice with him and be happy for him. This is a legitimate response. We do not have to believe he is "kooky". Many intelligent and sincere people have claimed to have mystical experiences. But at the same time our mystic cannot directly give his experience to us. His experience is subjective. And his interpretation of his experience is just that - his *interpretation* of his own subjective experience.

The mystic's experience, although it may be an ecstatic joy to him, is not very helpful to us in terms of the problem of evil. Even if we accept His interpretation of his experience we still need for him *to explain why we humans suffer* given that God's knowledge, power, and love are perfect. In other words, we still need help in resolving the contradiction between God's perfection and the suffering of His supposed creatures. We may not doubt that this person had an ecstatic and joyous experience, and even accept the idea that it was an experience of direct union with God, but we still need an account of human suffering if our mystic claims that the God He experienced is really God, One Who is perfectly knowing, loving, and powerful.

This brings us back to the significance of premises 3, 4, and 5. Each one contains an *implication* of the attribute it ascribes to God.

Premise 3 states: "(either) God does not know about the evil in the world, in which case God is not omniscient". This premise is logically equivalent to: "If God is omniscient then God knows about the evil in the world". Thus this premise claims that "God knows about the evil in the world" is an *implication* of the statement "God is omniscient".

The reason that most theodicists accept this implication of God's omniscience is that it seems to make sense that if God created the world and all living things in it then God would know about human beings and their suffering. Thus most theodicists would agree that "God knows about the evil in the world" is part of the meaning of "God is omniscient".

Premise 4 is logically equivalent to: If God is omnipotent then God can prevent the occurrence of evil in the world. The same points we made about premise 3 apply to this premise. Premise 4 claims that "God can prevent evil from occurring in the world" is an implication of the statement "God is omnipotent".

Again, most theodicists accept this implication of God's omnipotence because it seems to make sense that if God created the world and its inhabitants then "God can prevent evil from occurring in the world" - if God wants to. Having the power to do what you want to do (as long as the task itself is not inherently self-contradictory) is part of the very meaning of being "omnipotent".

Premise 5 is logically equivalent to: If God is omnibenevolent then He does not want there to be evil in the world. This premise claims that "God does not want there to be evil in the world" is an implication of "God is omnibenevolent".

Many theodicists accept this implication because it seems to make sense that if God is perfectly loving then He would not want His creatures to suffer, but would want them to be happy. Wanting His creatures to be happy is part of the very meaning of "God is perfectly loving"

Those theodicists who accept premise 2, that the evil in the world is real, must deny one of the premises on God's attributes if they would escape the conclusion of the AFE. In other words, if they accept premise 2, they must deny either premise 3, 4, or 5 in order to claim that their belief in God is a rational belief, a belief that includes nothing contradictory, but is, on the contrary, actually supported by reason.

In the next chapter we will examine three approaches to refuting the AFE. Each approach denies a different premise of the argument, and each constitutes a different theodicy. We will examine what premise each theodicy denies, and what justification is given for doing so. We will then decide which, if any, has provided an intellectually satisfying refutation of the argument from evil.

2

PREVIOUS ATTEMPTS
TO SOLVE THE PROBLEM

The problem of evil is the rock upon which
most religious thought systems are
shipwrecked.
Alfred North Whitehead[1]

Various approaches have been used in the attempt to
refute the argument from evil (AFE). Over the period of time
in which I was writing this book I had many conversations
with people who were gracious enough to ask me what my
book was about. Whenever I briefly presented the logical
problem of evil, almost invariably I received the response,
"Well, yes, but... when God created humans He gave them
free will or freedom of choice. And the cause of evil in the
world is our misuse of the freedom of choice that God gave
us."

This, of course, is the traditional response. It has long
been called "the free will defense". It supposedly defends
God's perfect love by attributing the moral evil in the world
to the fact that humans have freedom of choice.

The question is whether this free will defense really works. How does it provide an escape from the conclusion of the AFE? If it does provide an escape it must deny one of the premises. But which one?

In this chapter we will examine three main approaches, all of which acknowledge that humans have freedom of choice, but each of which denies a different premise of the argument. The theodicies we will examine are Classical Theodicy, Person-Making Theodicy (sometimes called Irenaean Theodicy), and Process Theodicy. Before we discuss each theodicy individually it is worthwhile to list the significant propositions all three theodicies assume as true.

1. God created the physical world including human beings.

2. Humans have free will whereby they can choose wrongly as well as rightly (i.e., contrary to or in accord with the Will of God)

3. God is aware of the choices humans make, and the good or evil effects of these choices for their lives here on earth.

4. After the human body ceases to function, some "part of human nature" -- the soul, the mind, or the spirit -- continues to live on, to be aware and feel in some sense. In colloquial terms, all three theodicies affirm there is an afterlife, or "life after death".

The first three of these propositions form the fundamental framework within which all three theodicies attempt to solve the logical problem of evil. In fact, these three propositions -- related to what God created, the human's freedom of choice, and what God knows or is aware of -- combined with the concept of God as a perfect being, *engender* the problem of evil. There would be no logical problem of evil if one did not try to affirm these propositions in combination with the idea of God as a perfect being. It may be fair to say that the logical problem would virtually dissolve if one did not accept these three propositions. Without these affirmations the whole issue of God and human suffering would appear quite different.

Furthermore, for each of these theodicies, once propositions 1 through 3 are accepted, proposition 4 is necessary for solving the problem. If one did not affirm that there is life after bodily death the problem would be even more difficult or even impossible to solve.

All four of these propositions, then, are part of most, if not all, Western religious belief systems. And all four are held by most theodicists who attempt to reconcile these beliefs with the proposition that God is a perfect being.

Which premise of the AFE a particular theodicy denies reflects the difference in its overall metaphysics and theology. Some of these differences will emerge as we discuss the premise each theodicy denies, and the justification each gives for doing so.

Classical Theodicy

This centuries old approach to the problem of evil has its roots in St. Augustine (354-430). Augustine was persistent in his attempts to solve this problem. He is perhaps the most influential theodicist in the Christian Tradition. His approach was further developed, refined, and somewhat modified by St. Thomas Aquinas (1225-1275), whose thought in turn has been carried on and refined by modern Thomists. This "Classical Theodicy" based on the Bible, and the works of Augustine and Aquinas, is defended by other contemporary philosophers of religion who, along with the

Thomists, make modifications here and there in light of contemporary science and philosophy.

Perhaps the most outstanding characteristic of Classical Theodicy is its conception of God as a "Perfect Being", Whose attributes include not only omniscience, omnipotence, and omnibenevolence, but also timelessness, changelessness, endlessness, formlessness, limitlessness, and perfect happiness.

Because of its insistence on maintaining the traditional attributes of God as a perfect being it seems that the only way Classical Theodicy can refute the argument from evil is to deny premise 2, the premise on evil. And this is what many forms of Classical Theodicy do. Others seem to implicitly, if not explicitly, deny premise 5. Let us begin with the first approach.

Classical Theodicy's First Approach: Deny Premise 2. What We Call Evil Merely Seems to be Evil but is Really Good.

In what sense does Classical Theodicy deny premise 2? Although there are various types of arguments used by classical theodicists to deny that the evil in the world is real, I will present only what I consider the best argument in this tradition. This will be enough to make the point that denying premise 2 is one approach theodicists have taken to escape from the conclusion of the AFE.

In its most general form the argument runs as follows: What we call "evil" in this world is not really evil, but good. Since all the attack and suffering is really good there is no evil in the world.

The claim is that if attack and suffering where seen from a universal perspective (e.g., from God's perspective) they would be seen as really good because they play a necessary part in the goodness of the whole of God's perfect creation.

When this idea is applied to our experiences in daily life it amounts to saying that all the attack and suffering we experience in this world can be seen as a means to a good end. And because it is a means to good, it is actually good. The evil, therefore is only *apparently* evil not actually evil. Thus all attack and suffering is good because it serves as a means to a greater good which would not have happened without the suffering.

Augustine himself saw all suffering as punishment from God for sin. And this is good because a world in which sin is punished is better than a world where sin goes unpunished. God's punishment follows from God's justice.

Augustine thus claims he defends God's goodness by showing that punishment of sin is merely part of God's justice, and God's justice is part of God's perfect wisdom and goodness, and yes, even part of His perfect love.

Even the evil of "original sin" -- the evil of Adam's disobeying God's Will -- turns out to be good, because, in Augustine's words, it was "a happy fault" that led to "so great and wonderful a redeemer" as Jesus Christ, who revealed God's mercy and His love for humankind.

By denying the premise on evil, then, Classical theodicy can affirm the premises on God's knowledge, power, and love, and still escape the conclusion of the AFE. God knows about the sin, attack and suffering, but in God's eyes none of it is really evil. It may seem evil to us, but in fact it is all good because in the end God brings good out of it. Thus, according to Classical Theodicy, the argument from evil fails in its attempt to prove that there cannot be a God Who is perfectly knowing, powerful, and loving.

According to this view, then, things are as we would expect them to be if a perfect God exists. If God wants there to be only good, and because of His perfect power, God can have what He wants, then there *is* only good; there can be no evil. And sure enough, there is none.

It may seem to us there is evil, but this is only because we have a limited point of view. What we call evil is only apparently evil. From God's point of view the suffering, and even the attack and sin, is good because ultimately it all leads to good. Thus in addressing God, Augustine says, "And to Thee is nothing whatsoever evil" (*Confessions*). And in the eighteenth century this view was put to poetic lines by Alexander Pope:

> All discord, harmony not understood;
> All partial evil, universal good;
> And, spite of pride, in erring reason's spite,
> One truth is clear, Whatever is, is right.[2]

At first the idea that suffering is a means for good looks like an acceptable way to view many of the "bad things" we humans experience. Perhaps one of the best examples of this is the visit to a dentist or a hospital for surgery. There may be some fear, pain and suffering involved, but ultimately the healthy tooth or the repaired heart is a good end.

This may lead us to agree that the suffering is not really evil because it was a necessary part of the means to a good end. The same idea is applied to the good results of a "just war", or the death of a loved one who was suffering terribly, or the lost of a job which later led to a better one.

We all have suffered from bad things that have happened in our lives and then later have been thankful for them because of the good result to which they ultimately led. We often use suffering as a means for learning, or for "growing spiritually". We have learned to "offer it up". This may be a good way of dealing with suffering. And experiences like this do add some support to this kind of argument which claims that evil can be seen as a means to good. We may be even tempted to accept the idea that "whatever is, is right", even though at the time it is happening it may not seem so.

Critique Of The First Approach

A great number of contemporary theodicists, including those who subscribe to the next two theodicies we discuss, do not find this argument -- or any other arguments which pretend to demonstrate that evil is good -- convincing.

These theodicists argue that even if evil events do turn out to have a good ending that still doesn't make the evil itself good. The best you can say is that the end is good, but the means is evil. And if there are evil *means* in the world then there is *evil* in the world. And if the end is real, the means to this end is also real. Thus the fact remains that *there is evil in the world, and the evil is real.*

Thus according to its critics Classical Theodicy is still implicitly admitting that there is evil in the world and the evil is real; there is attack in the world and the attack is real, there is suffering in the world and the suffering is real, there is sin in the world and the sin is real. After all is said and debated, suffering is still suffering; it is not happiness. And what is not happiness is evil. Suffering itself is evil whether it is a means to a good end or not. You can call it a necessary evil if you like, but it is still evil. If attack were good and suffering were happiness then "offering it up" would be wholly meaningless. Thus, in the view of these critics, premise 2 of the AFE still stands: "the evil in the world is real".

Furthermore, even if some particular evil was necessary to bring about some particular good, there is simply no evidence that this is true in every case of evil. What greater good necessitated the holocaust? What so called good purpose did God have in His Mind that required that six million Jewish people be murdered? How does this horrendous evil fit into the goodness of the whole of God's creation? Could not "God's creation as a whole" been good without things like the Holocaust, the Oklahoma City bombing, the destruction of the towers of the World Trade Center, or the massacre of one million Cambodians at the instigation of Pol Pot?

Harold Kushner, in his best selling book of the early 1980's could ask the question: what greater good necessitated that my son have a disease from birth that would lead to certain death by age 14? Am I supposed to see this evil as good? Good for whom? my son? his mother? me? God Himself? Or perhaps for the congregation to whom I preach of a loving and almighty God?

We all have questions like this. And we very seldom are convinced that every bad thing in our life had to happen in order for some good to be possible. In many cases the good that comes to us after experiencing some evil could have been ours without the suffering having occurred at all, especially when the good is "I learned something which is very helpful". Could you not have learned what you learned the easy way rather than the hard way, without having suffered so much? Most of us realize we could have, we simply made a mistake that led to the suffering. The suffering would have been avoided if we had not made the mistake. So we decide not to make the same mistake again.

This whole idea of calling evil good in order to save the idea that God is all-loving is tricky business, to say the least. At worst it is self contradiction or literally nonsense. For it states that what is not good is good, and what is not happiness is happiness.

For this and other reasons many thinkers, including many in the classical tradition itself, have tried another approach to escaping the conclusion of the AFE.

Classical Theodicy's Second Approach: Deny Premise 5 God Has A Good Purpose For Permitting Evil

In the face of such objections to their position that all evil is *only apparently evil*, but really good, modern theodicists in the classical tradition have tried another approach to escaping the conclusion of the argument from evil. In this approach their reasoning involves God's motive for creating the world. Their attempt, while acknowledging that sin, attack and suffering are evil, is to reconcile God's perfect love and power with the evil in the world He created.

This line of argument runs as follows: God created finite beings (read "humans") with freedom of choice whereby they can choose wrongly as well as rightly. Most human suffering (sometimes called "physical evil") is the result of the wrong choices (sin or "moral evil") of human beings.

The argument continues by placing great value on "morally good actions". But there cannot be morally good actions unless there was the possibility of morally evil actions. And this requires that the actor have freedom of choice.

A world with moral good, and thus with beings who have freedom of choice, is better than a world with no moral good and no beings with freedom of choice.

Thus God's goodness is seen in the fact that He created beings with freedom of choice rather than creating no beings with freedom of choice. The alternative is to create beings who always did right because they could not do otherwise. But then there would be no "morally good actions". Some claim that angels are such beings. They perform no *morally good* actions because they can perform no *morally bad* ones. They do only good because there is no other alternative for them given their nature as God created them.

This line of argument seems to gain even greater strength when it makes the claim that God could not have created at all unless He chose to create finite beings. And are we not glad He did create finite beings! For if He had not done so, we humans would not even exist! And it is better -- at least for us -- that we do exist rather than not. Isn't it?

In other words, this argument claims that God cannot create perfect and infinite beings. If He did then His creations themselves would be God, because they too would be perfect. And this, the argument goes, is absurd. Why it is absurd is not always explained, but I assume it is considered absurd because if God's creations were perfect there would be more than one God because there would be more than numerically one perfect being and that supposedly is impossible.

So, given that God has to create finite beings, if He is to create at all, and given that God is all-good and all-powerful, it follows that God would create the best kind of finite beings He could possibly create. And the best kind are those with freedom of choice, for this makes moral good possible. Beings who can do *morally good deeds* are somehow better than those who cannot.

Those who use this line of argument would claim that God is still all-powerful even though His creatures can disobey Him and chose what is opposite His will. In other words, although God could have prevented evil (by not creating at all, or at least by not creating a world of finite creatures with freedom of choice) He nevertheless still chose to create such creatures.

This supposedly shows His love, and we should be grateful for such love. For by it we live. And since God created beings with the power to choose He does not interfere with their freedom even though He could if He wanted to. Thus He is still all-powerful. But instead of intervening, God permits the evil because He respects the freedom of choice He gave in His creation of us.

Here, then, we see in classical theodicy a line of argument which does not deny premise 2 of the AFE, but instead denies premise 5, the one on God's omnibenevolence. In other words, they acknowledge that the attack and suffering is evil and the evil is real. They also claim that God is omnipotent, and that this implies that He can prevent any evil from occurring if He wants to. But they claim that He does not want to because He gave us free will. He would rather have the evil occur than to interfere with the freedom of choice He gave us. And ultimately, somehow (it remains a mystery how) "God's sovereignty" will win out over evil. Somehow God will bring good out of all evil that occurs in His creation.

All this denies premise 5 by saying it is not true that if God is omnibenevolent He does not want there to be evil in the world. For in a sense God does want there to be evil since He permits the evil that results from our exercising the freedom to choose which He gave us in His creation of us. Nevertheless, He still is all-loving because He created us, and gave us freedom of choice in the process. (*Why* God created finite beings with freedom of choice is one of the difficult questions that arises in all such theodicies that claim that God created such beings.)

As an added argument in its defense of God's love, Classical Theodicy includes the Christian idea that God gave His only Son to save us from the "just" consequences of the sin we committed in exercising the freedom of choice He gave in His creation of us. This redemptive love is God's love in the form of forgiveness and mercy towards us despite the mistakes or sins we make in exercising choice.

Even in this second approach, however, we can see a hint of the first approach that involves the denial of evil. Namely, although God permits the evil, He is willing and able to bring good out of it, and in fact "mysteriously" does so, even if it is not always clear to us at the time we are suffering just how He is going to do this. And many times it is never clear to us how God brings good out of some instances of evil. Supposedly, "in Heaven" we will understand why God permitted this or that instance of attack and suffering, even though He could have prevented it. According to Classical Theodicy, how God brings good out of each and every instance of evil in the world will remain a mystery until God in His own wisdom and good time reveals this to us. Why He keeps this secret from us is even more "mystery."

Critique of the Second Approach

Does this "free will defense" solve the problem? At first glance it may seem so. But there are other issues this solution raises within Classical Theodicy because there are other qualities it attributes to God as a perfect being which are difficult to reconcile with this solution.

For example, Classical theodicy claims that God is not only perfectly knowing, perfectly powerful, and perfectly loving, but perfectly happy as well. They also claim that God, being perfect, must be timeless, changeless, and eternal, or to put these last three attributes into positive terms, God is *always the same forever.*

It is also true that many theologians in this classical tradition claim that hell, a condition of eternal suffering (and thus eternal evil), is still a real possibility for some of God's creatures. They say that humans are not really free if they are not free to reject God forever. In other words, the possibility of unending suffering in hell must be taught as a religious doctrine if one also teaches that humans have *real freedom of choice* in relation to God's Will. It must be possible for one to eternally reject God's Will as one's own.

The teaching that God is timeless and changeless raises numerous unsolvable problems in Classical Theodicy. It is beyond the scope of this book to present the arguments used by some classical theodicists in their attempt to demonstrate that one can consistently say that God is both timeless and changeless, and yet, this same God is creator of, and thus aware of, a world of time and change. Here I will simply say that I do not find any of their arguments convincing, for none of them avoid running into contradictions. Part Two of this book will make it clear why no such arguments will ever be intellectually satisfying.

Let me simply point to a few examples where Classical Theodicy has unsolvable problems arising from its position that God is both a perfect being, and that God is the creator of us as human beings, i.e., creator of finite bodily creatures who live in a world of time, space, and bodies; a world of change and of beginnings and endings.

On the one hand, it is claimed that God's knowledge is immutable or unchangeable. What God knows He knows for all eternity. His knowledge is truth, and truth does not change. But on the other hand, God supposedly knows of everything that happens in the world and in the lives of every human. How can this be?

Supposedly God knows that George Washington is president of the United States, and then knows that George Washington is not president of the United States. This is not immutable knowledge. At one time God knows one thing is true, at another time He knows its opposite is true.

Another example: supposedly I am going to either heaven or hell (or purgatory first for a while) after my body ceases to function. Let's assume, for my sake at least, that I am going to heaven. Given that God's knowledge is timeless and changeless He knows *now*, and has changelessly known for all eternity, that I am happy in heaven with Him.

I may be willing to accept this conclusion, but Classical Theodicy does not offer any explanation of why this is not my present experience. Why am I not experiencing myself as in heaven and happy with God right now? If God knows I am in heaven, and what God knows is the truth, and the truth is timeless and changeless, then I am in heaven right now. It follows then that God does not know that I am here in the world, or that I sometimes experience attack and suffering. And thus it would be false that I am here in the world, for God forever knows the truth that I am in Heaven, happy at home with Him.

This objection gets even stronger when we assume the opposite scenario. Instead of supposing I were to go to heaven after my body ceases to function, suppose, instead, I were to go to hell. Since God's knowledge is timeless and changeless He has known for all eternity, and knows now, that I am in hell. And this will never change. This is not only contrary to my belief and experience, but even if it were true despite my experience, it would be difficult to affirm that God is perfectly loving given that He created beings who are eternally suffering in hell. Such a God would be cruel. (Certainly I could not help but think so!) It also seems very strange indeed to think that God is perfectly loving or perfectly happy when some of His creatures are experiencing unending suffering regardless of its form. Not to mention the fact that it is His responsibility since He put them there for all eternity, timelessly and changelessly. For how could they have *chosen* to go there if there was no time in which to make the choice, and no possibility of changing their mind from accepting God's Will to rejecting it!

Despite the strange logical conclusions of their position, theodicists in the classical tradition, nevertheless, insist that God's knowledge must be timeless and changeless otherwise He would not *be* perfect. Despite the strange conclusions to which this position leads, most classical theodicists refuse to draw back from their strong insistence that God is a perfect being and that He has all the attributes of perfection we have mentioned here, including immutable knowledge.

In spite of the ingeniousness of arguments that attempt to reconcile the idea that God's knowledge is timeless and changeless with the idea that this same God created the world, and is aware of and acts in human history (called "God's providence"), they have never convinced those who see that this mystery is not "mystery" at all, but pure and simple contradiction.

It has been said that Classical Theodicy in its attempt to solve the problem of evil, ends up either: 1) denying that the attack and suffering in the world are evil, or 2) implicitly denying that God is omnibenevolent, or 3) contradicting some other attribute they ascribe to God, (e.g., His immutable knowledge or His timelessness and changelessness[3]).

Many theodicists, including this author, have concluded that Classical Theodicy contains too many contradictions (dubbed "mysteries") for a sane and rational mind to tolerate. Its critics point to numerous contradictions which arise merely as the result of conceiving God as *both* having all the attributes of perfection, *and* being creator of this world, and therefore aware of finite bodily beings who sin and suffer.

It is fair to say, then, that Classical Theodicy fails to escape from the conclusion of the argument from evil. Its "solution" to the problem raises serious questions it cannot satisfactorily answer unless it changes some of its basic teachings about God and the world. In other words, if one claims that God is a perfect being and also claims that this same God is the creator of finite bodily beings who really sin and really suffer, he is implicitly contradicting himself. The contradiction lies in saying, "God is perfect and God is not perfect", or "God's knowledge is timeless and changeless and God's knowledge is not timeless and changeless." This is as much a contradiction as saying, "God is real and God is not real", or "God exists and God does not exist."

Therefore we must conclude that Classical Theodicy has not as yet offered an acceptable solution to the problem of evil. And it never will, unless it changes some of its basic concepts about God, humans, and the world. But if it does that then it is no longer *Classical* Theodicy!

For centuries classical theodicists have tried to escape the conclusion of the AFE while remaining within the traditional theological framework handed down through the Bible, Augustine, and Aquinas. But none have been able to avoid contradictions in making this attempt. Let us turn, then, to another approach to solving the problem.

Person-Making Theodicy:
Deny Premise 5
God Had A Good Purpose For Creating Beings
In An Environment Where
They Would Inevitably Sin and Suffer

Perhaps the best known contemporary theodicist is John Hick. Hick's book, *Evil and the God of Love*, published in 1966 and revised in 1977, was soon recognized by many in the academic community as a modern theological classic.

Hick's position centers on giving an explanation of how God benefits by creating creatures with freedom of choice. His theodicy can be briefly summarized as follows: To be "genuinely free" a being must be "out of the immediate presence" of God. God wanted to create beings who are genuinely free. Thus God created finite beings not in His immediate presence, but "at an epistemic distance". He did this by having persons "come into existence" by emerging to self-consciousness through the evolutionary process. Thus human beings were created "already as sinners", separated from and not immediately aware of God's existence. Since God's creatures, then, are not "overwhelmed" by God's presence, they are capable of choosing contrary to His Will, which would be impossible if they had been created in His immediate presence. Given the nature of the world -- highly competitive -- in which we came into existence as "persons" or "souls", it was inevitable that we would sin by acting out of "animal self centeredness", and thus suffer the consequences, not only of our own choosing wrongly, but also of the autonomous laws of the world in which we were created.

As we learn to have concern for others (the ethics of love) we "grow spiritually" and "come to freely trust, love, worship, and obey God."

This last line is the crux of Hick's theodicy. It gives the *purpose* for which God created us as human beings. He created us separate from Him so that we could come to *freely choose* to love, worship, and obey Him rather than love Him because we could not do otherwise, which would be the case if we were created in His immediate presence (i.e., in Heaven where God exists eternally).

Thus, since Hick admits that God is "ultimately responsible for evil" given our *nature* as He created us, and given the *environment* in which He created us, Hick cannot find a way of holding on to the concept of God as Love unless he posits that God included in His plan of creation a *guarantee* that all "souls" will be saved in the end.

This guarantee, however, requires "many lives", since it is obvious that some people have not grown to "spiritual maturity" in this one lifetime on this planet.

From this brief summary of Person-Making Theodicy (sometimes called Soul-Making Theodicy) we first notice that this theodicy eliminates eternal suffering in hell as a real possibility. Hick feels that the problem of evil is unsolvable as long as we accept the idea that eternal suffering is possible for anyone.

Notice that Hick is also advocating a modified form of reincarnation with his idea of "many lives". Hick feels that this idea of many lives is needed in order to solve the problem of evil.

In terms of the AFE, this theodicy affirms premise 2, 3, and 4. To avoid the conclusion of the argument, then, it must deny premise 5. And this it does. Person-Making Theodicy denies the premise on God's omnibenevolence by saying that a perfectly loving God may have a good reason for permitting evil, even though He can prevent it if He wanted to.

According to this theodicy, God is omnipotent even though His creatures can oppose His Will. God is all-powerful in the sense that God can intervene in the world to prevent evil if He wants to. Yet He does not always want to. Why? Because He has "voluntarily limited" His own power for the sake of His plan of creation, which includes that His creatures be *free to choose* to love or not love Him; to obey or not obey Him.

So what is the origin of evil according to Hick's theodicy? God is the origin of evil. *God Himself is responsible for evil* because He created us in such a way that we would inevitably attack and suffer. Evil could not be avoided given the way God created His creations and the environment in which He created them.

The question arises, why is it so important that God's creatures have freedom of choice vis-à-vis God? We humans, who seem to cherish our freedom of choice, may feel that this freedom itself is worth all the suffering it may cause. We would rather tolerate the suffering than not have freedom of choice. For some reason or other we think we cannot be fully happy if we were not free to choose wrongly as well as rightly. Some theodicist accept this idea, but some do not. Some theodicists seem to think that God should intervene when we go to excess in exercising our freedom of choice.

For example, some feel it would have been more loving of God to have interfered with Hitler's exercise of his freedom of choice. They do not understand why God did not do this if it is really true that He could have. And it is true that He could have if indeed He is perfectly powerful as Hick asserts.

Hick claims that the value of freedom of choice goes beyond any value for which *we* might cherish it. It is a value that exists for *God Himself.* Hick claims that creating beings at an epistemic distance so they could choose contrary to His Will has an "added value for God". Somehow the love and worship that God would receive from beings who freely choose to love Him even though they could choose otherwise, is more valuable to God than the love He would receive from beings who cannot choose otherwise. In other words, the love God receives from those who cannot but love Him because of His very nature, or because of their own very nature as God created them, is not as valuable as the love received from those who freely choose to love Him.

Hick seems to be saying that to have His creatures love and obey Him as an act of choice is much more valuable and pleasing to God than to have them do so necessarily or "automatically" as a result of the way He created them. In other words, if His creatures loved and worshiped Him, and always did His Will naturally, or because of "character determinism", this "would *lack for God* the value of a freely offered worship and obedience" (Evil and the God of Love, p.310, 1st ed.) (emphasis mine).

Hick seems to be saying that the "worship and obedience" simply would not be as satisfying for God if his creatures had no choice about it, but simply did His Will naturally because God created them as creations that cannot but love as He does. In colloquial terms Hick is saying that God's creations would be like robots who acted the way they do only because they were programmed to do so in God's creation of them. And such "automatic" (or natural) love would not be as valuable to God as a love that is freely offered by someone who could choose not to love Him.

Critique of Person-Making Theodicy

Person-Making Theodicy seems to solve at least one problem that arises in Classical Theodicy, that of reconciling the existence of a perfectly loving God with the idea that He would allow His creatures to suffer for all eternity. Hick solves this problem by denying that eternal hell is a real possibility. Hick claims that the problem of evil is unsolvable unless we allow for universal salvation, that all God's creatures will be saved in the end.

Some critics do not accept Hick's position on universal salvation, citing various reasons including that it is contrary to the teachings in the Bible. Since universal salvation is crucial to Person-Making Theodicy, anyone who cannot accept this teaching could not consistently accept its solution to the problem of evil.

Many critics, however, point out numerous other problems within this system. It is beyond our purpose to deal with all their objections and Hick's replies. For our purpose here we need but mention a few.

First there is the problem of God's motive for creating finite beings with freedom of choice. The question arises whether there really is any added value for God in creating beings at an epistemic distance so they can have freedom of choice. If God's power guarantees that all His creatures will come to love Him in the end, then in what sense are they really free to choose not to come to Him and love Him?

Secondly, if it is true that they will come to Him, God must know this already, since God is omniscient. So why not simply create them "in His presence" in the first place? Why make them go through all the suffering when in the end they will make it to heaven anyway? God might have just as well created them in His immediate presence where it would be impossible for them to oppose His Will.

There has been much debate on Hick's position that God created beings separate from Himself for the purpose of obtaining some added value due to the fact that His creations have the choice to love Him or not.

Another objection is that the motive for creating which Hick attributes to God is not consistent with God as a perfect being. For a perfect being lacks nothing, and therefore would not and could not create out of a sense of lack. A perfect being could not create for the purpose of getting something he does not have but thinks he would like to have. A creator who creates in order to get something instead of give something cannot be a perfect being who already has everything.

We need not be led astray from our purpose in this chapter in order to discuss in more detail other aspects of Person-Making theodicy. It does raise many issues which have been debated back and forth between Hick and his critics. Our main objective in this chapter is simply to show that theodicists have taken quite different approaches in attempting to escape from the conclusion of the AFE, even though they all accept the four propositions we mentioned in the beginning of this chapter. This shows that the AFE is not refuted simply by saying that humans have freedom of choice and that they therefore are responsible for the evil in the world.

We see in the present case that the approach to refuting the AFE is to say that God's "omnibenevolence" does not imply what the premise in the argument says it implies. The premise says that God's perfect love implies that He does not want His creatures to suffer. Person-Making Theodicy says that God's omnibenevolence does not imply this. It claims that we can consistently say, on the one hand, that God wants His creatures to suffer and wants there to be evil in the world He creates (for one reason or another, it matters not), and, on the other hand, God is perfectly loving.

Person-Making theodicy has been roundly and rightly criticized for its conception of God's perfect love. Many philosophers of religion reject the concept of God found in this theodicy because its God is not one who is really perfectly loving, given His responsibility for the evil that humans experience.

Some theodicists have repeatedly argued against attributing to God the purpose that Hick attributes to God for creating finite beings who are separate from Him. It seems that a perfect being would have no need for the "added value" which supposedly accrues to God as a result of creating creatures who are "already sinners" simply because of the way He created them.

In the process of denying premise 5, then, Person-Making Theodicy presents a concept of Love which is conditional and limited, at best, and at worst is not love at all, but cruelty and selfishness. One must admit, however, that the cruelty is less than that which would permit unending pain and suffering in hell. But being simply less cruel is not the same as being perfectly loving.

Along with its critics, this author concludes, then, that Person-Making Theodicy has not provided an acceptable escape from the conclusion of the argument from evil. Its attempt to deny premise 5 in order to escape the conclusion is done at too great a cost to the concept of God's Love. It is a difficult task to convince a rational person that, on the one hand, God is perfectly loving, and on the other, this same God creates creatures in an environment in which they cannot avoid suffering.

Process Theodicy:
Deny Premise 4
God's Omnipotence Does Not Imply That God Can Create a World without Evil or That He Can Prevent Evil from Occurring in His Creation.

David Griffin, the most prominent representative of Process Theodicy, attempts to escape from the conclusion by denying premise 4, the premise on God's omnipotence.

After all is said, Griffin concludes that God's omnipotence does not imply that God can prevent the occurrence of evil in the world. In other words, Process Theodicy rejects the traditional notion of God's omnipotence.

The traditional concept of God's omnipotence includes the following ideas: God has *all* power, God has *unlimited* power, God can do whatever He wants to do, God causes all things, God's Will is done, and finally nothing can really oppose God's will.

Process Theodicy accepts *none* of these ideas as true of God's power. Yet Griffin still wants to say that God is omnipotent!

In what sense, then, is God omnipotent according to Process Theodicy? The suggestion is that when we say God is "omnipotent", we should mean merely that God has the most power; God has more power than any other being.

That God has more power than any other being is demonstrated in the fact that it is God who creates the world. God's creating of the world is a process whereby God is attempting to bring order and harmony out of a pre-existing chaos in order to bring about higher and "more intense enjoyment" in His creation.

According to Process Theodicy we must acknowledge that other "actual entities" like human beings have some power too. Humans have freedom of choice or "the power of self-determination". Thus God's power is limited, He does not have "all the power"; there are wills other than God's, which have power to really oppose God's Will.

The other two theodicies we just discussed say that human beings have freedom of choice because God gave it to them in His creation of them. Process Theodicy, however, hypothesizes that humans have freedom of choice not because God gave them this power in His creation of them, but because of "the nature of things beyond God's control".

In other words, there has always existed some primordial stuff, perhaps some mass-energy in an original state of chaos, which has existed for all eternity alongside God, and which has "always posed some limitation on God's power." In bringing about beings of a higher level of complexity through the evolutionary process God has ultimately created human beings. But the long process has always included some resistance that posed a limitation on God's power.

There is no need to discuss here how Process Theodicy justifies this hypothesis of "pre-existing actual entities", but Griffin claims it makes more sense than the hypothesis that God created the world *ex-nihilo* (from nothing), a position held by the two previous theodicies.

Critique of Process Theodicy

Process Theodicy, which accepts premise 2, 3, and 5 explicitly denies premise 4 in its attempt to escape the conclusion of the AFE. But in the process it so dilutes the term omnipotence that it is without meaning. For this reason, among others, many philosophers of religion reject the concept of God presented by Process Theodicy. Its God is a "finite god", a "weak god", a god whose power cannot guarantee a positive outcome of his creative activity.

Although Process Theodicy offers many brilliant insights into our thinking about God and the world, its attempt to escape the conclusion of the AFE is done at too great a cost to the conception of God's power. For this reason many thinkers, including this author, believe that Process Theodicy has not provided an intellectually satisfying refutation of the AFE..

Person-Making and Process Theodicy are both products of the twentieth century. Hick and Griffin both have continued to defend the core ideas in their respective theodicies against objections that have been raised since their seminal works were first published. Naturally, there are some reconsiderations in light of criticism[4], but in both cases the basic teaching each relies upon to escape the conclusion of the argument from evil remains the same throughout. Hick denies the premise on omnibenevolence, and Griffin the one on omnipotence. Hick claims that Griffin's God is not "God", a perfect being, because He is too weak to be called omnipotent. And Griffin claims that Hick's God is not "God" because He is too cruel to be called omnibenevolent, (or in Griffin's words, "morally perfect").

Classical theodicists continue to deplore the weakness, helplessness, and finitude of the God conceived by process theodicists. They also feel no need to accept Griffin's hypothesis of pre-existing entities beyond God's control, for classical theodicists hold that God created the world *ex-nihilo*, and do not see as yet any good reason to give up this position in explaining the origin of the physical universe.

Classical theodicists also reject the conception of God as responsible for evil as found in Person-Making Theodicy. Furthermore, Classical Theodicy refuses to give up the traditional idea that God is timeless and changeless despite the logical problems this involves when it is claimed that this same God created the physical world. They are satisfied at this point to relegate the inconsistencies to the realm of "mystery", rather than accept, as Griffin does, that change and temporality are part of God's experience.

Classical Theodicy also affirms that God, being perfect, is also perfectly happy. Both Person Making and Process Theodicy present us with a picture of god who himself suffers due to the sin, attack, and suffering of his creatures. Their god is an "empathetic" god, and therefore "a suffering god."

In the next chapter we shall set forth the beginnings of a fourth theodicy, which we call "Miracle Theodicy". The chapter shall be devoted to setting forth an alternative refutation of the AFE. As we shall see, Miracle Theodicy denies a premise that is not denied by any of the theodicies we have discussed in this chapter.

Notes

1. This statement may be a paraphrase. It comes from my memory of reading Whitehead long ago. Any help in locating the reference will be appreciated. I suspect that any process theodicist will recognize it immediately.

2. Alexander Pope, *Essay on Man*, Epistle I, lines 291-294.

3. David Griffin, *God, Power, and Evil: A Process Theodicy*. Philadelphia: Westminster Press, 1976. pp. 76-77.

4. See, for example, Griffin's *Evil Revisited: Responses and Reconsiderations*, listed in the bibliography.

3

THE MIRACLE SOLUTION

Everything that God created cannot have an
end, and nothing He did not create is real.
A Course in Miracles (Q20,5:7).

In this chapter I will present a radically new way of
escaping from the conclusion of the argument from evil
(AFE). Like the other three theodicies examined in the last
chapter, Miracle Theodicy attempts to refute the AFE by
denying at least one of its premises.

This chapter, then, has a simple purpose: to refute the
AFE. In the chapters which follow I will fill in the details of
the new theodicy we are constructing.

Thus the central question we want to answer in this
chapter is: which premise of the AFE does Miracle Theodicy
deny, and what is its justification for doing so?

The answer to this question lies in the Course's
teachings on the nature of God and His creation. The Course
teaches that God is a perfect reality or being. And as such
God is pure Mind. As pure Mind God creates Thought or

spirit. God is not a body, nor does He have a body. The Course also teaches that what God creates is like Himself.

These ideas are not completely foreign to those of us who have been raised in the Christian tradition. What is surprising, at least on first glance, is what the Course infers from these statements.

The Course teaches that since God is pure mind, and since what He creates is like Himself, all God's creations are purely minds. God does not create bodies, nor does He create minds mixed with bodies or minds "in" bodies. What God creates is spirit or Thought Which is like Himself. And since it is like Himself it is a mind. Thus spirit, which is a Thought of God Which He created like Himself, is also mind since Mind is what God is.

The Course also teaches that God created "You". Therefore, you, as God created you, are spirit, or a Thought of God Which He created like Himself. And thus, you are "a mind, in Mind, and purely mind" (L158,1:2). You, as God created you, are not a body. Nor do you, as God created you, exist "in" a body or have a body. As God created you, you are a pure mind like Himself. According to *A Course in Miracles*, then, God did not create bodies or a world of bodies.

Of course, we as human beings do not think of our selves as pure minds. Suppose someone asked you "what are you, are you a mind or a body?" What would you say? If you are like most human beings you would most likely say something like: "I am both a mind and a body", or "I am a soul and a body", or "I am a spirit, mind, and body, with a will of my own".

Human beings perceive themselves in different ways. In terms of mind and body there are various ways you might perceive your self. I want to list at least four different ways a human might think of himself in terms of mind and body:

1) *I am a body*. This is the way a materialist may describe what he is. He identifies with the body. The mind is seen as nothing more than brain activity or the result of brain activity (neural firings, for example) and the brain, of course, is part of the body.

2) *I am a mind in a body*. This is the way many religiously oriented people describe their nature. They are interested in making clear that they believe their mind or soul lives on after their human or "fleshy" body ceases to function. When the body "dies" the soul leaves the body; somewhat in the manner depicted in movies like *Ghost*. The mode of existence the soul experiences after "leaving the body" is open to debate among those who hold this position. Some say, for example, that the soul goes to either heaven or to hell immediately after the human body ceases to function.

3) *I am a mind and a body*. Perhaps the main difference between this position and the previous one is the definite claim that *some sort of body* is an essential aspect of what I am *always*. In other words, if a *human* body is not part of what I am *always*, at least some kind of form or image or body is (e.g., a spiritual body or astral body). Various arguments are proposed to support the idea that some kind of form, or "individuating element" of the spirit (soul, mind) must be an *essential* part of our true and eternal nature. One such argument is that a form or body is needed to distinguish me (my unique self) from you, and from everyone else, including God Himself.

4) *I am a mind* (or spirit). Yet I am *temporarily using a body*. Here the emphasis is on the idea that one's true and eternal nature is as a mind and spirit (or soul, or Thought, or idea). In this view the body is merely something the mind is *using for a time, for one purpose or another*. This is the way the Course would have us perceive ourselves while we seem to be "in" a world of bodies or a world of perception.

Regardless of which view one holds, he will generally think of "human nature", or the nature of the human, as including a *human body*. As a "human" I have a body. The body is part of what I am; it is part of what it means to be "human". And if we believe in God, we usually think that the body is included among the things that God created. For God, as the Bible says, created human beings; He created the first man or "Adam".

The Course, however, teaches that God did not create us *as* human. "Human" is not what you are *as God created you*. God did not create "human beings". He did not create man as "man". He did not create a body, or a world of bodies. He created only spirit or Thought or pure mind. This is because *God* is pure Mind, and what God creates is perfectly like Himself.

In light of its teaching that God did not create us as "man" or as "human" the Course offers a reinterpretation of the well known Biblical passage about God's creation of man:

> The statement "God created man in his own
> image and likeness" needs reinterpretation.
> "Image" can be understood as "thought," and
> "likeness" as "of a like quality." God did
> create spirit in His Own Thought and of a
> quality like to His Own. (3.5,7:1-3)

Thus, as God's creations, you and I, and all truly living things, are spiritual. We are the creations of a God Who lovingly created us as spirit and "of a quality like to His Own". .

Consistent with this is the Course's further teaching that God did not create the world of bodies in which we seem to live. In other words, God did not create the physical world or the physical universe, the world of time, space, and bodies.

God did not create it directly, by speaking it into existence in 6 days as Genesis says, nor did God create it indirectly through the process of evolution as many contemporary theodicists hold, as a way of being more in line with contemporary physical science.

Every dedicated student of *A Course In Miracles* (ACIM) is familiar with its teaching that God did not create this world of bodies. The Course not only states this directly, and repeatedly, but this teaching logically follows from its more general teachings about the nature of reality, or the nature of God and His creations.

The Reality Formula

For our purpose of constructing a theodicy, then, perhaps the most significant statement the Course makes about the nature of reality, or about God and His creations, is contained in the following passage from the *Manual For Teachers:*

Forgive the world and you will understand
that everything that God created cannot have
an end, and nothing He did not create is real.
In this one sentence is our course explained
(Q20,5:7-8).

Notice that "in this one sentence" is contained the Course's criterion for what is *real*. This is the reason that the author says, "in this one sentence is our course explained".

Much philosophical discussion centers around the question concerning the nature of "reality", or the nature of "the real". In fact, one branch of philosophy is called "ontology", or "the study of being *as being*". The basic question of ontology is "What ultimately is *real*?

From this one sentence -- "in which our course is explained" -- we can infer that the Course teaches that *only what God created is real.*

We first notice that everything God created is eternal ("cannot have an end"). This is a repeated theme in the Course. What God creates is eternal like Himself. From other passages in the Course we learn that everything that has a beginning in time also has an end. Thus, if everything God created cannot have an end then it cannot have a beginning in time.

From this one sentence, then, we can deduce that *only the eternal is real.* The reasoning goes: what is not eternal was not created by God. What was not created by God is not real. Therefore, what is not eternal is not real.

From what we just said we can derive what I will call "the Course's reality formula". The reality formula states that what is real is eternal and was created by God. What is not eternal is not real and was not created by God. We can write this *reality formula* as a kind of equation:

real = eternal = God created.

Of course, included in "real" and "eternal" is God Himself as well as what God created. *Only God and His creations are real. Nothing else is real.*

Thus to the fundamental question of ontology, viz., what ultimately is real? the Teacher of *A Course in Miracles* would respond "Only God and His creations are real", or "Only the eternal is real". Thus, what is not eternal is unreal. What God did not create does not exist.

Applying the Reality Formula:
The Eternity Test

The Course often says of itself, "this Course is simple" (15.4,6:1). And here is one example of its simplicity; the reality formula: only the eternal is real.

Thus the Course implicitly offers a simple test to determine what is real. I call it "the eternity test". If you want to know whether anything you are aware of is real, ask yourself: "Is it eternal?" If the answer is "no", then it is not real. Nor was it created by God.

So we may ask, is the human body real? Well, is it eternal? No. Then it is not real. Nor was it created by God. Consider the house for which I make mortgage payments. Is it real? Well, is it eternal? No. Then it was not created by God. And thus it is not real, even though it seems real to me.

We can use this eternity test on anything to determine whether it was created by God or not, and thus whether it is real or not. We can, as another example, use our simple test on the entire physical world. Is the cosmos, - the physical universe of time, space, and bodies, of matter and energy, and the forces which govern them - real? Well, is it eternal?

Astrophysicists say the physical universe began with a "Big Bang" some 12 billion years ago as we count time. (It seems this number keeps changing. It once was 15 billion.) But despite the number of years, the significant claim is that *the physical universe had a beginning*. According to the Course, anything that has a beginning has an end. If the physical cosmos had a beginning then it will have an end. So the physical world is not eternal. Therefore, by our reality formula it was not created by God, and thus it is not real, since "nothing God did not create is real" (Q20,5:7)

Perhaps the Course's most direct statement that the physical cosmos has an end and thus is not eternal is the following:

> What *seems* eternal all will have an end. The stars will disappear, and night and day will be no more. All things that come and go, the tides, the seasons and the lives of men; all things that change with time and bloom and fade will not return. Where time has set an end is not where the eternal is. (29.6,2:7-10)

So even though the physical universe may seem eternal, the Course would teach us it is not. And since it is not eternal, it is not real. There are many other passages in the Course which state straight out that God did not create the world we see, that it is not eternal, is not real, does not exist, and therefore is an illusion. For example:

> The world you see is an illusion of a world. God did not create it, for what He creates must be eternal as Himself. Yet there is nothing in the world you see that will endure forever. Some things will last in time a little while longer than others. But the time will come when all things visible will have an end (C4,1).
> What God did not create does not exist. And everything that does exist exists as He created it. The world you see has nothing to do with reality (L14,1:2-4).

This teaching may be surprising at first. It may even seem to be "heretical" to anyone raised in the theological tradition which uses the canonical Jewish and Christian Scriptures as the basis for assertions about God. If you have been raised in this tradition, and nearly all people in the Western world have, you have been taught that God created the physical world including the human body. So it is no surprise that this teaching may seem radical to you. It was to me when I first read it. Now, however, after considering it seriously more and more, I have come to accept it. It makes sense to me. We will have much to say about this specific teaching, but we reserve our discussion for later, since we want to keep our focus in this chapter on the direct path to refuting the AFE.

The Solution to the Problem:
God Does Not Know about the Evil in the World

Based on the ideas we have just discussed concerning God and His creations we can now construct a deductive argument by which we arrive at a conclusion which serves to refute the argument from evil. Here is the argument constructed on the basis of relevant teachings of the Course:

1. Everything God created is eternal.
2. This world of bodies is not eternal
3. Therefore God did not create this world of bodies.
4. Nothing God did not create is real.
5. Therefore this world of bodies is not real.
6. God knows only what He creates (i.e., only what is eternal, only what is real)
7. Therefore God does not know about this world of bodies.
8. If God does not know about this world of bodies then He does not know about the attack and suffering (evil) in this world of bodies.

9. Therefore God does not know about the evil in this world.

We now have an answer to the question we posed above, namely, which premise does Miracle Theodicy deny in order to escape from the conclusion of the argument from evil? Yes, it is premise 3.

Premise 3 implies that, if God is omniscient then He knows about the evil in the world. We deny this premise. The conclusion of the argument we just constructed states that God does *not* know about the evil in the world.

Does this mean, then, that the God of ACIM is not omniscient? The Course claims it does not. According to the Course, even though God does not know about the evil in the world it is still true that God is omniscient. This, then, is our next task: to show that it makes sense to say that God is omniscient even though God does not know about the evil in the world.

Before we begin this task it is worthwhile to point out that we are attempting to refute the argument from evil in the same manner as Person-Making and Process Theodicy attempt to refute it. We claim that our conception of a particular attribute of God, in this case "omniscience", *does not imply* what the relevant premise says it implies. We are saying that our conception of God's "omniscience" does not imply that God knows about the evil in the world; just as Person-Making theodicy claims that its conception of God's "omnibenevolence" does not imply that God does not want there to be evil in the world, and just as Process Theodicy claims that its conception of God's "omnipotence" does not imply that God can create a world without any genuine evil, or that He can prevent the occurrence of evil in this world which He created, and is still "creating".

In the last chapter we claimed that the concept of omnibenevolence in Person-Making Theodicy, and the concept of omnipotence in Process Theodicy, were so diluted or weakened that these two theodicies are actually denying that God possesses the attribute in question. Our task then is to show that the concept of omniscience in Miracle Theodicy is not so diluted and weakened that we are in effect denying that God really has this attribute.

Miracle Theodicy claims that the conditional statement: "If God is omniscient then God knows about the evil in the world" is not necessarily true, but in fact, is false and not true at all. The Course teaches that God is omniscient even though He does not know about the evil in this world. Is this a diluted concept of omniscience, or does it contain the full meaning of the term, that God knows everything knowable?

Does It Make Sense To Say That God Is Omniscient Even Though God Does Not Know About The Evil In The World?

How does the Course justify its position that God is omniscient even though God is not aware of the evil in this world? The key to answering this question lies in what the Course teaches about the *reality status* of what God did not create, namely, "Nothing God did not create is real" (Q20,5:7).

Since the world of bodies was not created by God *it is not real*. It is not eternal, it does not exist in reality, or in God's creation. Since the world of bodies is not real to God, it does not exist in God's Mind. God is not aware of it, God does not know about it.

Yet since God created everything that is eternal and real, He is aware of, and does know about, everything that is real. God is aware of everything that *is*, everything that exists in reality, everything that He created, everything eternal, everything real. And everything He created exists forever and always as He created it. (In chapter 5, we will discuss in detail just what God did create and therefore *what* God does know).

This can be put another way by looking at what the Course says about "innocence". According to the Course, innocence is forever the state of God's Mind, and of every mind as God created it. The Course says, "Innocence is wisdom since it is unaware of evil and evil does not exist. It is, however, perfectly aware of everything that is true" (3.1,7:4-5).

In other words, the Course is saying *both* that God is unaware of evil, *and* that God is omniscient. An Innocent Mind is omniscient because It is "perfectly aware of everything that is true". God is perfectly aware of everything that is true. He is perfectly aware of everything He created, everything that is eternal, everything that is real.

To be omniscient means to know everything that is knowable. Only reality or the truth is knowable. And God knows the truth. God knows everything that is knowable. That is perfect knowledge. That is what omniscience means. God is omniscient means God is perfectly aware of everything that is real and true; He knows everything that is able to be known, and only reality can be known.

God is not aware of evil because evil is not true, evil does not exist in reality. It may "exist" in this world of bodies, but this world of bodies is not real because God did not create it. This world is a dream, and evil exists only in dreams. In later chapters we shall discuss in detail the Course's teaching that this world of perception is a dream. It is a dream of bodies and of attack and suffering and death. It is a dream of separation, sin and evil.

Notice that what we are saying here does *not* mean that we as humans, as minds with a body, do not sometimes perceive or experience evil. We do perceive attack and experience suffering. Nor does the Course mean that evil is not at times real to us, that it does not exist for us as humans. It does exist for us as humans. Humans do perceive and experience evil. The Course does not deny this.

It is essential to understand that *the Course does not deny that we humans sometimes perceive and experience evil*. Thus I repeat this point again. When the Course says that evil is not real it is not denying that evil is real to us while we are using a body. It is not denying that we perceive attack and experience suffering sometimes. *Sometimes evil is real to us*. Sometimes we see ourselves as attacked and losing by attack, and suffering pain by attack. And the attack, loss and suffering are evil; for what is not happiness is evil. We do at times experience unhappiness and misery.

Therefore, when the Course says that the evil in the world is not real it is saying that it is *not real to God* because God did not create the world. And since "nothing God did not create is real" the world is not real, and thus all the attack and suffering in the world are not real either. Evil is not real to God, because God is not aware of anyone who attacks and suffers. Nor is evil real to you *as God created you*. But it *is* real to "you" who believe you are something other than what God created you as. It is real to "you" who believe you are human. But God did not create you human. "God did create spirit in His Own Thought, and of a quality like to His Own". God did create you as spirit, as pure mind.

In other words, the Course is not denying what premise 2 in the AFE is intended to convey, namely, that we humans experience suffering and that the suffering is real to us. We believe there is suffering in the world and we have lots of "evidence" for our belief. What the Course denies is that *God* perceives or experiences attack and suffering. It denies that God is aware of limited and separated selves in a body who attack and suffer and die. How could He be aware of such beings, not having created them?

Notice also that the Course is *not* teaching the same thing that Classical Theodicy teaches. Classical Theodicy teaches that *God is aware* of the attack and suffering, but that He does not consider these things *as evil*. Classical Theodicy would have us believe that God somehow perceives the attack and suffering that humans experience, but from His point of view the attack and suffering is good because ultimately it leads to a greater good which God has in Mind, some purpose for which all the suffering was necessary. This view of the human experience of attack and suffering, as we have discussed in Chapter 2, is not only associated with Classical Theodicy, but also appears in a slightly different version in Irenaean Theodicy (Person-Making) as well. According to Miracle Theodicy this is a pervasive error; a terrible mistake.

It is important that we be clear on this difference between Classical and Miracle Theodicy with regard to the relation of God and evil, so I will repeat it again. The Course is teaching that God Himself is not aware of attack and suffering at all. Attack and suffering are meaningless to God Himself. God is not aware of "suffering sinners". He is not aware of humans or any other kind of beings who attack and suffer. Classical Theodicy, on the other hand, says that God is aware of the attack and suffering; He is aware of suffering sinners, of humans who attack and suffer. It merely claims that God does not judge all this as evil, because from His point of view it is not evil, but good, and if we saw it from His point of view we too would see that it is good.

In fact, according to the Course, God does not perceive at all. Perception involves the use of a body. Since God is pure Mind, and does not have a body, He does not have perceptions. God does not *perceive* but only *knows*. God is not aware of attack and suffering in any sense. Thus He is not aware of the evil we experience in this world, nor even that anyone is in a physical world, as we believe we are. God, the Father, is not aware of sinners or sufferers, victors or victims, predators or prey.

This can be put another way. God is not aware of evil because God is not aware of anything which happens in a world He did not create. Evil exists sometimes for us who seem to live in this world of bodies, but the world of bodies is not real, and so the evil is not real either. All of it is but a dream, existing in our minds apart from God's Mind.

We may be tempted to say that such a God, who is unaware of evil, is not very wise or sophisticated, but rather naive. But the Course points out that "innocence is wisdom". It is wise to be unaware of evil *because* evil does not exist. It is *not wise* to be aware of something that is unreal and does not exist. It is wisdom to be perfectly aware of everything that is real or true.

If you are aware of "something" that does not really exists you are not wise but deceived, or delusional, or hallucinatory, or dreaming. You are perceiving illusions as true, a dream as reality. God knows the truth. He does not perceive illusions. That is wisdom, that is perfect knowledge. We will have much more to say about God's knowledge of reality and our perception of illusions in the upcoming chapters.

At this point we now have an answer to the question which introduced this section. We now have shown that *it does, indeed, make sense* to say that God is omniscient even though God does not know about the evil in the world. We are not stating a contradiction when we say God is omniscient but He does not know about the evil in the world. When we say God is omniscient, or that God "knows everything", we mean that God knows everything that is true, everything that is real, everything that exists in reality, in His creation. God knows everything that is knowable, and only reality is knowable, only truth is knowable. A mind using a body can perceive illusions and be deceived they are true, but God is not a mind with a body and thus He does not perceive at all.

It is no more legitimate to deny that God is omniscient because He does not know illusions, than it is to deny that God is omnipotent because He cannot make a square circle. All theodicists agree that we cannot deny that God is omnipotent simply because He cannot make a triangle with four sides, or do some other task that is self-contradictory.

So too, we should not deny that God is omniscient because He cannot know what is not knowable or what is not true, or because He does not know about what does not exist, or what is not real. We should not deny that God is omniscient because He cannot be certain of the truth of what is not true. To know something that is not knowable, or that does not exist in reality, is self-contradictory; it is wholly meaningless. Our perception of illusions, which God neither perceives nor knows about, does not make God ignorant; it makes us deceived and delusional. In fact, as we shall see later, it makes us sick.

If we grant that God is omniscient although He knows no evil, then we can legitimately claim that the evil in the world does not constitute proof or evidence against the existence of a God Who is perfectly loving and perfectly powerful. It is clear that *only if one claims that God must know about the evil* can he legitimately use the evil as evidence or proof against God's perfect love and power.

It is surely apparent at this point why the argument from evil has for so long been the source of doubt in the minds of thinking men and women about the existence of an all-powerful and all-loving God. For the argument begins by stating the obvious - that we humans experience attack and suffering, and this attack and suffering is evil, and this evil is real to us. Then it claims that God must know about the evil we experience because He is omniscient. Given that God knows about the evil, it then goes on to argue, correctly and irrefutably, that God cannot be both omnipotent and omnibenevolent.

Thus, once we accept premise 3, once we grant the argument's claim that *God* must know about the evil, we cannot escape its conclusion without diluting the meaning of God's perfect love or God's perfect power to the point that they no longer convey the meaning they are intended to convey.

But by denying premise 3, we can affirm that God is perfectly loving and perfectly powerful in the full meaning of these terms, namely, that there is no limit to His love, there is no limit to His power.

IS THIS AN INTELLECTUALLY SATISFYING SOLUTION?

At this point we can claim with confidence that *the AFE has been refuted.* We have actually escaped the argument's conclusion that there is no God. We have done this by denying premise 3. We declare that *God's omniscience does not imply that God knows about the evil in this world.*

Incidentally, as an attentive reader, you may have noticed that we have, by implication, also denied premise 2. Since neither the body nor this world of bodies were created by God, neither is real. And thus the evil in this world is unreal as well. We will discuss the illusory status of this world, and of the self that attacks and suffers while it seems to live in it, when we arrive at Part Three of this book.

We see, then, that Miracle' Theodicy's solution to the theoretical problem of evil is based on the Course's teaching that God did not create us as minds with bodies. He did not create us *as humans.* Nor did He create a physical world.

And, as we have seen, this means that the evil we as humans experience is not real to God; God Himself "knows no evil". God Himself is not aware of beings who attack and are attacked, who hurt and are hurt, who suffer and cause suffering, and who kill and are killed.

Can we claim, then, with full confidence, that we have solved the problem which has for centuries been "the most powerful objection ever raised against belief in God"? Can we claim we are rational people even though we believe that a God of perfect love and power exists *while acknowledging that* humans beings perceive and experience evil? Have we shown that faith in an "almighty and loving God" is not irrational, but rational? Have we really escaped from the conclusion of the argument from evil in a way that any rational person can accept?

Well, I believe we have. But you may not think so. At least not yet. Many readers, especially those strongly identified with traditional Christianity, Judaism, or Islam -- or even atheists for that matter -- may find this solution too radical to accept. Unless there is further explanation.

Any reader who has followed the argument to this point has a few questions which beg for answers! And they are questions that must be answered before this solution can be fully understood and accepted. We turn now to some of the more obvious ones.

QUESTIONS RAISED BY THIS SOLUTION

In this chapter we have presented a solution to the logical problem of evil based on the teachings in *A Course in Miracles*. As we have seen, the key to this solution is the idea that God does not know about the evil in the world because He did not create the world. And since this is the case, any argument against the existence of God which contains the premise that God knows about the evil in the world is unsound. The evil we experience and perceive, then, cannot legitimately serve as proof or evidence against the existence of an all-loving and all-powerful God.

Obvious questions, however, are raised by this solution. In this, the last section of this chapter, we will merely raise those questions. In the chapters which follow we will attempt to answer them.

What immediately follow are three general questions that must be answered in order for this solution to be fully understood and accepted. Within each of these general questions is a whole set of specific questions and issues which must be - and will be - dealt with as we proceed with our theodicy project.

Question 1: If God created neither the body nor the physical world, what did He create?

The brief answer is spirit. We have already mentioned this when we quoted the Course's reinterpretation of the Biblical statement about the creation of man. There we learned that "God did create spirit in His Own Thought and of a quality like to His Own" (3.5,7:3).

However, there is much more that needs to be said about the nature of God's creations. First, we need to look at the Course's teachings on the nature of God Himself as a perfect being. What are the attributes of a perfect being? Chapter 4 will be devoted to answering this question.

Then in Chapter 5 we will discuss what the creations of God must be like given that God has the attributes of perfection we described in Chapter 4. We shall see that the Course's conception of what God created is quite different than the one found in traditional Western religions.

Finally, in Chapter 6 we set forth some of the more significant implications of the conclusions we reached in chapter 4 and 5. We will focus particularly on those implications related to the possibility of attaining true and lasting peace, joy, and happiness, both in this world and the next.

Question 2: If God created neither the body nor the world, who did?

Part 3 will be devoted to dealing with this question about origins. In chapter 7, we will discuss the nature of the self that both attacks and suffers. This chapter includes a discussion of the conditions necessary for the possibility of experiencing evil. Chapter 8 contains the direct answer to the question, who made the world? In this chapter we set forth the sequence of events which led to the making of the body and the world. In Chapter 9, the last chapter of Part 3, we will attempt to answer what is perhaps the most powerful objection that can be raised against our explanation of the origin of the world of bodies.

Question 3: Given that God Himself does not know about this world, its inhabitants, or their suffering, in what sense, then, is Divine Help available to us?

This third question points to the most difficult problem for any theology that holds to an uncompromising view of God's perfection. If it is impossible that God as a Perfect Being could be creator of this world, and thus impossible that He be aware of us who suffer in this world, then what hope for salvation can we possibly have? Is there any way that we can receive divine love, at least in some form that would be helpful, whether in the form of guidance, or comfort, or forgiveness?

In Chapter 10 we answer this question. There we set forth the sense in which Divine Help *is* available to us. In this same chapter we also deal with the issue of free will. We make a significant distinction between true freedom and freedom of choice. We will see that Miracle Theodicy's understanding of the free will with which God endowed His creations is quite different than the understanding of freedom found in the other theodicies we discussed in chapter 2.

In Chapter 11, we show how our solution to the logical problem of evil provides the foundation for teaching that forgiveness is *always* justified, and attack is *never* justified. This chapter also makes clear why forgiveness is the solution to the practical problem of evil.

We turn now to Part Two, which provides an answer to our first question, the one concerning the nature of God and His creations.

PART TWO

GOD AND HIS CREATION:
YOUR PERFECT SELF

PART TWO

GOD AND HIS CREATION:
YOUR PERFECT SELF

This [the extension of the joint Will of the
Father and of the Son] is perfect creation by
the perfectly created, in union with the
perfect Creator.
A Course in Miracles (8.3,3:3)

Introduction to Part Two

From Part One we learned that our *conception* of
God is crucial in responding to the argument from evil
(AFE). In other words, how we conceive God, including
what attributes we conceive Him to have, and what we
conceive these attributes to imply, determines whether we
are trapped by the AFE, or can escape from its conclusion
instead.

In chapter 3 we presented our way of escaping the
conclusion. Although at this point we have indeed refuted
the AFE, some serious questions remain. One of these

questions is: given that God did not create the world we see, what did He create? And a corollary question is: if God does not know about this world and its evil, what does He know?

We said that God is omniscient because He is perfectly aware of everything that is real and true. And only what God created is real. Well, what is it that God created? What is it that is real and true? What is it that God knows? These questions are all the same. Here in Part Two of this book we will answer this question.

Part Two is organized as follows: In Chapter 4 we discuss the attributes of God as a perfect being. The attributes which *ACIM* ascribes to God are similar to, if not the same as, those which Classical Theodicy has for centuries ascribed to God as a "perfect being".

In Chapter 5 we examine the nature of God's creation; not only the nature of what God creates but the nature of God's creative activity as well. We will see that the nature of what God creates logically follows from the nature of God Himself. In short, since God is perfect, everything God creates is perfect as well.

Thus, even though the list of attributes Miracle Theodicy ascribes to God is in close agreement with the list offered by Classical Theodicy, the two theodicies, nevertheless, are quite different because they draw different implications from these attributes, especially with respect to what God creates. For, as we have seen already, Classical Theodicy maintains that God created the physical cosmos, whereas Miracle Theodicy maintains not only that God *did not* create the physical cosmos, but that He *could not* have, given that He is a perfect being with all the attributes of perfection.

It is in chapter 5, then, that we offer the most direct answer to the first of the three questions we raised at the end of chapter 3.

In Chapter 6 we will examine some of the implications of the idea that everything God created is perfect like Himself, particularly those which provide the theoretical foundation for forgiveness, the one choice we need make in order to escape from all loss, grief, pain, suffering and fear of death.

4

GOD IS A PERFECT BEING

What is a perfect being? It is that than which
none greater can be thought.
St. Anselm (1033-1109)

In chapter three we presented and discussed the key
idea which provides our solution to the problem of evil;
namely, *God does not know about the evil in the world.* This
is true because God did not create the world. God knows
only what He creates, and only what God creates is real and
true. Only the real is knowable.

In this chapter we will explore the attributes which
the Course ascribes to this God Whose creations are eternal,
and therefore are the only things real.

Traditionally God has been said to be "a perfect
being". Philosophers of religion have long agreed with this
notion of God. The idea is that if any being or reality is
worthy to be called "God", it is because that being is perfect.
The Course agrees with this. In fact, all of the Course's
essential teachings can be seen as conclusions which

logically follow from its fundamental teaching that God is a perfect being.

What Does It Mean To Be
A Perfect Being?

For centuries theologians have accepted and used St. Anselm's definition of a perfect being. Anselm defines a perfect being as: "that than which none greater can be conceived."

A few comments on Anselm's definition will be helpful. First, we point to what it does *not* say. It does not say that a perfect being is one which is merely greater than *any other being* we have seen. For example, we might show great respect for space beings or "extraterrestrials" who happened to come to our planet. We may even consider their leader a "God" and love, worship, and obey him or her because of his or her obvious superiority to us. He or she may be the greatest being we have ever seen.

This is not exactly what Anselm means by a perfect being. To say that God is a perfect being, does not mean merely that God is a "supreme being" or the most superior being. The idea of being "supreme" *in itself* is not what is meant by "perfect". It may be true that a perfect being is also the supreme being, but being the supreme being does not in itself imply perfection. Supremacy, then, in itself, does not quite catch the full meaning of "perfect". Perfect means having and being everything real and good without limit, and lacking nothing.

I also want to make explicit at least two things Anselm's statement implies which may not be obvious on first reading. First, that as far as our discussion of a perfect being is concerned a perfect being is one that we *conceive.*

This means that we *logically construct* it. And this is true regardless of the sources we use as aids in constructing our concept of God as a perfect being. The source may be our personal experience, or it may be what we read in great and inspiring literature, which may include "holy scriptures", the writings of well respected theologians and philosophers, poets and novelists, saints and mystics. It may be psychic sources like the Edgar Cayce or Seth readings, or the works of Rudolf Steiner and the like. Or it may be *A Course in Miracles* as is the case here. Or finally, it may be a combination of all of these. Regardless of the sources which may serve as aids in our conception of God, it is still true that while we seem to live in this world our idea of God is something we *conceive* God to be.

This point is especially significant in dealing with the topic of this book. Anselm's definition requires that the being we conceive God to be should be *the greatest that can be conceived*. Some philosophers of religion have dubbed this perfect reality or perfect being as the "GCB", the "Greatest Conceivable Being".

Secondly, it is important to notice that it is *we* who do the conceiving, regardless of any sources we use. Philosophers of religion would agree that in His reality, or as He defines Himself, God is very likely to be even greater than any concept of Him we can construct. But while acknowledging that this is so, it is still true that the God we speak of is an idea of God as *our minds* conceive Him to be. Anselm's definition merely requires that our concept of this being be the *greatest* we can conceive. God, then, must be the GCB - the Greatest Conceivable Being; He must be "that than which none greater can be conceived".

This means that if we presently can conceive of a being greater than one we have conceived in the past, or greater than one conceived by someone else, we should accept the newer conception of God, and discard the older one. This, of course, is what most of us do presently. How many of us have the same concept of God we had when we were 6 years old? Or 14? or 21? or 35? or even 5 years ago? Hopefully, our newer conception of God is closer to the GCB, for it will be closer to what God really is. It is, then, the GCB that we refer to in using the word "*God*".

The Criteria For Conceiving
A Perfect Being

No one has ever seen a perfect being. So describing God's attributes is a process different from that of describing the properties of something in this world, like a mountain, a tree, a dog, or even a human, wherein one makes empirical observations and then describes the characteristics of the thing observed. No, it is not like that at all. Rather we come to affirm the qualities of a perfect being by *conceiving* the attributes which the GCB would have.

Since no one in this world can literally see God, since He is not an object of the body's senses, we cannot use empirical observation as the basis of our description of God's attributes. What basis, then, can we use? Most if not all contemporary philosophers of religion agree that one of the criteria for an acceptable concept of God is that of *consistency*. Our conception of God must be internally consistent; it cannot be self-contradictory. We cannot say one thing about God and then turn around and say another thing which contradicts the first thing we said. All the attributes on our list of attributes must be consistent with one another; they must be able to "stand together", with no one attribute lacking agreement with another.

A second criterion is that our concept of God should be relevant to our experience, either directly or indirectly. It should have some implication for our daily lives and choices. The point here is that our idea or concept of God should have some influence on our values and our thinking, on our feeling and experience. Our concept of God may explain or illuminate our experience, or it may help change our experience and perception of ourselves and others.

If our concept of God as a perfect being would have no implications for our lives here in this world, then there is no value in conceiving it, unless we merely enjoyed playing with words and ideas in a game of make believe. The goal of such a game would be simply to conceive of the greatest being you can think of without contradiction, and then your opponent would point out at least one contradiction in your concept, and he would win a point. Then it would be his turn to build his conception of the GCB, and the game goes on.

Recognizing that we are not merely playing a game of words and ideas, let us turn to a discussion of the Course's conception of God as a perfect being. It is more than a game. Those who are familiar with other theodicies will recognize the similarities and differences between the attributes the Course ascribes to God and those ascribed by Augustine, Anselm, and Aquinas, and many other traditional Christian philosophers and theologians. For the sake of keeping this book short, while at the same time giving its subject matter fair treatment, I will not point out these similarities and differences unless it serves a purpose beyond such a purely academic one.

The Personal Attributes of God
As A Perfect Being

I have already stated that the Course agrees that God is a perfect being. And it would accept the idea that a perfect being "is one than which none greater can be conceived". The Course would also agree that our concept should be internally consistent, and would also agree that God, as He really is, is beyond what words can say. Nevertheless, God must be *at least as great* as we can consistently conceive Him to be. In other words, words and concepts themselves will not give us a complete understanding of what God is. Nor do they give us direct awareness, knowledge, or experience of God. But a proper *concept* of God can serve to correct an improper one. And this is crucial for our purpose here, namely, the construction of a theodicy. And, in fact, the Course itself implies that it is crucial for attaining happiness while we are using bodies and seem to be living in the world of time, space, and bodies.

As we shall see in Part Four, a proper *concept of God* is of great value in bringing us peace and joy in our daily lives. It can eliminate the doubt and fear, loneliness and misery which come from a mistaken concept of God. The word "God" appears 3638 times in the Course. This does not include the many pronouns and other terms like "Creator" or "Father" or "Mind" which refer to God. The word "God" appears throughout the Course in many and varied contexts. But in no one place does the Course simply list and discuss all the qualities it attributes to God. Nor does it offer only one definition of the attributes it ascribes to God. However, everything it says is consistent with everything else it says about God. As mentioned in the Introduction of this book, the Course itself is not a book on theodicy. And thus it does not explicitly focus on God's attributes with the aim of refuting the argument from evil.

Thus the list of attributes offered here, as well as the "definitions", or various understandings of these attributes, are gleaned from different places in the Course. The following attributes are ones I have extracted from the Course, and which I consider crucial for understanding the solution to the problem of evil found in its teachings.

Let us turn, then, to listing and describing the various attributes of God as a perfect being; "a being than which none greater can be conceived."

Happiness. God is perfectly happy. This is not a surprise. For what value is there in being "perfect" if you are not happy? A perfect being must be perfectly happy or It would not *be* perfect. Can you conceive of a being who is "perfect", yet unhappy and sad? A suffering, fearful, angry, and sorrowful being is not a perfect being.

God is perfectly happy because His perfectly loving will is done. And He knows It is done. As a perfect being, then, God is perfectly happy and full of joy. As the Course puts it, "God, being Love, is also Happiness" (L103). God not only *has* happiness; God *is* Happiness! In fact, the Course teaches that, in reality, at the spiritual level of experience, *having* and *being* are one, they are the same.

Mind. God has a Mind. God is Mind. In the previous paragraph while discussing happiness as an attribute of God we mentioned or implied other qualities and characteristics. We shall list and discuss each attribute separately even though it has already been mentioned. It will soon be obvious that it is difficult, if not impossible, to discuss one attribute without mentioning another since they all imply one another, they all come together and go together. This is what we would expect if all God's attributes must be consistent with one another.

To say that God is Happiness already implies other things. In other words, we can deduce from the concept of happiness other qualities and characteristics which can be attributed to God. One of them is Mind. Since happiness means "a state of being happy" we can ask, *what* is in a state of being happy? The Course's answer would be "a mind".

So the Course teaches that God is Mind. He is a reality that has awareness or is in a state of being aware. To say that God is aware is not enough. He is Self-aware. He is aware of Himself. He knows Himself. God is not like a stone or a marble - assuming that a stone or a marble have no self-awareness. God, being perfect, knows Himself perfectly. He also knows Himself *as perfect*, that is, as having everything without limit, and lacking nothing.

Sometimes the Course uses simply the word "Mind", with a capital "M", to refer to God. At times, in this book, we too will follow this practice of capitalizing words that refer to God or His creations or Sons.

Thought. As a Mind God has Thoughts. In fact, it is His Thoughts Which forever secure His perfect happiness. His Thoughts are His creations; they are extensions of Himself which are like Him. The Course uses the phrase "God's extensions" as another phrase for "God's creations", "God's Thoughts", "God's Effects", or "God's Sons". God's creations or extensions, are *in* His Mind. They never leave His Mind, for "ideas leave not their source" (26.7,4:7).

Will. God has a Will. Will is of the Mind. We can and do speak of "God's Will" or "the Will of God". The Course is no different. It has a lot to say about God's Will.

There are at least two meanings of the term "Will" in the phrase "God's Will" as the Course uses it. The term is used as a verb or a noun, just as it is commonly used in English.

Used as a verb, as in "I will this", the term "will" refers to the mental act of "wanting", or "desiring". We "want" or "desire" something. We will it.

But the term "will" is often used as a noun as well. When so used it can refer not only to an aspect of mind in the sense that will is of the mind, but also to *"the thing"* the mind wants or wills, and then *has* when its will is done.

It can refer to the result of my will. In other words, to "the thing" or state of mind that I will or want. For example, I could say, "I want to be happy". I could just as well say, "happiness in my will", or "my will is happiness for myself".

If my will is done, then, I have happiness, I have this state of mind. In this sense my "will" is the thing, or quality, or situation, or state of mind which I want to be true, or to exist, or to occur.

"What is God's Will for me?" you may ask. And the author of the Course answers, "perfect happiness". In this example, happiness is the state of mind God wills to be true of you, or real for you. As we shall discuss later, the question is whether you share God's Will for happiness for you, and for everyone.

It is in this second sense that the Course says, "God's Will *is* Thought" (8.6,7:3). In other words, God's Thoughts *are* His will. They are the things He wills. They are *what* He wills. They are *what* He wants to be real, to exist, to be true. And, because God's Will is done, God's Thoughts *are* what is true and real. So the Course says, "You *are* the Will of God" (7.7,10:1). You are What God wills, you are what God wants to be true, to exist, to be real. You are God's Thought. You are God's Creation. Your are God's Effect. You are God's Son. You are God's extension of Himself. As He created you, His Son, You are what He is.

Lesson 101 states, "God's Will for me is perfect happiness." Your happiness is God's Will. And as He created you, you are perfectly happy, for God's Will is done. We will discuss this in more detail in the next chapter where we talk specifically about the nature of God's creations.

Experience. God has experience. God experiences. Experience is awareness and feeling. This means that God has awareness and feeling. Mind has awareness and feeling. God is aware of the perfect oneness of Himself and His creations, because He created Them one with Him. *Joy* is the main term the Course uses to describe God's feeling. In this sense, Love *is* joy. Joy is the feeling that comes with loving and being loved. You cannot have the one without the other. "There is no difference between love and joy" (5.IN,2:3) The

Course calls love an *emotion*. And joy is an essential aspect of love. Pure happiness and joy is what God experiences in sharing Himself with all His creations. It is also what you experience when you share yourself with all your creations when you co-create with your Creator.

Emotion. God has emotion. God emotes. The Course uses the term *emotion* in its etymological sense of a "moving out" or "giving away". It actually refers to the Mind expressing or extending Itself. When you are emoting you are expressing your self and your state of mind. You are attempting to share yourself, your thoughts desires and feelings. God emotes in this sense. He shares Himself with all His creations. He shares His Thought and Feeling, His Mind and Will, and His power to create. He shares His peace and joy and love and happiness. All this He shares with all His creations by extending His Spirit, His Self, His Thought of What He is.

God's creations, as we already mentioned, *are* extensions of Himself, and thus they are what He is. The Course says love is the only real emotion, because it is the only emotion God has. In this sense, to create is to love. God creating is God loving. And since God is Love, God creating is Love loving.

Creator. God is a Creator. God is the creator of all that is. Thus God has the power to create. Mind creates. Mind causes to be. Since God is perfect He is a perfect creator. And as a perfect creator God creates perfect creations. In the Course's language, God's act of creating is virtually synonymous with His willing and emoting. God's creating is God's extending of His Self. This is how God creates. He extends Himself; His extensions are His creations. We will discuss this in more detail in chapter 5.

Knowledge. God has knowledge. Pure Mind knows. God, being perfect, has perfect knowledge. He knows all His creations perfectly. He knows all reality. There is no limit or lack to His knowledge. God knows everything that is knowable, everything that is true, everything that is real. He knows everything that exists in reality, in His creation, in Heaven. He knows everything He creates, and knows of nothing He does not create, for what He does not create is unreal.

Love. God has love. God is Love. God loves. Being perfect, God loves Himself and His creations perfectly. There is no lack or limit to God's love. God *is* Love. "There is no love but God's" (L127). To say God's love is perfect is to say that God wills only happiness for all His creations. In His perfect love God wants to share everything He has and is with all His creations. This makes all His creations one with Him. Thus the Course says, "love's meaning lies in oneness" (L127,3:3). God wants to share everything He is with His Son. God wants to share everything He has and is with You. His Will for You is perfect happiness. God's love, indeed, is perfect; it has no lack or limit. Nor is it mixed with its opposite. His love is pure and unambiguous. God is pure love and happiness, pure peace and joy.

It must be clear by now that the term "love" as used by the Course is conceived from various perspectives. As a "thing" or being, Love is a Loving Mind; as an act of mind or mental act, love is giving everything to everyone; as a thought, love is the idea that everyone has everything; as a state of mind, love is happiness; as a condition of mind, love is peace; as a feeling, love is joy; as a relationship, love is oneness, including sameness and equality as well as unity. As an awareness it is the awareness of perfect oneness. In this sense Love is Heaven, and love is all there is.

Power. God has power. Being perfect, God's has perfect power. There is no lack or limit to His power. His power is the power to create. His power to create is so perfect, so without limit, that He can give everything He has to all His creations. He wants to do this. And He can. In other words, God, being perfectly loving, wills to share everything He has with all His creations, and, being perfectly powerful, God can share everything He has with all His creations.

Has He done it? We need another attribute to affirm that He has. Timelessness. God is timeless. So, "God's Will is done" (13.11,5:4). God does not have to wait on time for His Will to be fulfilled. It is already accomplished in reality, in His creation, in eternity, in Heaven.

According to the Course, then, God has already, in reality and in truth, given everything He has to all His creations. This is His Will. And His Will is done. You, as God's creation, already, now and forever, have what God *wants* to give you and *can* give you, because God is timeless, changeless and eternal, and so are you as God created you. God's Will is done. It cannot be changed or opposed. This is what it means to say God is perfectly powerful. And given that God is also perfectly loving, you as God created you, have and are everything God is. This is eternally true and is therefore true *now*. For what is eternal must be now. You simply have forgotten the truth -- but only for a time. You will remember. It is the purpose of the Course to help you do so.

In the next chapter we will say more about the Self God created you as; in Part Three, how you forgot it; and in Part Four, how to remember it.

As I mentioned God's perfect power not only means that His will is done, but also that His will cannot be opposed. As the Course puts it "God's Will is wholly without opposite" (Q20,6:2), and again, "Nothing God created can oppose His Will" (8.4,6:1). There simply cannot be, in reality, in eternity, in truth, in God's creation, in Heaven, anything opposed to God's Will. Nor can there be anything that can change it.

God's perfect power also means that God is the cause and creator of everything that is, everything that is real or that exists in reality. God wills or causes all things. Nothing exists in reality that was not willed, or caused, or created by God. If there seems to be something that God did not create, this "something" is not real. It *cannot* be real. It must be illusion. For as we saw in the last chapter, "nothing God did not create is real". It must, therefore, be illusion. It may seem real or true, but it is not.

So far, then, in our conception of a perfect reality we have conceived of God as a Mind Who shares everything He has and is with all His creations. Because He is perfectly loving, He wants to do this. Because He is perfectly powerful, He can do this. And because He is timeless and changeless He has done this. And because He is perfectly knowing He knows that all His creations have everything because He shares everything with Them. Thus God knows all His creation as perfectly happy like Himself.

The Metaphysical Attributes of God As A Perfect Being

At this point we can say that God is a perfectly happy and creative Mind Whose knowledge, power, and love are perfect. But there are a few more attributes we need to discuss in order to complete our conception of "that than which no greater can be thought".

I call the following set of attributes "metaphysical" for two reasons. First, to distinguish them from "personal" attributes. The terms used for the following attributes do not in themselves connote something personal, although it may be true that only something "personal" or mental or spiritual could have these attributes. Secondly, I call these attributes "metaphysical" because they are attributes that

normally do not apply to anything physical, material, or
bodily; or to anything phenomenal or perceptual or worldly.
They apply to what is "meta-physical" or "beyond the
physical" or to what transcends the physical and even the
perceptual.

The attributes to be discussed in this section are the
following: eternal, changeless, timeless, formless, and
limitless. I will discuss them in order, giving a brief
explanation of each as it is applied to a perfect being. Later,
we will see the full implications of these attributes as we
focus on God's creation(s) in the next chapter.

Eternal. God is eternal. This means that God is
without beginning or end. He is always and forever. God
cannot die. God simply is. And God remains forever as He
is. God's eternity includes His timelessness. It not only
implies that God has no beginning or ending *in time*, but that
God is in no way governed by or subject to time. Time is not
an aspect of God's experience. There is no temporal before
or after to His Mind or His Thoughts or His knowledge or
His Will. There is no temporality involved in His loving act
of creation. Everything God creates is eternal and eternally
present to God always. Nothing of God has a temporal
before or after. Eternity is God's reality. Nothing temporal is
God's reality. If there is any sense in which the idea of
eternity can be stated in terms of time it is that "eternity is
one time, its only dimension being "always" (9.6,7:1). And
"The only aspect of time that is eternal is *now*" (5.3,6:5).

Changeless. God is changeless. Nothing about God
changes, has changed, or is changeable. He remains always
the same forever. He is never different than what He always
is. He is not one thing at one time and another thing at
another time. He is always perfect, and always perfectly
creating His perfect creations, always and forever extending
His Self, His Thought, His joy and happiness. Nor do His
attributes change. His perfect love does not change. His

perfect power does not change. His perfect knowledge does not change. His perfect creation does not change. His perfect happiness does not change. He is forever and always happy and full of joy eternally sharing all He has and is with all His creation.

It makes sense that God is changeless since by definition He is perfect. If God changed He would have to change either from being imperfect to perfect, or from being perfect to imperfect. If He changed in the first way then He was not perfect in the first place. And if He changed in the second way then He is not perfect now and forever. If God is perfect and were to change, He would have to change from a condition of having everything and lacking nothing, to *not* having everything and lacking something. If He changed He would no longer be perfectly knowing, perfectly powerful, perfectly loving, and perfectly happy. Thus if He changed He would not be "God"; He would not be a perfect being. Changelessness, then, must be an attribute of God as a perfect being.

Timeless. God is timeless. We have mentioned this already. The idea of God being timeless is consistent with the idea of God being eternal and changeless. "Time is inconceivable without change" (15.1,10:1). God is non-temporal. There is no chronological before or after in God's experience. God's experience is beyond time. Neither His knowledge, His love, His power, nor His happiness is subject to laws of time.

God does not know one thing at one time and the opposite thing at another time, like we do. For example, God does not know that George Washington is president of the United States, and then at another time know that George Washington is not president of the United States. God's knowledge is non-temporal, changeless, and eternal. God's reality, His creation, His Heaven, is timeless; it has no past or future. Time does not apply to anything of God. What He lovingly creates, wills, and knows is beyond time.

Formless. God is formless, without form. God Himself has no form. His knowledge is pure and formless. There is a close connection between God's formlessness and His limitlessness (the next attribute we will discuss). To be perfect is to lack nothing and have everything without limit. Because God is without limit, He cannot be a form or have a form. He must be without form, formless. This means that God is not a body, nor does He have a body. God Himself, God *as God*, has no bodily form. God is pure Mind, or pure Thought. God is not material or physical or bodily. God is not a mind with a body. God Himself neither perceives nor is God Himself perceivable. He only knows and is known. God is not something that can be perceived or seen with the body's eyes, for the body's eyes see only form and God is formless.

Because God is formless He is not spacial. He is non-spacial. Space concepts do not apply to God as they do to us who experience a physical world. He is not a body nor is He like a body which can be limited to one place at a time. Even heaven is not a place in a spacial sense. "Heaven" certainly is not a term which refers to a place in the spacial sense; it is not the sky or something up in the sky. Heaven, as the Course uses the term, is simply "awareness of perfect oneness, and the knowledge that there is nothing else; nothing outside this oneness, and nothing else within" (18.6,1:6). Heaven, then, is a kind of awareness, a kind of state of mind, a kind of experience, the experience of perfect happiness. It is the state of a mind that is timeless, changeless, and eternal, formless and limitless, perfectly knowing, loving, and powerful.

Limitless. God is limitless, without limit. He is infinite, and not finite. As we stated above, limitlessness and formlessness go together. God's limitlessness entails He must be pure mind not a mind with a body. But His limitlessness applies to His other attributes as well. His knowledge, power, and love are limitless. And His happiness and joy have no limit. God's limitlessness implies His timelessness. He is not limited by time. God is not limited by space. God is not limited in any way that a body might limit a mind. The Course says the body places a limit on awareness. There is no such limit on God's awareness. God is perfectly aware of everything that is true, and nothing He does not know is real or true. He knows only what He wills for only what He wills or creates is real. The Course also says that God's creations are limitless. There is no limit to the number of God's creations. His Thoughts are infinite in number. In this sense too, God is limitless.

General Remarks On The Attributes of God As A Perfect Being

Before we move to the next chapter to discuss what these attributes imply about the nature of God's creative activity and the nature of what He creates, I want to make a few general remarks about these attributes.

Notice that what I have called the "metaphysical" attributes of God, namely, eternal, changeless, timeless, formless, and limitless, are terms which *deny* something of God. Theologians have long recognized that much of what we say about God is stated in negative terms. This way of talking about God is called the *via negativa*, or "negative way". In speaking of God's attributes we use terms which deny the attributes of the things we see in the world. For example, we perceive that things in this world, including our own bodies, have limits. Then we deny that God has limits. So we say God is limitless. We notice that all "living" things we see in this world seem to die; they corrupt and decay, and are no more. We see this and we say to our self, "a perfect being would not be like that". A perfect being would not die. Its life would not end. Its life would be eternal. A perfect being would be infinite, without end or limit. It would live forever. Thus we say of God that He is infinite. He is not finite.

This is the way our thinking moves with regard to the other metaphysical attributes as well. Things in this world change, so we deny that God changes. We say that a perfect being is changeless. We see that we, and all other things in this world, are limited by and subject to time. A perfect being would not be limited by or governed by time. So we say that God is timeless. We say that time does not apply to His personal attributes. His knowledge is not governed by time. His will is not restricted by time. His love is not changed by time.

We notice that everything in the world has form or is a form. It is limited and has boundaries. There is a place where it ends and something else begins. Its form seems to make it the kind of thing it is, and makes it different and separate from other things which too have form. So we say that God, Who is limitless, does not have a form. He must be formless.

Another way of putting this is to say that everything we see in this physical world is an opposite to God. Very generally we could say God is perfect and everything of this world is imperfect. If the beings in this world have "positive" qualities they have them to a limited degree. But God has them to an unlimited degree, or better, there are no degrees or levels to God at all. God is "degree-less", "level-less", limitless.

For example, humans in this world seem to love, but their love has limits. In fact, sometimes their "love" seems to turn into its opposite, fear or hate. This is not true of God. People seem to know, but their knowledge has limits; they don't know everything. People have power, but their power seems to be limited. It seems they cannot do everything they want to do, or to have everything they want to have. They seem happy at times, but their happiness can suddenly change to unhappiness and misery. These things are not true of God. Finally, the beings we see in this world are physical or bodily, they are spacial and temporal. None of this is true of God.

I have called the first set of attributes "personal". I want to make clear what I mean, and what I do not mean, by naming these attributes of God "personal attributes". For by naming them as such, I am implying that in some sense God can be called "a personal God".

By "personal" I simply mean that God has some of the qualities or characteristics that we attribute to "persons". We say that persons experience, they are aware and have feeling. We say that they are minds, or have a mind and will. When we call something "a person" we usually imply that it has thoughts and feelings, purposes and emotion. We say of persons that they are creative, and that they know and love and will. We say they are happy or unhappy. We don't call a stone or a marble a "person" because we do not think of them as being happy or unhappy. Happiness and unhappiness are terms which do not properly apply to stones or marbles. Since we consider persons or minds greater than non-persons or mindless things, we attribute to God the positive attributes of a person.

Thus I call God "personal" in this sense. It is the sense in which the terms used to describe the attributes of a "person" or a "mind" can be used to speak of God, even though when they are applied to God they are not applied with exactly the same meaning as when applied to human persons. For example, we can say that God, as a Mind "thinks" or has "thoughts", but the manner of God's thinking may be different than the manner of our thinking, and the nature of His Thoughts may be different than that of ours. In this sense, then, God is a "personal" being in the Course's view. The important difference is that God, being perfect, is perfectly knowing, perfectly loving, perfectly willing, and perfectly happy. His Mind, Thoughts, and Will are perfect. He is a perfect Creator, perfectly creating perfect creations.

When we say that God is personal in this sense, we intend to deny that God is "impersonal". In some thought systems God is not thought of as a "personal" being, but as an impersonal force or energy. The term "impersonal" as used is such systems implies that this energy is not aware of itself, nor does it have feeling, knowledge, or purpose. It is as if love and happiness are not terms that are correctly applied to God conceived of as impersonal in this sense.

Such thought systems tend to identify this impersonal God with the energy physicists talk about. The "oneness" of everything is understood merely as everything being constituted by the same atomic or subatomic particles or waves or physical energy, rather than an awareness of the perfect oneness of all minds and thoughts.

The Course does not identify God with the physical energy or forces of the physical universe. In fact, I think it is fair to say that the Course denies any identification of God Himself with the energy or forces of the physical universe. If there is anything close in other thought systems to the way the Course speaks of God Himself it would be the way Aristotle speaks of God as a "Self-Thinking Thought" or Plotinus speaks of God as "the One". In other words, in the Course's view, God, the Creator, *totally transcends* the physical world. The physical universe, and what happens in it, including human history, has no part in the experience of God Himself, in the experience of God, the Father of all. He is totally unaffected by it because He is totally unaware of it.

If all this is true, and I believe it is, then it is easy to see why our solution to the problem of evil is entirely different than any solution which has hitherto been explicitly set forth in the literature of Christian philosophy or theology.

All this can be put another way. The Course talks about God in terms a psychologist might use rather than in terms a physicist would use. For example, the term "mind" or "minds" appears 1813 times in the Course, whereas the term "energy" or "energies" appears only five times, and not once in these five times is it used in the same sense it is used in theoretical physics. This reflects the fact that, in the Course's thought system, "mind" is the "basic unit" of all reality. Thus "mind" is the basic unit of discourse. "Mind" is most often *the thing the Course is talking about*. It is constantly referring to your mind and God's Mind, for Mind is *what God is* and what you are as God created you.

In other words, the Course's teachings center around the mind; the structure and the function of the mind; the mind's activity, its purposes or goals, its thoughts and feelings, its awareness, its perceptions, and its state. This is its central concern. According to the Course, the mind's experience is determined by the thoughts the mind thinks and holds as true, especially the thought of what it (the mind itself) is. In fact, according to the Course, the most essential thought in any thought system is what the mind which made the thought system thinks *it* is. In other words, the foundational thought in your belief system, or the thought system you live by, is the thought you think and hold of what you are. Furthermore, every decision and response you make is determined by what you think you are.

Thus, for the Course, reality *is* mind and *in* Mind. Specifically, reality is the Mind of God and His Thoughts Which He created like Himself. *God and His Thoughts, then, are the totality of reality.*[1] There *is* nothing else.

There is another meaning often given to the term "personal" which I want to talk about here. The term is commonly used by some Christians when they say they believe in "a personal God". This is the sense in which God is thought of as "a person" who is *separate and different* from other persons. In other words, God is spoken of as one among many persons who themselves are separate and different from God and from each other.

In this view of God as personal, these "other persons" are not what God is. They have a different nature than God does, and God knows them as beings who have a nature different from His Own. Furthermore, these other persons or souls will *always* be different than what God is. Each one will always be an "individual soul" that is a whole in itself different and separate from other individual souls. Even in Heaven they will be different from God and one another, for each one is a "unique" creation of God. None of them will ever be exactly the same thing that God is.

When we think of God as "a being" or "a person" who is up in heaven observing the rest of us down here on earth, we are thinking of God as personal in this sense. He is a person separate and different from us but "watching us from a distance" as a once popular song puts it.

The Course considers this a mistaken concept of God. It denies that God is personal in this sense. In fact, it maintains that it is essential that such a concept of God be eliminated from our thinking. For the Course, reality does not consist of separate and different persons with God as one among the many different kinds or levels of beings. All God's creations are the same and equal and joined in one nature or Self. They are all alike and they are all perfectly like God. They are all one with each other and with God as well. They share His life as one. "There is one life, and that I share with God" (L167). Would a perfectly loving God create any differently? And is it not possible that a perfectly knowing and powerful God be able to create this way?

There is, however, one sense in which God as a Mind *is* something different and separate from us as persons.

It is the sense in which *we believe* that He is different and separate from us. In other words, God *is* Something separate and different from *what we mistakenly believe we are*. Each of us believes he is a *human*, a mind and a body. As such we are something different and separate from God. Our ego-body is not like God or one with God. It is separate and different from Him. It is not something He created. We who mistakenly think we are ego-bodies are, *as ego-bodies*, separate and different from God. God is Something separate and different from ego-bodies. He is separate and different from our false thought of what we are. But when we think and hold the true Thought of what we are, we are not separate from Him nor is He separate from us.

In other words, we have a tendency to think of our self as a body or at best as a mind and a body. We think that a body is an essential and real part of what we really are, and even that God originally created us possessed of a body. But this is a mistaken idea of what we really are as God created us. Given this mistake, however, it is inevitable that we will think of God as a person separate and different from us, and in so doing we will say that we believe in "a personal God", all the time thinking of God as "a person" different and separate from us, with whom we have "a personal relationship" of one kind or another. In this way of thinking of God as a personal being we do not think of ourselves as having a relationship of perfect oneness with God in which we are equal, the same and united with Him. We would not thing of our relationship with God as being one which would support such statements as "what God is, is what I am, because my Father created His Son perfect like Himself. And I am His Son."

This leads us to the topic of our true nature as God created us, a topic we will discuss in the next chapter. The discussion will take place within the framework of asking what kind of creations a perfect being *must* create, given that a perfect being has the attributes we listed and described in this chapter.

Notes

1. Readers who are familiar with the history of philosophy will recognize that the metaphysics of the Course is in the tradition of "idealism". Idealistic philosophers answer the question "what ultimately is real?" by saying that only mind and ideas are real. Everything is an idea or a mind in which ideas exist. These philosophers, then, hold that matter or bodies are unreal and do not really exist other than as thoughts or ideas in the mind.

It is beyond the scope of this book to enter into the philosophical debate over the strengths and weaknesses of idealism as opposed to realism, or idealism as opposed to materialism, or monism as opposed to dualism. I simply state here that any questions which may arise in such discussions find a satisfactory answer in the Course itself. This may become clear as we proceed with our presentation of its teachings.

It may already be clear to some readers that the Course's brand of idealism is different from that of the famous German and British idealist, i.e., the philosophical systems of Hegel, Fichte, Shelling, Berkeley, Bradley, Royce, Brightman, and the like. Here I mention one significant difference. Unlike German and British idealism, the course would *not say* that the world, or "nature and its laws," are *in the Mind of God* – as ideas or in any other sense.

The Course does teach, however, that the world you see is *in your mind*. It is not outside your mind. It seems to be outside your mind only because the mind is identifying with the body. However, although the world is in your mind, it is not in God's Mind; it is *in your mind apart from God's Mind.* In other words, like all idealistic thought systems, the Course would say that the world has no reality or existence other than its existing in a mind. But since it does not exist in God's Mind (since God did not create it), it is not "really real". The things of this world are only apparently real; they seem real to you, but they are mere appearances; they are ultimately unreal and thus are illusions, as is everything in a world of perception (vs. the realm of knowledge in which no Thoughts exist apart from God).

The world, which is in your mind apart from God's Mind (as a dream exists only in the mind of the dreamer) includes your body. The mind is not *in* the body. The body is *in* the mind (as a figure in the dream with which the dreamer identifies). The body is but a false idea or image of what you are, with which you as mind are temporarily identifying. This false self-identification is the basis of all your suffering.

This is a crucial teaching in the Course's account of *our experience* of evil, or attack and suffering. This teaching and its implications for our daily life will be discussed in great detail throughout Part Three and Part Four of this book.

One more thing should be mentioned. The Course obviously rejects epiphenomenalism, the theory of mind which holds that the mind is merely an "epiphenomenon", nothing more than the result of the functioning of a complex brain. Epiphenomenalism implies that when the brain stops functioning the mind "goes out of existence" since no mind exists where there is no brain. The Course rejects this theory of mind as well as the philosophical materialism with which it is closely associated.

5

GOD CREATED YOU PERFECT
LIKE HIMSELF

You have not only been fully created, but
have also been created perfect.
ACIM (2.1,1:3)

We turn now to a deeper examination of the Course's
teaching on the nature of God's creations. In this chapter we
give the most direct answer to the first question raised at the
end of chapter 3, namely, if God did not create the body and
the world, what did He create?

Keep in mind that what we are attempting to do in
this chapter is to represent in concepts and words a reality in
which there are no concepts and words. This reality cannot
be directly experienced while we still seem to be using a
body in this physical world. The reality we are attempting to
describe is not something that is perceivable but only
knowable. As the Course puts it: "No one on earth can grasp
what Heaven is, or what its one Creator really means"

(Q23,6:1). And since Heaven and its one Creator *is* reality, no one on earth can grasp what *reality* is.

The body represents a limit on our awareness, making us perceivers who are not directly aware of our function in Heaven as co-creators. Nevertheless, we can say enough about what God created to make it clear that a perfect being, although He did not create the physical world, did create *something*. We can also, despite our limited awareness, understand the idea that God is a *living* being, a *creative* being, a dynamic being, and that His creative activity is in fact a dynamic process. We can understand and accept these statements as true, even though while on earth, we cannot fully understand or directly experience God's activity of creating.

We can, for example, realize that even though God is changeless, this does not imply that He is merely "a static blob" -- as more than one conversational partner put it. After all, if God is said to be a perfect being Who is timeless, changeless, and eternal, and unaware of the world and the suffering of its inhabitants, we might be tempted to think He is a thing that does not "do" anything. We might be tempted to think that a being with such qualities is merely an inactive blob of stuff, rather than a dynamic and creative Mind Who thinks and is aware of His Thoughts Which increase His joy to no end.

The conception of God found in *A Course in Miracles* is not one of a static being. The idea of "changelessness" as applied to God simply means that He is forever the same as He always is. He is always and forever creating, in union with the Sonship, perfect creations like Himself. This creating is an eternal dynamic with no beginning and no ending; a dynamic activity which always remains the same. Creating is what God does, and this creating *is* His loving. It is a function He shares with all His Sons as co-creators. It is Their pure and unending joy.

Thus we can use concepts and words, as the Course most certainly does, to help us understand what a perfect Mind creates, although we as minds using bodies cannot fully grasp what Heaven and its one Creator really means. While we seem to be in this world of perception - a world of time, space, and bodies - our understanding of God and His creation is limited, yes, but nevertheless, we can make statements that are *in accord with* what His creation is; and we can recognize statements which *contradict* what it is.

Let us explore, then, what the Course does teach about God's creation. Although our discussion, of necessity, will be somewhat abstract this does not imply that it is meaningless. As the Course says, "Complete abstraction is the natural condition of the mind" (L161,2:1).

THE NATURE OF GOD'S CREATION(S)

A persistent theme runs through the Course: everything God creates is like Himself. In fact, God's creative activity is one of Self extension. "He [God] has no Thoughts except the Self extending" (21.5,6:2). As we have already mentioned, God is Mind. And Mind creates Thought. What God creates is Thought. This Thought is an extension of Himself. Since God's Thoughts share His power to create They also are minds, as God is a Mind. They too can create as God creates.

God is perfect. So what God creates is perfect. The Course teaches that God created "you". Thus you are perfect. As God created you, you are a mind which co-creates with God's Mind; you extend His Thought, His Self, His Being. In this sense you think with God. This is your function in Heaven. Thus You are a Thought of God, an extension of God. And your co-creations are extensions of your Self Which is perfect like God. What you are is What God is.

The phrase, "The perfect Son of God", then, is an accurate verbal expression of the true thought of what you are as God created you. Your true Self, then, is perfect in exactly the same sense that God is perfect. As the perfect Son of God you are perfectly knowing, perfectly powerful, and perfectly loving. And thus you are perfectly happy co-creating with God your Father - eternally, timelessly, changelessly.

The Course calls your true and eternal Self "the Christ".

> "Christ is God's Son as He created him. He is the Self we share, uniting us with one another, and with God as well. He is the Thought Which still abides within the Mind that is His Source" (Th6,1:1-2).

Another term the Course uses for a "Thought of God" is "spirit". "*Spirit* is the Thought of God which He created like Himself. The unified spirit is God's one Son, or Christ" (C1,1:3-4). Thus you are spirit, you are part of Christ. You and I, and all God's creations, as unified, are God's one Son, the Christ. Christ is the perfect Self we all share. Christ is your true identity, Jesus' true identity, and my true identity.

All of what we just said, then, is the answer to the first of the three questions we raised at the end of chapter three, namely, If God did not create the physical world and its human inhabitants, what did He create? God created Christ, His perfect Son. And you are His Son. As such you create perfect creations in union with your Father a perfect Creator. This function of "creating the perfect" is your function in Heaven. It is love, and it is pure joy and happiness. In fact, your free will was given you for your joy in creating the perfect.

Obviously, if God created you as His perfect Son, then God did not create you as a mind with a body; He did not create you as a "human". In Part Three of this book we will discuss how and why we seem to be something different than the Self Which God created us as.

God's Son is One in Nature, but Infinite in Number

Let's explore a little further what the Course says about the Son God created like Himself. When referring to God's creation as "God's Son", the Course sometimes uses the singular term "Son", sometimes the plural term "Sons". This is because there are an infinite number of God's Sons (Thoughts), but They all have the same nature, they are all united in one Self:

> It should especially be noted that God has only *one* Son. If all His creations are His Sons, every one must be an integral part of the whole Sonship. The Sonship in its oneness transcends the sum of its parts. (2.7,6:1-2)
> The Sonship is the sum of all that God created. (1.1,19:2)
> Creation is the sum of all God's Thoughts in number infinite and everywhere without all limit. (Th11,1:1)
> God, who encompasses all being, created beings who have everything individually, but who want to share it to increase their joy." (4.7,5:1)

When the Course uses the singular "Son" as a term for what God created it is generally referring to the Christ, the unified spirit, the unified Thoughts of God all of Which share one and the same nature or Self.

When the Course uses the plural "Sons" it points to the fact that, even though all God's Sons (Thoughts) are one in *nature*, they are infinite in *number*. "Creation is the sum of all God's Thoughts *in number infinite* and everywhere without all limit" (Th11,1:1) (my emphasis).

Thus, even though God's Thoughts (Sons, creations, effects, extensions) are *infinite in number* they also *share the same nature* or Self, and so they are God's *one* Son, perfect like Himself. Obviously, if all God's Son's are *perfect*, they would have to be *the same and equal*.

I already mentioned that all God's Thoughts are also *minds* because They share in God's power to create; they are like God in this respect because they are like God in every respect. Therefore you, as God created you, "are mind, in Mind, and purely mind" (L158,1:2). Thus, just as we can say there are an infinite number of Thoughts in God's Mind, we can say there are an infinite number of minds in God's Mind, and each and all of these minds are perfect like God Himself is perfect. Each has all the attributes of the whole. In fact, each part *is* the whole. And all these minds *as unified* are God's *one* Son, God's one Thought of What He is. They all are God's extension of Himself. And thus They all are what He is.

The Course also calls these infinite number of minds as unified "the Mind of Christ" (C1,1:2). The term "Mind of Christ", then, applies to all and to each mind as God created it. My true mind is Christ's Mind, Jesus' true mind is Christ's Mind; your true mind is the Mind of Christ. Christ is the true nature of everything God created. He is the Self shared by all God's creations. The Christ Mind creates in union with His Father. Thus, you, as a creator like God, always create in union with His Mind and Will. In this sense you think with God. And thus your thoughts are God's Thoughts. *In reality* you have no thoughts but His, just as you have no Will but His. "There is no will but God's (L74).

It is important to understand that, although the minds God created are united with one another and with God, they are not one mind in the sense of *numerically one. They are not one in number. They are infinite in number.* There is not a finite number of them. There is no end to the number of them. Their number is endless. Creation continues forever, it never stops. It is an eternal ongoing process, ongoing dynamic.

If you thought of counting the number of God's Thoughts (creations, Sons) you never would come to an end in your counting. They cannot be counted. They are not counted. There is no need, purpose, or reason to count them. Not even God knows how many there are because the concept "how many?", insofar as it implies a finite number, is meaningless to Him, and to everyone in creation. The increase in number of creations is simply a property of the very nature of God's creating. In this sense, then, God's activity of co-creating with His creations is one of *causing His Self to grow in number by causing another one of His Self to be.* This is a dynamic process that is always and forever the same. This increase does not constitute a change, because this Self is forever created to increase. It does not change by increase because it was forever created to increase, to create, to extend. God created you to create, to extend His Self by extending yours. In creation nothing is added that is different. Yes, it is simply more of the same. The same perfectly happy Self. The Father simply fathers a Son Who fathers and Son Who fathers etc.. And all Fathers and Sons are perfect. This Self-extension increases the joy of God and His Kingdom, the Domain in which His Will is done. It is the Domain of His infinite number of Sons Who are perfect creators like Himself.

In extending His Self God shares everything He has and is with His extensions. This is how God's Kingdom increases; God and His Sons cause another one of Their Self to be thus causing Their Self to grow in number. In doing so, then, They share everything They have and are. This is how the joy of Heaven increases. The joy is increased by the more who share everything. But this increase is not a spacial increase, nor does it involve time, nor is there really any change at all. Because you were forever created to create there is no change in what you are when you create, you are simply doing what you were created to do; you are doing what God does eternally and changelessly, extending both your Self and His Which are the same. You are what He is. Thus there is no change in what creation is. It is always the same forever: the joint Will of the Father and of the Son co-creating perfect creations thus increasing their joy by sharing everything they have and are with Their creations in the very act of creating Them. This is an unending process. It never stops; it continues forever. It is Love, perfect Love.

The minds God created *are* "one" in the sense that every one has everything and thus they all are *equal and the same*. Their "oneness" lies in their equality and sameness. It lies in their perfection. No one mind has something which another does not have. Nor does one mind lack something which another has. Thus there is a perfect equality among all the Sons of God, among all the members of the Sonship, among all the parts of Christ. We all share the same Self, the same nature, the same attributes of perfection. We share the same Thought of what we all are. And what we are is what God is. In this sense all minds are "one mind". No mind is greater than or less than another. No mind is better than or worse than another. Every mind is the same as all minds, because every mind has the same attributes of perfection. All the minds God created are equal because They all share the same thoughts, and They share an "equal number" of thoughts, namely all thoughts, an infinite number of them.

All Minds are Joined as One

All minds are one in another sense; they are *joined*; they are united. "Minds are joined; bodies are not" (18.6,3:1). How are minds joined? They share the same thoughts. "To share is to make alike, or to make one" (L45,2:4). In reality, any thought in my mind is in your mind. And any thought in yours is in mine. And any thought in God's Mind is in both our minds. In this way we are all alike. We are all the same, and equal. We are all joined and united. We are of "one mind". We share the same thoughts all of which are Thoughts of what we are. We are joined in the same Self, the Christ, God's one Son.

One of the most enlightening passages on this point of the likeness and oneness of minds which share the same thoughts is found in Lesson 45 entitled: "God is the Mind with which I think." Paragraph 2 in the Lesson is as follows:

You think with the Mind of God. Therefore you share your thoughts with Him, as He shares His with you. They are the same thoughts, because they are thought by the same Mind. To share is to make alike, or to make one. Nor do the thoughts you think with the Mind of God leave your mind, because thoughts do not leave their source. Therefore, your thoughts are in the Mind of God, as you are. They are in your mind as well, where He is. As you are part of His Mind, so are your thoughts part of His Mind. (L45,2)

What does it mean to be "a part of" a mind? It means to be a thought "in" that mind. If you are part of God's Mind then you are a Thought in God's Mind.

Let us note from this passage the lines: "your thoughts are in the Mind of God, *as you are*. They are in your mind as well, *where He is.*" In other words, you are in the Mind of God and God is in your mind. The Course also makes this point when it says, "every mind contains all minds" (L161,4:2). Thus God's Mind contains your mind, and your mind contains God's Mind. This, then, is another sense in which all minds are joined. They each contain the other, and they each contain all. Thus every mind, as God created it, has within it all minds, and thus all minds are united and joined by being "in" one another and a part of one another.

This also implies that each mind has all the thoughts that are in every mind. For if every mind contains all minds it also contains all thoughts in that mind. Thus every mind shares every Thought with every mind. Every mind then is perfectly knowing or has perfect knowledge, like God. God in His perfect love and power shares His perfect knowledge with every one. Every mind knows the truth and is perfectly aware of everything that is real and true. And all are perfectly happy doing what God does, creating as He creates, extending Itself and God as well. In other words, the function of each and every mind is to cause another one of Itself to be, thus causing itself to grow in number. This in turn causes another one of God's Self to be, and thus God's Thought of Himself increases in number, *ad infinitum*. "God has no Thoughts except the Self-extending" – forever, without end.

Another way the Course puts all this is to say that every mind is part of God's Mind. "My mind is part of God's" (L35). This means, as I have already said, that every mind is *in* God's Mind. It is in God's Mind as a Thought of

What He is. All of us as minds, then, are *part of* God's Mind, *in* God's Mind, and *one with* God's Mind. We are all God's Thought of What He is, namely, a Mind. And we "think with Him" thus extending His Thought, His Self, His Being. This process of extending or creating increases the joy of the Kingdom.

Furthermore, all thoughts are in minds, whether we are talking about God's creation, or about our experience in this world. "In the mind" is where thoughts or ideas exist. And everything is an idea. God is an idea, you are an idea, I am an idea. Thus God, you and I, and everything exists "in" a mind.

Thus since "every mind contains all minds", God's Mind is in every mind. God's Mind is in your mind as the true Thought of What He is, and thus as the true Thought what you are. You think with God's Mind. His Mind is what you are as His co-creator. This is why the Course says that in God's creation "every aspect *is* the whole" (13.8,5:3). Each part of creation *is* the whole of creation, because each part of creation (each mind) contains the whole of creation (the Mind of God and all His Thoughts). Each part of creation contain all the parts of creation as well. Every part of Christ contains all parts of Christ. As God created us each one of us has all of us within himself. "One brother is all brothers" (L161,4:1). One Son is all Sons, because every Son contains all Sons. And even though I, as a Son of God, may be your immediate Father in creation, and you my immediate Son, I am just as much your brother since I created you *with* the Prime Creator, God, the First Father. He is as much you Father and I am.

We can summarize what we said so far about God and His creation by saying that *everything God creates is perfect like Himself.* Because God is perfectly loving He *wants* to share Himself completely with His creations, and because God is perfectly powerful He *can* share Himself completely with His creations, and because God is timeless His Will *is* already done; He has already and eternally shared Himself completely with His creations. As a perfect being, then, God shares everything He is and has with all His creations. And since He is timeless all His creations eternally *have* and *are* everything God has and is. This is eternally true and therefore it is true *now*. We are all the Christ, now and forever. "Christ is God's Son as He created Him. He is the Self we share, uniting us with one another, and with God as well" (Th6,1:1-2).

Like God Your Father, You, as His Son, are perfectly happy because You are perfectly loving, perfectly powerful, and perfectly knowing. And like Your Father you are timeless, changeless, and eternal, formless, and limitless. Your function in Heaven is to extend God's Being by extending your Own. You share everything you have and are with all your creations as God shares everything He has and is with you. This is your "joy in creating the perfect". As the Course says in another context:

> The world has not yet experienced any comprehensive reawakening or rebirth. Such a rebirth is impossible as long as you continue to project or miscreate. It still remains within you, however, to extend as God extended His Spirit to you. In reality this is your only choice, because your free will was given you for your joy in creating the perfect. (2.1,3:9-10)

Of course, what we have just described is not an accurate description of our current experience. It is not what we directly experience ourselves to be in this world of bodies. We experience ourselves as "humans", as minds with a body. And as humans, we are, to say the least, imperfect, and lacking.

Our experience of being limited and separated selves, different from one another, of being born in a body and limited in awareness, of being ignorant, hateful, and weak; of being subject to attack and fear, and vulnerable to pain, suffering, and death - our experience of all this must be explained. And it will be in Part Three.

Meanwhile, there is still more to say which is directly related to the theme of this chapter, namely, the nature of God's creations, given that He did not create finite bodily beings who experience themselves inhabiting a physical world.

EVERYTHING GOD CREATED IS PERFECT

At this point I think it is fair to say that we have answered our first question, the first of three we need to answer in order for Miracle Theodicy's refutation of the argument from evil (AFE) to be credible. Giving a satisfactory answer to this first question is the aim we set for Part Two of this book. Clearly we have achieved this aim.

We need now to reflect, as it were, on this answer, and discuss it in light of what we have formerly believed. We also need to answer some questions which arise from this answer. As always, it seems that the answer to one question leads to another question which itself needs answering.

We now have a conception of God and His creation which serves as an alternative to the traditional conception of God and His creation, the conception that God created us as minds with a body in a physical world. It is this traditional concept of God's creation which, in fact, has engendered the problem of evil - "the most powerful objection ever raised against belief in God".

It should be clear that if any thinker supposes that God created the physical world he does so only by pre-supposing that a perfect being could create something imperfect. The Course's teaching that what God creates is perfect like Himself makes the conception of God as creator of the world of bodies a logical impossibility. To say that God created the world is equivalent to saying that God is not God. It is like stating the contradiction that God is a perfect being and God is not a perfect being, or God is changeless and God is not changeless. In other words, to conceive of God as *both* a perfect being *and* as maker of the world results in an inherently self-contradictory concept of God. To be consistent in our thinking we must avoid self-contradictory concepts, including a self-contradictory concept of God.

Thus we see that the Course's teaching that everything God created is perfect like Himself is crucial in Miracle Theodicy's solution to the problem of evil. As far as God is concerned all His creations are perfectly happy, and eternally happy. This can never change. There is no one suffering in Heaven, in God's creation, in reality. God does not know of evil for He knows of no attack and suffering. God gives only happiness, and thus all His creations are perfectly happy like Himself.

But are we, who have been raised in the Christian theistic tradition willing to accept this teaching? What does it require of us? It obviously requires we give up what we were taught in grade school. Ever since elementary school, or even before then, we may have believed that the world was created by God because that is what we were taught, and that is what we learned.

Perhaps, like me, you have been through what is commonly called a "crisis of faith". You may have given up belief in God altogether. Perhaps (again like me), you have used "the problem of evil" as the intellectual support of your unbelief, regardless of what the "real reason" for your unbelief was, whether some suffering or loss, or some pattern of behavior you were unwilling to give up, but must, if you were to honestly believe there is a God, a heaven, and a hell.

The general human complaint, "how could God, Who by definition is perfectly loving and powerful, allow *this* terrible evil to happen", is one always available to us to buttress our unwillingness to accept that there is a God.

But despite this unanswered complaint, you may have your own personal reasons for believing in God. Perhaps (yes, again like me), you had a "born again" experience or some other experience you would describe as a "religious conversion". Perhaps the realization that death will inevitably come to you personally has led to a "re-conversion", to an acceptance that there is a God and an afterlife.

Despite any or all these experiences, there always remains, for the thinking believer, the problem of reconciling human suffering and fear of death with the idea that humans are the creation of a God Who is supposedly perfect; perfectly knowing, perfectly loving, and perfectly powerful. In other words, the problem of evil is always lurking in the background of our belief system, ready to raise its ugly head at any opportunity.

The idea that everything God created is perfect like Himself may not be as difficult for traditional Christians to accept as it might first appear. One does not have to give up thinking of himself as a "Christian" just because He believes that God as a perfect being creates only perfect creations. The idea that what God created is perfect is not really a new idea in Christian philosophy or theology. It appears in the writings of the first great theodicist, Saint Augustine, as well as in other theodicies written since, including Person-Making Theodicy.

The crux of the matter lies in what is meant by the statement "what God creates is perfect". Other theodicies interpret this statement differently than does Miracle Theodicy. Augustine, for example, believed *both* that what God created is perfect *and* that God created this world of bodies including us as human. Thus Augustine did his best to argue that this world is perfect, including that God created Adam with a "perfect" nature, and only after his sin did Adam's created nature become imperfect, even "corrupt".

The world is perfect, Augustine argued, because each of the different and various kinds and levels of being God supposedly created -- minerals, plants, animals, humans, and angels -- plays its own special and unique part in the perfection of the whole of God's creation. Like a work of art the world as a whole is good, beautiful, and perfect even though any particular part considered in itself is may be evil, ugly, and imperfect. The parts must of necessity be unequal, and some parts must be better than other parts, like a man is better than a dog, a dog better than a tree, a tree better than a rock, or an angel better than a man. But the different parts, though imperfect in themselves, when considered all together make up a perfect whole. Furthermore, to strengthen his argument, Augustine says that God created all these many separate and different kinds of beings in order to display and reveal His abundance, His "plenitude" of being.

This argument was Augustine's attempt to reconcile the idea that God is a perfect being, on the one hand, and the biblical doctrine that "in the beginning God created the heavens and the earth", on the other hand. It is an ingenious argument, and it has been repeatedly used throughout the history of Christian philosophy and theology. The negative aspect of it, as we have seen, is that it has engendered a problem that Christian theism has never been able to resolve

- the problem of evil; a problem whose solution has eluded
us simply because *there is no solution,* as long as we try to
hold *both* that God is perfect and that God created this
world.

Person-Making Theodicy also teaches that this
world, as God's creation, is perfect. But it is perfect in a
sense different than Augustine interpreted "perfect". In
Person-Making theodicy this world is perfect because it
perfectly serves the purposes for which God created "finite,
morally free beings". The "harsh and cruel environment" of
the world provides a "perfect" environment for the
development of those virtues and characteristics which make
for "spiritually mature persons", who ultimately will "freely
come to love, worship, and obey God."

And finally there is Leibnitz (1646-1727) whose
theodicy would best be classified as a Classical Theodicy.
Leibnitz accepted the idea that God is a perfect being, one
than which no greater can be conceived, but he also accepted
the biblical doctrine that God created the world. Leibnitz
thus reasoned that since God is perfectly loving, powerful,
and wise, He would create the best world He could possibly
create. And so, by hypothesis, since God did create this
world, this world must be "the best of all possible worlds".
In this sense it is a "perfect" creation, because it is "the best"
of all worlds God as a perfect being could possibly create.
Like Augustine, Liebnitz subscribed to the idea that the
"perfection" of the world, as God's creation, lay in the
"universal harmony" it displayed. Thus the passage from
Alexander Pope, which we quoted in chapter two, aptly
describes Leibnitz's theodicy - "all partial evil, universal
good."

To debate the strength and weakness of arguments
used to defend the idea that this world is "perfect" will serve
no purpose here. Our point here is simply the fact that the
statement "what God created is perfect" is not one which is

foreign to the thinking of those who call themselves Christian. Stated in this abstract and very general way, the statement has consistently been accepted throughout the history of Christian theism. It is not a new or "heretical" idea to state that "what God created is perfect". The simple fact is that it has been interpreted differently by different philosophers of religion.

A Copernican-Like Reversal

The meaning and the implications which *A Course in Miracles* draws from this statement, however, *is* new for many Christians today. And it may, at first glance, be considered by some as too radical. Few, if any, thinkers in the Christian tradition have drawn from the idea that "everything God created is perfect" the implication that since this world is imperfect, it cannot be a creation of God.

In relation to the traditional view, then, this new interpretation of the idea that what God creates is perfect is indeed a 180 degree turn around! Just as the Copernican revolution of the sixteenth century reversed our conception that the sun revolves around the earth, to the conception that the earth revolves around the sun, so too, the Course reverses our conception that since God created this world, it must be perfect, to the conception that since this world is not perfect, it could not have been created by God!

When carefully considered, this "Copernican-like reversal" makes eminently good sense. This new and radical implication of the idea that "what God creates is perfect" is more coherent than the traditional interpretation. In fact, it seems to me, and to at least a million other students of *A Course in Miracles,* to be more coherent, more reasonable, more logical, and more easily understood and accepted than the traditional view. To say that this world of bodies, space, and time is perfect, as some philosophers of religion purport, is to so dilute the notion of perfection as to make it wholly meaningless. In fact, it is *because* this world is imperfect that the problem of evil has arisen in the first place! How can there be complaint about the evil in the world, if the world is perfect? If the world is perfect, the complaint makes no sense. The fact that we complain about the attack and suffering in the world, and that we have a need to explain it in light of the existence of God, belies our statements that the world is perfect. Somewhere deep within us we wonder how a perfect being, who is perfectly happy, would create such an imperfect world inhabited by such imperfect and unhappy creatures as we see around us.

Thinkers in the Christian tradition have for centuries understood that this teaching, namely, that what God creates is perfect, is a legitimate implication of God's very nature, a legitimate implication of all the attributes He has as a perfect being. But the thinkers in the tradition have for some reason not been willing to explicitly accept the idea that God shares *everything* He has with *every one* of His creations in the very act of creating Them, and that therefore the "creatures" of this world, who do not have everything God has, cannot possibly be God's creations.

One of these reasons is that theologians in the theistic tradition have for centuries been taught by their teachers, and have in turn taught their students, that God created the world and human bodies. This teaching is based on statements in Genesis like the following: "In the beginning God created the heavens and the earth" (Gn 1:1). "Then the Lord God formed man of dust from the ground, and breathed into his nostrils the breath of life; and man became a living being" (Gn 2:7).

Obviously, if one accepts these statements from ancient Jewish scriptures as literal statements of truth, he cannot accept the Course's teaching that everything God created is perfect like Himself. For if God created this world of bodies, then it is not true that what God created is perfect in the same sense that God is perfect. Nothing in this world is perfect in the same sense that God is perfect.

An Uncompromising Notion of Perfection

Surely, the Course's idea of a God as a perfect being lives up to Anselm's requirement that a perfect being is "that than which none greater can be conceived". The author of ACIM does not compromise on the notion of perfection. Can you conceive of anything greater than the Course's concept of God? Can you conceive of anything greater than a perfect Creator of an infinite number of perfect beings like Himself? Can there be anything greater than a perfectly loving God Who eternally and changelessly shares everything He has and is with every one of His creations? And could all His creations be perfect if one had something another did not? They all must be equal and the same, joined and united in one Nature, in one Mind and Will, in one Self, happily co-creating the perfect in union with Their perfect Creator. And think of this: this process of creating, of causing the Self to grow in number by causing another one of the Self to be, is one that never ends; it is an everlasting and changeless activity of the Mind of God and of His perfect Sons. This is one sense in which God is indeed infinite, limitless.

Can we agree that the Course's idea of a perfect being far exceeds the ideas we so often hear and read? I believe we can. The Course's concept of God as a perfect being cannot help but amaze us -- as perfection should! It is wonderful! It is marvelous! It is truly awe-inspiring!

In fact, as we shall see in the next chapter, the idea that "everything God created is perfect like Himself" is the foundation not only for our perfect happiness in heaven as pure minds, but also for our salvation, our peace and joy, and our happiness here on earth, while the body is still part of our experience in a physical world.

DOES AN INFINITE NUMBER OF PERFECT BEINGS IMPLY THERE IS MORE THAN NUMERICALLY ONE GOD?

One may be tempted to think that if there was an infinite number of perfect beings, this implies that there is more than numerically one God. And the idea that there is more than numerically one God is an idea that no Jew, Christian, or Muslim would seriously consider. Nor, in fact, would the author of *A Course in Miracles.*

The Course clearly teaches that there is only numerically one God. But we may ask, how can it *consistently* teach this, when at the same time it teaches that there is an infinite number of perfect beings? Well, it does so by saying that there is a sense in which God, the Father, is "greater than" God the Son, while at the same time maintaining that both Father and Son are perfect. Yet, the fact that the Father is "greater" than the Son does not force us to say that the Son must be imperfect, or not "as perfect" as the Father. Nor does the fact that the Father is greater than the Son imply that there is only one in number of perfect beings. It simply implies that the Father is "greater" than the Son *in some sense* even though both the Father and His Son are perfect.

As we mentioned in Chapter three, there is a difference in meaning between "a perfect being" and "the greatest or supreme being" among any particular group of beings. We used the hypothetical case of extraterrestrials visiting this planet. We pointed out that "supremacy" is not the same thing as "perfect".

In examining the notion that God the Father *is* greater than His creations, even though all His creations are perfect like Himself, we are, in a sense, providing an interpretation of what Jesus meant when he said, "I and the Father are one" (Jn 10:30), and also said, "The Father is greater than I" (Jn 14:28).

In fact, this combination of statements also appears in the Course itself. In the context of describing his relation to us here in this world, on the one hand, and his relation to God, on the other, the author of the Course (who identifies himself with Jesus) concludes his remarks by saying:

> This may appear to contradict the statement "I and my Father are one", but there are two parts to the statement in recognition that the Father is greater" (1.2,4:7).

But if God the Father *is* greater than God the Son, we may ask whether this implies that there is something the Father has and is, which He did not give to His Son. If so, what is it? And how does it make the Father "greater" even though both He and His creation are perfect? Does the fact that He did not give this "something" imply that the Son is not really perfect? Does the fact that the Father did not give this "something" to His Son constitute a limit on the Father's love? Does it constitute a limit on His power? Or is it something He could not give because it was impossible to do so? It is to answering these questions that we now turn.

The One Distinction between God and His Creation(s)

The Course teaches that there is one distinction between God and His creations. The distinction is that God the Father is the Creator, and God the Son, although he too is a creator, *was created*. God is the one Cause and His Son is the one Effect. The Mind of God is the one Cause and the unified Thought of God is the one Effect.

> "*Cause* is a term properly belonging to God, and His *Effect* is His Son. This entails a set of Cause and Effect relationships totally different from those you introduce into miscreation" (2.7,3:11-12).

Thus, insofar as the Father is the Creator, the Cause, He is not the created, the Effect. And insofar as the Son is the Effect, He is not the Cause. In other words, the Father created the Son, but the Son did not create the Father. This is the only sense in which the Father is greater. And it is for this reason that "awe" is a proper response to God. It is this *relation of creation*, and only this relation of creation, that distinguishes God as a perfect being from His Son as a perfect being. It is also this relation of creation that is the ground for the *numerical distinction* between Father and Son and between a Son and his Son. The numerical distinction does not lie in a difference in *nature*, or in *qualities* of their very nature. In all senses the Father and the Son are one *in nature*. They are the same, equal, and united. The Son *has* and *is* what the Father has and is.

The Father did, however, give the Son the power to create as He does:

> "The Father must give fatherhood to His Son, because His Own Fatherhood must be extended outward. You who belong in God have the holy function of extending His

Fatherhood by placing no limits upon it"
(8.3,3:4-5).

There are two obvious implications of this relation of
creation, the idea that God the Father created God the Son,
that the Father is Cause and the Son is the Effect: 1) The Son
is not cause and creator of God (the Father), and 2) The Son
is not cause and creator of himself (the Son).

Neither of these implications, however, imply that
the Son is imperfect. He is neither an imperfect creation nor
an imperfect creator. He is not imperfect in any sense. He is
neither an imperfect effect, nor is he a creator of imperfect
effects. He still has everything His Father has, and can create
the perfect just as His Father creates the perfect. And it can
still be said that God gave His creations everything. He gave
them everything He could possibly give Them without
contradiction. The Father shares everything He can possibly
share with His Son, His one creation. He shares His
perfection with him.

In other words, we do not have to concede that God's
love or power is limited because He did not give the Son the
attribute of being his Father's father, or his Cause's cause, or
his Creator's creator. Why? Because the task itself is
impossible; it is self-contradictory. And, as such, it cannot be
said to be something that the Father could have given His
Son, but instead held it back from him, and kept it for
Himself alone. No, the Father held back nothing in giving
His Son everything in His creation of him. Thus this does
not constitute a limit on God's love.

It is also clear that it does not constitute a limit on
God's power. It is not a legitimate objection to say that since
God cannot do this God's power is limited. We cannot
legitimately say that God's power is limited because God
cannot do what it is impossible and logically contradictory to
do. Nor can the Son's "lack" of a self-contradictory attribute

constitute a reason for saying that the Son is imperfect or lacking. We cannot meaningfully say that the Son is imperfect because He cannot create his Creator, or cause his Cause, or father his Father.

Furthermore, God could not give the Son, His creation, His effect, the attribute of being cause and creator of himself. This too is a self-contradictory task, like making a triangle with four sides. Just because God did not (since He cannot) make the Son his own creator does not mean God's power or knowledge is limited. Nor does it imply that God's love has a limit, as if God held back for Himself alone something He could possibly give His Son in His creation of him. He shares with His Son everything He could possibly share with him. Thus the Son lacks no attribute which He can possibly have as a perfect creation. He is perfect like His Father, because He shares everything with Him. His perfection is not less than His Father's simply because he did not create himself. If he were to create himself, he would have to be his own creator, and this is an impossibility, a self-contradiction. Thus the Son cannot be said to be imperfect simply because he was created and is not his own creator. The Son is perfect because his perfect creator created him perfect like Himself.

This can be put another way. What is creat*ed* cannot, by definition, be creator of its own creator. And what is Effect cannot be cause of its own Cause. Nor can what is created be creator of itself. Nor can what is effect be cause of itself.

God simply *is*, forever, always, and eternally. He has no creator. He is First Cause. He is First Cause and Prime Creator of *all* that is, without exception. He is the one and only Uncaused Cause, Uncreated Creator. The Son, on the other hand, was caused and created by the Father. He is a caused cause; he is a created creator; He is a fathered father.

As his Father's Son he creates exactly like His Father does, and in union with His Father:

> "This [the extension of the joint Will of the Father and of the Son] is perfect creation by the perfectly created, in union with the perfect Creator" (8.3,3:3).

In the context of explaining creation as extension, the Course alludes to this distinction between God and His Son:

> In this sense the creation includes both the creation of the Son by God, and the Son's creations when his mind is healed. This requires God's endowment of the Son with free will, because all loving creation is freely given in one continuous line, in which all aspects are of the same order. (2.1,2:7-8)

This distinction between God and His Son, then, helps us to see that even though there may be an infinite number of perfect beings this fact does not imply that there is more than numerically one God. We can still say there is only *numerically one God* because there is only numerically one Being that is *both* perfect *and* is First Cause and Prime Creator of everything that is. There is only numerically one Being Who is Creator of *every and all* Thought-minds. Only *God, the Father*, is Creator of *both* the Son *and* Their co-creations.

The Son, on the other hand, is creator only of co-creations; of what He creates in union with His Father. The Son has no creations in reality which He did not co-create with His Father. And the Father has no creations in reality which He did not co-create with the Son - *except* the Son himself.

Thus, even though there is only numerically one God, Who is Prime Creator of all, this does not imply that there cannot be an infinite number of perfect beings who have the same attributes of perfection that God the Father has. The fact that there is only numerically one God Who is perfect does not imply that the creations of this one God cannot also be perfect, and have the *same Nature* as Their Creator, and the same qualities He has. The distinction between God and His creations does not imply that what God creates must be imperfect. It does not imply that the Son must be imperfect. The Son is perfect. All God's Sons are perfect. In fact, it is precisely *because* God is perfect that all His creations must be perfect. A perfect being *cannot* create imperfect creations. Thus you, as God created you, are perfect; I, as God created me, am perfect; Jesus, as God created him, is perfect. All God's creations are perfect like Himself. Again this is so because God, as God, must have created Them that way, for if He didn't, He Himself would not be a *perfect* Creator, and thus not a perfect being. God would not *be* God if He had not created creations perfect like Himself.

As God's perfect Son you share in everything Your perfect Father has and is. For "Only Love creates, and only like Itself" (Th11,1:2). Thus, we find in the Workbook the following "idea for today" that the Course would have us say, and repeat whenever we are tempted to believe otherwise: "Love, Which created me, is what I am" (L229). And, for ten days in a row, as part of a review session, we are to say, "God is but Love, and therefore so am I" (R5,4:3). This means that God is a perfectly loving Mind. And so am I as He created me, and so are you as He created you. And so is your mother as He created her! Despite your beliefs to the contrary.

SUMMARY

The purpose of this chapter was to give an answer to the first of the three questions we raised at the end of chapter three. All three of those questions immediately arose once Miracle Theodicy's solution to the problem of evil was offered. Miracle Theodicy dissolves the problem of evil by maintaining that God did not create this world, and therefore is not aware of the evil - the attack, pain and suffering, sickness and death - we perceive and experience in this world.

But if God did not create this world, what did He create? In this chapter we gave our answer. God created a spiritual realm of pure minds and Thoughts which are perfect like Himself. You and I and everyone are part of that creation, not as humans, but as spirit. And although it may be impossible for anyone on earth to grasp what heaven is, and what its one creator really means, we have done our best to hint at what it means, and hopefully have provided enough light so that the reader need not reject Miracle Theodicy's solution to the problem of evil by objecting that there is no answer to the first question. We have indeed provided an answer, and it is one which lends strong support to the solution offered in chapter 3.

Before we begin Part Three of this book, where we shall answer the second question raised at the end of Part One, I want to discuss some practical implications of the idea that what God created is perfect like Himself. In the next chapter I do this, and I include some implications directly related to understanding the single lesson we need learn in order to experience the love which is our natural inheritance as God's Son.

I will close this chapter with a passage from the Course, which expresses more succinctly more beautifully and more profoundly what we have said in this chapter about the nature of God's creation(s):

> Creation is the sum of all God's Thoughts, in number infinite, and everywhere without all limit. Only Love creates, and only like Itself. There was no time when all that It created was not there. Nor will there be a time when anything that It created suffers any loss. Forever and forever are God's Thoughts exactly as they were and as they are, unchanged through time and after time is done.
>
> God's Thoughts are given all the power that their own Creator has. For He would add to Love by its extension. Thus His Son shares in creation, and must therefore share in power to create. What God has willed to be forever one will still be one when time is over; and will not be changed throughout the course of time, remaining as it was before the thought of time began.
>
> Creation is the opposite of all illusions, for creation is the truth. Creation is the holy Son of God, for in creation is His Will complete in every aspect, making every part container of the Whole. Its oneness is forever guaranteed inviolate; forever held within His holy Will, beyond all possibility of harm, of separation, imperfection and of any spot upon its sinlessness.
>
> We are creation; we the Sons of God.
>
> (Th11,1-4:1)

6

GOD KNOWS YOU AS PERFECT

God knows but His Son, and as he was
created so he is.
ACIM (Q29,7:10)

In the last chapter we kept our focus on the nature of
God's creation, and learned that everything God created is
perfect like Himself. In this chapter we will discuss several
implications of this teaching. I want to draw out these
implications because they have great significance for our
discussion in later chapters.

Our focus in this chapter will center on three main
ideas. The first is that our happiness rests on a sure and
unshakable foundation. It rests on truth, the truth of what we
are; it rests on an unchanging and eternal reality. In other
words, from our point of view in this world we have good
reason to believe that peace and joy is possible even while
we seem to be in this world of bodies. We can indeed
experience "heaven on earth".

The second idea we will focus on is the reality formula introduced in Chapter 3. We are now ready to extend the reality formula and expand and deepen our understanding of it. And finally we will discuss the Course's teaching that reality, or God and His creation, is not at all affected by our mistakes. Let us turn now to a discussion of each of these ideas in order.

Our Happiness Rests on a
Sure and Unchanging Foundation

The Course teaches that the guarantee of happiness lies in the fact that God created us as His perfect Son, and that we remain forever as He created us. There is no one statement the Course has us repeat more often than "I am as God created me". This phrase, for example, is part of the daily review lessons for 20 days in a row. The entire statement in the review is: "I am not a body. I am free. For I am still as God created me" (L201-220).

There is good reason for the centrality of this statement in the Course's Workbook training. It serves to help undo our false self identity and to awaken our mind to our true identity as the Christ. And as the Christ we are perfectly happy. This Identity as the holy Son of God, then, is the sure foundation for our certainty of salvation, and our return home to Heaven. But it is also the sure foundation for the possibility of happiness while we seem to dwell in this world of bodies.

The eternal Self we share with God and with each other has never changed. We remain forever as God created us. And what is eternal is *now*. Even now our true identity is as the Christ, even though we have forgotten It. And awareness of our true identity is still available to us for the asking. This means that we can remember God and our true

Self. We can, even while we seem to dwell in this world, experience at least a reflection of the love, power, knowledge, and happiness we have as Christ. But first we must *want* it. We need a "little willingness" to accept ourselves as the holy Son of God.

This fact that the perfect Son of God still remains as our true identity, then, is a significant implication of the Course's teaching that everything God created is perfect like Himself. And this fact cannot be overestimated in understanding, not only Miracle Theodicy, but more practically in understanding why we can attain happiness even while the body is part of our experience in a physical world.

This world is one of seeming attack and suffering, of seeming hate and fear, of seeming pain, loss and death. But there is no necessity that it be perceived or experienced this way. Instead we can let our minds be trained by *A Course in Miracles*. In the Introduction to the Workbook we read:

> "The purpose of the Workbook is to train
> your mind in a systematic way to a different
> perception of everyone and everything in the
> world" (W-IN,4:1).

And this different perception has its basis in an identity different than that of the ego-body, since all perception is determined by what you think you are.

As we shall discuss in great detail in Part Four of this book, the idea that the choice for happiness *is* the choice of self-identity as the holy Son of God is crucial to understanding what forgiveness really is. Forgiveness involves a choice of what I want to be, and what I want to be *is* what I think I am.

If our happiness depends on making the choice that we are as God created us, then obviously we must understand that *identity as the holy Son of God is a real alternative for choice.* In other words, if we do not believe that identity as the holy Son of God is a real alternative for choice then we will not believe that true happiness is a real possibility while we seem to be in this world of bodies. And thus we, who seem to live in this world, are doomed to suffering, to sickness and pain, loss and grief, death and fear of death.

Many readers may not be ready to make the choice for happiness, for they do not as yet realize that identity as the holy Son of God *is* really one of the alternative identities from which they can choose. You may have never thought you could be anything other than something different from what God is. You may believe that you are a human being, or an ego-body, or a soul who will always be something different and separate from God. Even if you accept the idea that you were created by God, to you this may mean only that God created you as a human, as a mind *and* a body, or a mind in a body, but never as spirit or as pure mind which is His perfect Son, the Christ.

We who have been raised in the Judeo-Christian tradition were taught that Jesus of Nazareth was the only Son of God, that only he was the Christ, and there was (is) no other Son of God. But, as I have already said, and repeatedly, the Course teaches that Christ, the Son of God, is not only Jesus' true identity as God created him, but that Christ is our true identity as well. The present difference between us and Jesus is simply the fact that he recognized this, he remembered it and accepted it and lived in this world as if he were not an ego, but the holy Son of God. As the Course puts it, Jesus, as a man, was the first to complete his part in the Atonement. He accepted Atonement for himself. In other words, he rejected the idea that he and everyone around him were really separated from God, as they appeared to be. He accepted that God was his Father, and accepted that he was at-one with Him. In the writings about Jesus, which have come to be known as "the New Testament", Jesus acknowledges that in reality, in spirit and truth, we all have the same relationship with God that he has. For example, when he teaches his disciples to pray he tells them to address God as "*Our* Father". Here Jesus implies that God is not only his Father, but God is our Father as well. Our Father created us perfect like Himself, just as He created Jesus perfect like Himself. But it is not the *man* Jesus, but the Christ, the Christ *Mind*, that God created perfect like Himself. As the Course says, in pointing to this all-important distinction between *Jesus* and *the Christ*:

> The name of *Jesus* is the name of one who was a man but saw the face of Christ in all his brothers and remembered God. So he became identified with Christ, a man no longer, but at one with God. The man was an illusion, for he seemed to be a separate being, walking by himself, within a body that appeared to hold his self from Self, as all illusions do....In his complete identification with the Christ...Jesus became what all of you must be....Is he the Christ? O yes, along with you (C5,2:1-3,3:1,5:1-2).

Some readers of this book have already accepted, at least intellectually, the idea that their true identity is as the holy Son of God. In their perception, identity as the holy Son of God is a real alternative for choice. Dedicated students of *A Course in Miracles,* for example, have often said and repeated to themselves, "I am the holy Son of God himself" (L191). Saying this to oneself is part of the training the Course offers. Although the following passage is found in another context, it applies to many other things the Course teaches, including the idea that you are the holy Son of God:

> "This is the truth, at first to be but said and then repeated many times; and next to be accepted as but partly true, with many reservations. Then to be considered seriously more and more, and finally accepted as the truth" (L284,1:5-6)

Some other readers may not as yet be able to even speak these words to themselves, much less mean them. To such readers these words, although they should be good news, may be considered at best arrogance and at worst blasphemous. But the author of ACIM asks us to reconsider. For what could be more arrogant than to think you can oppose God's Will and succeed? Can God be wrong about what He created? Can He be wrong about what you really are? Or is it possible that you are wrong in thinking you are something else?

I would hope there are none that find the idea that they are the holy Son of God so difficult to accept that they can not even say these words. For, according to the Course, your happiness depends on accepting the truth that you are the holy Son of God. This truth is the only sure foundation for constant happiness. And only constant happiness is true happiness. Only happiness based on a certain and unchanging truth is true happiness. Happiness which is not constant, but changes with changing circumstances of the world, is not true happiness. True happiness is not something that comes and goes; happiness is not based on a whim, on chance, or on lucky fortune, or even on hard or smart work in getting what this world has to offer. Elusive happiness is not happiness. True happiness is a state of being that cannot be lost because it is inherent in what you are as your loving

Father created you. The Self God created you as is not only eternal, He is eternally happy. It cannot be otherwise.

The following passage, taken from Lesson 66, "My happiness and my function are one", is perhaps the Course's most explicit and direct argument that God gives His creations only happiness. For the sake of brevity I will quote only a syllogistic argument found in this lesson, and only one of several paragraphs which constitute its discussion of this syllogism. If you have the Course itself available to you I urge you to read the other paragraphs that relate to this syllogism:

> *God gives me only happiness.*
> *He has given my function to me.*
> *Therefore my function must be happiness.*

> The first premise is that God gives you only happiness. This could be false, of course, but in order to be false it is necessary to define God as something He is not. Love cannot give evil, and what is not happiness is evil. God cannot give what He does not have, and He cannot have what He is not. Unless God gives you only happiness, He must be evil. And it is this definition of Him you are believing if you do not accept the first premise (L66,6).

Let's assume, then, that we are willing at least to *accept the idea* that Christ is our true identity and therefore we are truly happy simply by being what we are and fulfilling the function God would have us fill. What can we do to *experience* this truth? How can we attain this new experience, this new feeling and awareness? In other words, how can I, while I seem to be something different than the holy Son of God, learn to make the choice for happiness by making the choice for Christ identity?

The only honest answer to this question that I personally can give, based on my own experience and the experience of others, is: *do the lessons in the Workbook.* The Course aims at this happy experience for all its students, and says that this experience is not only possible for everyone, but in fact is necessary (C-IN,2:5-6). But it also says, "Yet it is doing the exercises that will make the goal of the course possible" (W-IN,1:2)

The Course's training helps us to be willing and able to make this choice for Christ Identity. And if this book serves to motivate its readers to begin the Course's training, or to continue once they have started, it may have helped them in a way that is just as valuable as the help it provides in offering a solution to the logical problem of evil.

Short of actually doing the exercises in the *Workbook*, it may be helpful at least to mention and briefly discuss the one lesson that must be learned - a lesson for which the Course provides ample training - in order to experience the true happiness which comes with identity as the holy Son of God.

First let me mention that the Course uses various verbal expressions to refer to the goal it would have its students attain while they seem to be in a world of bodies. All these verbal expressions refer to nearly the same thing, but described from a different point of view. I will simply list some of these expressions here.

The phrases the Course uses to express its goal for us include the following: Atonement, salvation, healing, sinlessness, guiltlessness, fearlessness, the peace of God, the awareness of love's presence, joy, happiness, the remembrance of God, the remembrance of your true Self, Christ's vision, true perception, seeing the face of Christ, seeing your brother sinless, and perception of the real world.

There are others expressions that relate more to the means of attaining this goal - like the holy instant, the holy relationship, and receiving and giving miracles - but this is enough for now.

The phrase *"the peace of God"*, or simply the term *"peace"*, is perhaps the most used phrase the Course employs to describe its goal for us. In any case, we can talk about the Course's goal for us in terms of peace and joy, love and happiness, and in the long run we will be talking about all the other things mentioned above, for all of them imply a mind that is certain rather than doubtful about what it is, a mind at peace rather than at war within itself; a mind feeling love and joy rather than fear and pain; in short, a mind that is happy rather than miserable.

The one lesson we must learn in order to attain the peace of God is *forgiveness*. It is through forgiveness that we attain happiness in this world. Forgiveness is the one lesson around which all the lessons in the workbook are centered. In this sense *the choice for happiness is the choice to forgive*. Forgiveness then is our only function in this world! For it is only through forgiveness we can attain happiness. This relation of means and end, the relation between forgiveness and happiness, is expressed in many passages and lessons in the Course including:

> Forgiveness is the key to happiness (L121).
> Forgiveness offers everything I want (L122).
> I want the peace of God (L185).
> What is the peace of God? Nothing more than this: the simple understanding that His Will is wholly without opposite (Q20,6:1-2).
> God's Will for me is perfect happiness (L101).
> I share God's Will for happiness for me (L102).

My happiness and my function are one (L66).
Forgiveness is my function as the light of the
world (L62).
Forgiveness ends all suffering and loss (249).

In Part Four of this book, where we focus on
answering our third question, which relates to the *practical*
implications of our solution to the logical problem of evil,
we will discuss the Course's own definition of what
forgiveness really is. And thus we will more fully understand
why it is true that *only through forgiveness* can we
experience the peace and joy, love and happiness which is
our natural inheritance as God's Son.

In this chapter and section our purpose is simply to
make clear that true happiness is a real alternative for choice,
and that the possibility of making this choice for happiness
rests on a sure and certain foundation, namely, *eternal and
unchanging truth; the reality and truth of our eternal Self,
the Christ.*

Our true Identity is eternal, timeless, and changeless.
We have, however, forgotten It. But forgetting this does not
mean It is gone. It merely means we have lost awareness of
It. But we can regain this awareness; we can remember.

It is through forgiveness that we will remember God
and our true Self as He created us. "The way to God is
through forgiveness here. There is no other way" (L256,1:1-
2).

We can see that, ultimately, the certain and secure
foundation of our happiness lies in the fact that God is a
perfect being. And that out of His perfect love and power He
has created you and me perfectly happy like Himself. Thus
we can see the relationship between our happiness and our
solution to the logical problem of evil. Both depend on our
concept of God as a perfect being -- and the consistent

implications we draw from this starting point of our thinking about God, ourselves, and one another.

Let us turn now to a deeper discussion of the reality formula which we introduced in chapter three. There are some things we can now add to it as a result of our discussion on the nature of God and His creations.

Extending the Reality Formula

In chapter three we introduced what I called the Course's *reality formula*. This formula can be used to test whether something is real or not. We stated the formula as an equation: *real = eternal = God created.*

We used this formula to help us determine whether the body and the world of bodies is real. We concluded they are not. Since neither is eternal, neither was created by God, and thus neither the world nor the body is real.

We can now extend the reality formula to include the idea that everything God creates is perfect like Himself. Thus we have the following expanded reality formula:

real = eternal = God created = like God = perfect.

It has always been accepted by philosophers that one has the right to define the terms he uses in developing his philosophical system. There are, however, at least two important requirements one must follow in order to be understood, and to be credible. The first is that once you have defined a significant term, it must consistently be used with the meaning you gave it. And the second is that there must be some reasonable basis for using the term as one uses it. In other words, there should be some recognizable connection between the way you use the term and the way it is generally used in the given language you speak. Let us discuss these two requirements with respect to the Course's use of the terms *"real"* and *"reality"*.

We said that the first requirement in defining and using your terms is that once you have defined a significant term in your thought system, you must use it consistently throughout the discussion. It cannot imply one thing here and not imply the same thing there. If you do use it in a different sense than as you defined it, this must be pointed out to avoid confusion and inconsistency.

In our case, then, when we are using the term *real*, or the term *reality,* we are referring to those things defined as real by the reality formula. When the term *real* is used in this sense it is true to say that what is real "exists", and what is unreal "does not exist". The Course points to this fact when it says, for example, "This Course can therefore be summed up very simply in this way: Nothing *real* can be threatened. Nothing *unreal* exists. Herein lies the peace of God" (T-IN,2; my italics).

The Course does, however, use the term *real* in another sense. It sometimes uses the term *real* to mean "real to you", and actually uses this phrase quite often to indicate that something may be real to you, or seem real to you, but, in fact, is not real in terms of the reality formula. When it uses the term "real" in this sense it is generally very careful to let the reader know that it is doing so. I know of no case where the Course is ambiguous in this regard, even though it does this frequently.

What the Course is doing when it uses the term *real* in this second sense is that it is acknowledging that something may seem real to you, even though it is not real to God, and therefore not real at all. In fact there are a lot of things that seem real to us which are not real according to the reality formula. In fact, everything in this world! So all the things we see in this world may seem real, but are not real in terms of the reality formula. What seems real, but is not, the Course calls an *illusion*. This world is an illusion in that sense, because it seems real to us, but it is not. And it is not real because it is not eternal and therefore was not created by God. Neither is it like God and His creations, nor is it perfect.

The body is an illusion as well. Your body seems real to you. You are aware of it, it seems to tell you what to feel. You experience your body. You perceive other bodies and they seem real to you. At times your experience seems to be caused by what other bodies say and do. It is in this sense that the body is "real to you". You believe the body is real, but it is not. The body is an illusion, because it was not created by God. It is in this sense, then, that bodies *"exist"*. They exist for you. You believe that bodies are real. You may even believe God created them. If God did create bodies they would be real. But He didn't, so they're not. They must, then, be illusions.

The world and its evil seem real to you. The world exists, and the evil in the world exists, in this sense. They exist for you. You "see" the world and you perceive and experience things which you rightly call "evil". The attack and suffering is real to you. And thus you would affirm "evil exists in the world, and the evil in the world is real".

The Course says that even false ideas "exist" in some sense because they are thoughts. Your thoughts "exist" in your mind. Your thoughts about yourself and your brother, about God and the world, even though they may be false thoughts, "exist" in the sense they are *in your mind*. But they "exist" in your mind apart from God's Mind. You believe them, you live as if they are true, and thus you experience their effects as if they were true.

You perceive what you call "the world". It is a world of many separated beings, including human beings, people. This "people world" is important for you. Each person seems to be a separate mind in a separate body. All this seems to be part of "reality" for you. And others might agree with you that it is reality. A world of many imperfect, limited, separated, different and special persons seems to be "reality" for nearly every human being. But it is not reality according to the reality formula, because such a world is not eternal, was not created by God, is not like God, and is not perfect.

The Course points to these two fundamentally distinct uses of the term *real* when it says, "The separation is a system of thought real enough in time, though not in eternity. All beliefs are real to the believer" (3.7,3:2-3).

This distinction between "real" according to the reality formula (in this passage "real in eternity"), and "real" in the sense of I believe it, or I perceive it, or I experience it (in this passage "real enough in time"), has led some students and teachers of the Course to talk about "levels" in the Course's discourse, or levels of the things the Course talks about. These "levels" could be understood as two different levels *of* mind or levels *of* experience. I have found this distinction very helpful, and think it is worthwhile to discuss here.

"Level One and Level Two"

Dr. Kenneth Wapnick, a long time student and teacher of the Course, has used the terms *"Level I"* and *"Level II"* to represent this fundamental distinction between the real and the unreal, between knowledge and perception. In other words, we can use these terms "Level I" and "Level II" in a general way to indicate the distinction between real according to *the reality formula* and real in the sense of real to you but not real to God. The second sense of "real" simply acknowledges that beliefs are real to the believer, perceptions are real to the perceiver, dreams are real to the dreamer, and experiences while using a body are real to the experiencer, the self that feels and is aware of something or other in this world.

According to Dr. Wapnick, most misunderstandings about what the Course teaches result from confusing Level I and Level II. Ken discusses this distinction in the introduction to his *Glossary-Index for "A Course in Miracles"*, where he briefly presents the Course's Theory.[1]

The Course is speaking of Level I, the level of reality or of the spiritual level of experience, when it is speaking about God and His creation. As we have already discussed, God, Christ, and Their Co-creations are the only things that are real and true. Thus when the Course is speaking of Level I things it is speaking of the spiritual level of experience, or the realm of Heaven, or the realm of knowledge and truth. Discussions about the nature of reality and the spiritual level of experience rather than of illusion and the bodily level of experience, are called "Level I discussions" It could correctly be said that most of my discussion in the last chapter referred to Level I things -- things not of this world, things at the level of reality, of knowledge, of spirit, of pure mind -- rather than Level II -- things of this world, things at the level of the dream, of perception, of the mind using a body.

Obviously, the Course does at times speak of the nature of God and His creation *as They are in reality and truth*, as opposed to how *we think* of God while in this world. When it does so it is speaking "on Level I". And even though we, while seeming to be in this world, have no direct knowledge or experience of reality as it is, the author of the Course can speak of reality in terms that we in this world can understand. Thus, even at Level II, the level of perception, we can get some hint of what it is like at Level I. We can experience what the Course calls a "reflection of truth". In other words, our Level II perception and experience, although it can never be exactly the same experience we have at Level I, can be *in accord with* the experience of Love we have at Level I, rather than in direct opposition to it.

The Course speaks at Level II when it speaks of our function and experience in this world, or how they compare with our function and experience in heaven. It speaks of the way we think while using bodies, the things we value and want while in this world. It speaks of the way we think of our self, of others, and of God. It speaks of how we think about and perceive the world, and it speaks of how we can change our perception of everyone and everything in the world. It speaks about its own training program and how and why it works to bring us the peace of God, and what choices we need to make to experience the peace which reflects our state of mind in reality.

When the Course speaks of these things it is speaking about Level II things. When it speaks of Level II things it focuses mostly on our mind, its activities, its thoughts, and its state. It is concerned with our mind while it is functioning as a perceiver, while it is using a body in a physical world. It is concerned with helping us to ultimately return to our original state as God created us, by preparing us to be ready for this return to a home we never really left. In other words, it is preparing us to awaken from the dream, not only by helping us to first understand that we are dreaming, but teaching us what we need to learn in order to have a "happy dream" which is a necessary step before we can awaken from all dreams to direct awareness and knowledge of reality.

The Course, then, speaking of Level II things speaks of the dream, and the dream contents; it speaks of the body itself, and its role in our perception of our self and the world, as well as the role it can play in the healing of the mind of God's Son. In short, when the Course speaks of our experience in this world it is speaking of Level II things.

Another way to put this is to say that the Course talks about both the dream -- this world of perception, a world of minds with bodies (Level II), and about reality -- the realm of knowledge, a world of pure minds without bodies (Level I). At the level of reality and knowledge there are no bodies and no perception. Thus, there are no images, no sights, no sounds, no touch.

When the Course does speak of Level II things it speaks of wrong-mindedness and right-mindedness, as opposed to the One-Mindedness of Level I. Wrong-mindedness and right-mindedness are two alternative ways of thinking while we are in a world of perception. They are alternative ways of thinking of yourself and God, of your brother and the world. These alternative ways of thinking lead to, among other things, two different ways of perceiving the world; one which the Course calls false perception, the other true perception. So sometimes the Course describes the world as it seems to be when we are perceiving falsely. At other times it describes the world as it seems to be when we are perceiving truly. (The world as perceived truly is called "the real world"). When we are perceiving falsely we see attack, pain, suffering, and death as real. When we are perceiving truly we recognize that evil cannot be real, but must be illusion. This recognition is crucial. For "illusion recognized must disappear" (L187,7:1). The disappearance of evil is the result of forgiveness. "I will forgive and this (evil) will disappear" (L193,13:3).

Right-mindedness then is the result of the correction of wrong-mindedness. True perception is the result of the correction of false perception. And identification with our true Self is the result of correcting our identification with a false self, the ego-body.

These alternative ways of thinking about and perceiving the world correspond to other pairs of alternative experiences associated with either wrong- or right-mindedness. We need not discuss these here. For our purpose we need but recognize that even though there is a distinction between true perception and false perception, a distinction that has meaning at Level II, neither kind of *perception* is the same thing as the *knowledge* of reality.

True perception, however, does reflect knowledge, and has many elements that are like knowledge (5.1,7). Knowledge, however, is something we share with God as He created us. Perception is a term that does not apply to God at all, nor to us in the condition in which God created us. God does not perceive at all, and neither do we when we are as God created us.

Let us turn now to the second requirement one must fulfill in order for one's definition of a term to be understood and accepted. The second requirement is that there should be a reasonable basis for defining a term as one does. There should be some recognizable connection between our use of the terms *"real"* and *"reality"* and the general use of these terms in our language.

This second requirement should pose no problem for us. Philosophers of religion have long been willing to ground "reality" or "the real" in God, and in what God creates and knows. So our use of the terms *reality* and *real* as applying to only God Himself and what God creates should pose no difficulty.

Of course, it is true that Miracle Theodicy has a conception of God and His creation which is quite different from that of the other theodicies we discussed in chapter two. These other theodicies would agree that God, and what God creates and knows, is real, but they include the world of bodies in what God created and knows, and thus they say this world of bodies is real or is reality. It seems that these other theodicies, however, especially Process Theodicy, are also willing to say that even things *God did not create* are real. And I am referring here to things that even Process

Theologians would say God did not create, not merely what the Course says God did not create. For example, most Process Theologians would say that God did not cause or will or create the holocaust, yet they would say that the holocaust was real. Thus it is not clear whether they even have a criterion for what is ultimately real. Certainly their criterion for what is ultimately real is not so explicitly expressed as it is in the reality formula we set forth in this book.

And so, although most philosophers of religion would accept the equating of the real or reality with God and His creation(s), they have a different understanding of precisely what it is that God created. Nevertheless, I think it is fair to say that we have fulfilled the second requirement for the use of the terms *real* and *reality*.

We will close this chapter with a discussion of one more crucial implication of the Course's teaching that everything God created is perfect like Himself.

God and His Creation
Remain Unaffected by Your Mistakes

That God and His creation are completely unaffected by your mistaken thoughts is another implication of the fact that God created you perfect like Himself. Your true Self is eternal and changeless. God created you perfect and this is how God knows you eternally, always and forever. To Him you are always His perfect Son co-creating with Him in gratitude for your creation, and this is so regardless of what you mistakenly think you are.

The Course says that the way we think about ourselves and this world is mistaken. We think of ourselves as egos, as a mind in a body. "The ego is idolatry; the sign of limited and separated self, born in a body, doomed to suffer and to end its life in death" (Th12,1:1).

Thus we think of our self as imperfect, not as perfect; as egos, not as holy Sons of God. As the Course's description of the ego implies, when the mind identifies with the ego it is perceiving itself as limited and separated, as in a body, and as vulnerable to attack and loss, pain and suffering and death. This way of thinking of ourselves leads us to think that, even if God did create us as His perfect Son, we are not perfect anymore. We have been changed. We have lost our original perfection and God knows it. And He probably doesn't like it. In fact He is probably very angry about it, and in His "justice" will punish us in return. And thus we fear God.

The Course says that although you do believe all this, and it seems very real to you, none of it is true. You are mistaken. You are deceived in yourself. You, as God created you, have not changed. You are still God's perfect Son, and He knows you only as such. He loves you. You are His joy. This means that God Himself is not affected by your false beliefs about yourself. Nor is your true identity as Christ changed by your false self-concept. Reality is not affected by your illusions of what you are. Reality remains as it always was, is now, and forever will be. You are free to believe what you think reality is, but you are not free to change it. "God knows not of your plans to change His Will" (L136,11:1)

This can be stated in terms of our last chapter. God is perfectly loving and perfectly powerful. And as such He shares everything He is and has with all His creations. You are one of His infinite number of creations, and as such you are perfect. Thus you are and will always be perfectly happy co-creating with your Father in eternal and unending joy. Neither your Father nor you, as He created you, is affected by your experience of evil, of attack and suffering and fear of death.

Yes, it is true that as humans we do perceive and experience these evils. What then must we conclude? We must conclude that our experience of being human and being in a world of bodies must be a *dream*. None of it can be reality. It is a dream in which we seem to be something we are not. While you are dreaming you think you are what you are not. It is a dream of being a body, of being limited and separated, of being different than God and His Son. It is an evil dream, a fearful dream, a nightmare, a dream of pain and death. How right we are when we sometimes exclaim, "I must be dreaming. This can't be real!"

A dream is not reality. Nor does it affect reality. Creation continues unabated despite your dream. What happens in a dream seems real to the dreamer while he is dreaming. But what happens in dreams is not what is happening in reality as God created it. The only thing happening in reality is what God wills, and that is the creation of the perfect, the extension of His perfect Self. God, then, is not aware of the contents of anyone's dream. The whole dream of time, space, and bodies exists in the mind of the Sonship, exists in your mind, apart from God's. When you wake up you simply awaken to "the knowledge of where you are always and what you are forever" (8.6,9:6). You are always at home in God, and you are forever His perfect Son creating in union with Him. A dream can never change that.

In Part Four, we will discuss in detail what is necessary before we can awaken from the dream. Here we can but repeat what we said earlier, that the first step in the awakening is to have our nightmare changed to "a happy dream". And this is done through forgiveness. The happiness of the dream reflects the natural condition of perfect happiness which is the inheritance of every Son of God as He created him.

Before we discuss the awakening, however, we must first understand why and how we put ourselves to sleep and dreamed a dream. Why did we, who were created perfect, make up a dream as a substitute reality? Why does it seem as if each of us is an ego-body, when the truth is that we are a pure mind, the holy Son of God Himself who cannot suffer, cannot be in pain, cannot suffer loss or experience evil in any form? (L191,7:3-4)

We turn, then, to Part Three where we deal with this all important question of the origin of limited and separated selves in a body. There we answer the second question we raised at the end of chapter 3, the second of three questions which must be answered if we are to fully understand and accept the solution to the logical problem of evil offered by Miracle Theodicy.

Hopefully at this point we are beginning to see the relationship between understanding and accepting this solution and making the choice for happiness. To put it another way, hopefully we are beginning to see the relationship between the solution to the *logical* problem of evil and the solution to the *practical* one.

Note

1. Kenneth Wapnick, *Glossary-Index for "A Course in Miracles."* New York: Coleman Graphics, 1982. p.4.

PART THREE

MISCREATION:
EVIL AND
THE SELF YOU MADE

PART THREE

MISCREATION:
EVIL AND THE SELF YOU MADE

The world of bodies is the world of sin, for
only if there were a body is sin possible....
Only the body makes the world seem real, for
being separate it could not remain where
separation is impossible.
A Course In Miracles (C4,5:5,9)

Introduction

In Part One we made clear the contradiction involved
in believing that both God and evil are real. We then
presented those teachings in *A Course in Miracles* which
provided us a way out of being so irrational that we insist a
contradiction is true. We then recognized that this escape
raised three general questions which must be answered
before we can fully understand and accept this solution to
the logical problem of evil.

In Part Two we answered the first of these questions, namely, if God did not create the body and the world of bodies, what did He create? Our answer was that He created You as spirit, as His Son, as a pure mind perfect like Himself. As He created you, you are one of an infinite number of God's Thoughts, and you still remain in His Mind as your Source, for what God created can never be separate from Him. You are spirit, and the unified spirit is God's One Son, the Christ. All of us are part of Christ, for Christ is "the Self we share, uniting us with one another and with God as well" (Th6,1:2).

In the upcoming Part Three we look at the Course's teaching on why each of us seems to be, not the perfect Son of God, but rather an ego, "a limited and separated self, born in a body, doomed to suffer and to end its life in death" (Th12,1:1). In other words, if God did not create us as humans, then how did we come to seem to be humans?

In Chapter 7 we examine the nature of the self to whom evil is real, the self that experiences evil; the self that attacks and suffers pain and loss, sickness and death. We not only look at the ways we as humans suffer, but we examine the conditions which are necessary for the possibility of attack, pain and suffering. We then answer the question of *why we seem to be an ego-body*, rather than the perfect Self God created us as.

In Chapter 8 we set forth the logical order of steps which led to the making of the ego, the body, and the world we see. In doing so we will answer the second question we raised at the end of chapter 3, namely, if God did not create the body and the world, who did? And, of course, this answer makes our position quite different from the other theodicies we have considered, all of which begin with the supposition that God did create the body and the world, and is thus aware of the evil that is part of it.

In Chapter 9, the last chapter of Part Three, we attempt to answer what is perhaps the most difficult question one could ever raise against the theodicy we are presenting here, and thus against the teachings of the Course itself. It is a question that seems to throw doubt on everything we said in Chapter 5 about God's creations being created perfect like Himself. Unless this question is answered our solution to the problem of evil will appear to be inconsistent, and therefore unacceptable to any rational person. We will not raise the question here in this introduction but reserve it for the point in our discussion at which it becomes meaningful.

Let us turn, then, to the next chapter where we begin our discussion of the Course's teachings on the origin of the ego, the body, and the world of space, time and bodies; a world in which evil seems real to those who made it, and who seem to live in the world they made.

7

WHO IS THE "YOU"
WHO SUFFERS?

*The ego is idolatry; the sign of limited and
separated self, born in a body, doomed to
suffer and to end its life in death.*
ACIM (Th12,1:1)

At this point we recognize that the most powerful
objection ever raised against belief in God *is* raised because
of our experience of evil. When we consider, on the one
hand, our experiences of evil, and on the other hand, the idea
that God created us as humans and must therefore be aware
of our suffering, we run smack into the contradiction clearly
displayed by the argument from evil (AFE).

In chapter 3 we set forth Miracle Theodicy's way of
avoiding this contradiction. We deny that God created us as
humans, and therefore deny that God Himself knows of
humans and their experience of evil. In this way we escaped
from the conclusion of the AFE by denying premise 3, the

one which states that God's omniscience implies that He is aware of the evil in the world.

I already mentioned that in denying premise 3, we are by implication denying premise 2, namely, that the evil in the world is real. Premise 2 can be seen as consisting of two statements: 1) There is evil in the world, and 2) the evil is real. We interpret the phrase "there is evil in the world" to mean that human beings experience attack and suffering and death, and that the attack, suffering, and death is evil; for "what is not happiness is evil" (L66,6:3). We do not deny that there is evil in this world. We acknowledge that humans do experience attack, suffering and death, and we affirm that the attack, suffering and death is indeed evil.

It is clear, however, that Miracle Theodicy does deny the second statement above, viz., the evil is real. We say that the evil is unreal because it is not real according to the reality formula. And since it is not real, the evil must be illusion. It is something that seems real to us, but it is not. We are deceived.

In other words, since God did not create this world of bodies, this world of bodies is not real. And since this world is not real, the evil in it is not real either. The evil in the world is illusion because it is merely part of the contents of a dream, and a dream is not reality. This world is a dream world. It is a dream of separation. Evil does not exist in reality, but only in an illusory world, a dream made up by a mind apart from God's Mind. This mind is the mind of God's Son mistakenly identified with the ego. Evil does not exist in God's Mind. God knows of no one who suffers. In short, evil is not real to God. Nor is evil real to you *as God created you.* For as God created you, you are perfect like Himself. You share His perfect happiness, love, knowledge, and power.

All of this implies that we must be *deceived* in believing that this world, and the evil we perceive in it, is real. We must also be deceived about *what* we are, and about *where* we are. The self that experiences evil *must be* an illusion, since our true Self cannot attack, suffer, or die. Let us look a little closer at the nature of the self that suffers. It is this self that claims evil is real.

THE SELF THAT EXPERIENCES EVIL

We said that in reality there is no evil. There is no one in God's creation who attacks or suffers. In fact, evil is impossible in reality as God created it. This is what we would expect if God is perfectly knowing, loving, powerful and happy. In fact, this is why the argument from evil (AFE) seems to prove that there is no God. It basically says if there was a perfect being there would be no evil in the reality He created. And this is the truth. The problem with the argument is that it assumes that this world is God's creation, that this world is reality.

The fact that there is no one in God's creation who attacks and suffers leads us to examine the nature of the self that does experience evil. What is it about human beings which makes their experience of evil possible? What is it about "the human condition" that makes it possible for us to attack and be attacked, to hurt and be hurt, and to die and fear dying? What is it that makes it possible for us to perceive others as attacked and attacking, as hurting and being hurt, as suffering and in pain, as sick and sinful, guilty, and afraid?

The first thing that comes to mind is that we as humans have *bodies*. We are minds using bodies. We each have a body, and we tend to identify with it. It seems as if we live within the body, or even that we *are* the body. As bodies we can attack and be attacked, kill and be killed, destroy and be destroyed. "Bodies attack, but minds do not" (L161,6:1).

When some other body attacks our body we usually suffer in some way. We feel pain or hurt. We may be physically injured or seriously harmed. For example, as a Vietnam vet I have seen fellow veterans who no longer have legs on their body. They lost their legs as a result of being shot by a North Vietnamese soldier, or by having stepped on a land mine, or by having fallen into a "pongee pit". Some of these veterans suffer long after the attack is over due to the disability that is a consequence of their injuries.

There are, of course, numerous ways we as humans may suffer as the result of a physical attack, by either another human body or some other animal body, or even by an inanimate body such as occurs in natural disasters like hurricanes, floods, earthquakes, and fires.

It seems that because we have a body we are also vulnerable to many forms of disease and sickness. "Little bodies", like viruses and bacteria, attack our bodies and we suffer discomfort, weakness, sickness and pain. We suffer losses as a consequence of the sickness. We might, for example, lose the money we would have earned by working, but we couldn't work since we had been attacked by the flu virus; or we lose out on the "fun" we would have had at the super-bowl party we planned to attend but couldn't because we had a cold.

There are many ways our bodies are attacked and we suffer as a result. We can add to our list things like cancer and heart attacks, pneumonia and AIDS, strokes, emphysema and muscular dystrophy, not to mention all the "accidents" like car, train, and plane crashes that occur every year. The list of diseases and other sources of suffering is indeed a long one. These attacks, and the pain and suffering which often result, are possible only because we each seem to be a body, or to live within a body. It is because we have bodies that attacking and being attacked seems to be an inevitable part of the human condition.

Furthermore, when we identify with the body we believe our life can end in death. Death is the end of life. If we believe that a functioning body is life then we must believe that life ends when the body stops functioning. We do believe this when we identify with the body. Since so many identify with the body the fear of death seems to be universal among humankind. This fear of death is another way we suffer. And we believe in death as long as we think we are a body. But there is no death. There is only a belief in death. There is no end to life, there is only a belief that life ends.

When one body attacks and kills another most of us would consider this the ultimate attack. And perhaps that is why murder is generally considered the worst of all crimes. The thought of being killed by another human being is a terrifying thought for most humans. The experience of somebody killing a loved one can seem even more terrible. Many people to whom this has happened suffer extreme horror and anger, loss and grief, and even a deep emptiness and deprivation after somebody killed their spouse or child, their parent or a dear friend. They have felt as if there own life became meaningless without their loved one. Death sometimes may seem more desirable to them than living without their loved one. This grief can be one of the most terrible forms of suffering. This kind of suffering too, however, is possible only because we have bodies, or think we and our loved one are bodies.

Having a body, then, is the condition necessary for the possibility of evil. Without a body the mind is unlimited, and is not only perfectly aware of everything that is true, but is perfectly happy. If we did not have a body we could neither attack nor suffer. Minds cannot attack. Nor can minds without a body suffer. It is because we have bodies we as human can attack and be attacked. And since attack always produces fear, and since fear is suffering, we can suffer and cause suffering because we can attack and be attacked.

We can name other conditions necessary for the possibility of evil. Each one we mention, however, is related to having a body. Another condition is *separation*. The idea of separation is directly related to having a body. In fact, as we shall see the idea of separation produced the body and is always associated with it. Because we seem to live in a body, we experience our self as separate from others, and different from them. Your mind seems to be in your body, and another mind seems to be in another body. You can point to your body and say, "This is me", and point to another body and say, "that is you". So you can say, seeming to speak the truth, "I am not you and you are not me. You are there and I am here."

Space is a form of the thought of separation. It seems to place a gap between you and me. Time is also a form of the thought of separation (26.8,1:3). I might say, for example, "Moses lived more than 3800 years ago, but I am living now, about 3800 years later. Moses is not me and I am not Moses. This is because "Robert Hellmann" and "Moses" are different labels for different bodies. In reality, which is timeless, what Moses is, as God created him, and what Robert Hellmann is, as God created him, are the same; we both are pure minds perfect like God, our loving Father.

Space and time and bodies are merely forms of the thought of separation, and the thought of separation exists in our mind, where all thoughts exist. "Only by assigning to the mind the properties of the body does separation seem to be possible" (18.6,3:2). In other words, I could never believe that I am a separate self unless I assign to my mind the properties of a body. By identifying with the body, by making ourselves be a body, we not only make separation seem possible, but as we have seen, we make attack and suffering seem possible as well.

When you attack you seem to be attacking someone different and separate from your self. And at those times when you are attacked you seem to be attacked by someone different and separate from your self. This is because you perceive your self as a body and thus you perceive your brother as a body. As a pure mind you cannot do this. A pure mind recognizes everyone as its Self, and perfect like Itself. And because no one seems separate or different from its Self, it attacks no one nor is attacked by anyone. There is no attack in reality, and thus there is no suffering either. God has given only happiness to all His creations. And, as we have seen, He has given us the power to extend this happiness to our own creations which we create in union with Him.

Another condition for the possibility of evil is *limitation*. Like separation, limitation is directly related to being or having a body. "The body is a limit" (L199,1:2). Because we are using bodies our awareness is limited (18.6,8:3). We are not perfectly aware of everything that is true. We do not experience ourselves as knowing everything. We often make mistakes. Yet, as the Course says, "The mind without the body cannot make mistakes" (L192,5:1). A mind with a body can make mistakes, for being a perceiver it is always subject to mistaking appearances for truth. We suffer because we can and do make mistakes.

We can summarize what we said about the self that experiences evil by saying that such a self must be an ego, a limited and separated self in a body. The self that suffers is an ego. Only the ego can suffer, for "only the ego can be limited" (L319,1:4).

From the above discussion it is clear that imperfection is a necessary condition for the possibility of evil. The perfect and unlimited cannot suffer. Finitude makes attack and suffering possible. This is not a new idea. Finitude, or the condition of being limited, has long been recognized by theodicists as the condition without which evil would be impossible. "No finitude, no evil", would be a short way of expressing this insight. It's that simple: no limitation, no evil; no limitation, no attack or suffering; no imperfection, no unhappiness.

Since limitation is the foundation of all evil, limitation itself is a kind of evil. In fact, theodicists have long given a special name to this kind of evil to distinguish it from other kinds of evil. They call it "metaphysical evil" to distinguish it from "moral evil" (sin or attack with the intention to do harm) and "physical evil" (pain and suffering and death) - sometimes called "non-moral evil".

WHY DO YOU SEEM TO BE A LIMITED AND SEPARATED SELF IN A BODY?

We are now ready to begin offering an answer to the second question raised at the end of chapter 3. As I have mentioned often, it is but one of three questions that must be answered before our solution to the problem of evil can be fully understood and accepted. Recall that the second question is: if God did not create the body or the world, who did?

It will be helpful to distinguish two aspects of this one question. The two aspects can be stated as different but closely related questions contained in this one question about origins. The first question seems to be more personal. It has to do with our experience of being an ego, or a limited and separated self in a body. This question can be stated as: what is the origin of the ego? The second has to do with what may seem to be a less personal question. It has to do with the origin of the physical world. This question can be stated as: what is the origin of the world we see and in which we seem to live?

In the next chapter it will become clear that these two questions are more closely related than one might at first think. In other words, in order to describe what led to the making of the world we must first describe what led to the making of the ego.

The first question we just raised can be stated in various ways because it can be framed differently: If God did not create each of us as a limited and separated self born in a body, then how did we get this way? In other words, if God created us as pure minds that live forever, why do we each seem to be an ego, a mind living within a body that must die? If God created us perfect, why do we seem to be imperfect? How did we come to believe that we are really humans, separate and different from one another, even though in truth we are really the perfect Son of God united as one Self, the Christ?

The second question, closely related to the first, can also be stated in various ways: If God did not create the world we see, how did it arise before our sight? Who made this world of bodies, and why? What is the origin of the physical universe, given that God did not create it? What is the purpose of the world of bodies? Whose purpose does it serve?

In this chapter I will simply *begin* the process of answering these questions. In the next two chapters I will complete the answer. Here in chapter 7 I will merely introduce what the Course calls "the request for special favor". It is this request that is the ultimate explanation of the origin of the ego, the body, and the world we see.

After introducing the idea of the request for special favor, I will use the remainder of this chapter to discuss what specialness entails and what it means for you who identify with the ego.

So let us begin. The question we have before us is: Why do you seem to be an ego, a limited and separated self in a body? The Course gives a simple, but provocative answer to this question. It says that you seem to be an ego merely because you believe you are. And you believe you are an ego because *you as a mind want to be!*

In other words, the Course would have us recognize that our mind is more powerful than we generally acknowledge. We are denying the real power of our own mind and will! The fact is that you believe you are an ego merely because *you want* to believe it. That is the power of your wanting! What you want to believe you do believe. And if you believe it, it is true for you. What you believe is real, is real for you. And because you believe it, you perceive it. You find evidence for it because you make the "evidence" which witnesses to your false belief about yourself.

As we mentioned earlier none of this changes reality or the truth. It does not change reality as God created and knows it. It does, however, change your experience. You can believe that reality is what you think you want it to be, but you can never change it. "Truth is unalterable, eternal and unambiguous. It can be unrecognized, but it cannot be changed" (Pref.3,1:4-5).

Thus, the Course asks us to recognize that we each believe we are an ego because we *want* to believe it, whether this wanting is conscious or unconscious. We who seem to be in this world are afraid to give up ego identity because we believe our ego self is our life, and that the end of our ego means the end of our life - it means death.

Just think of this for a minute. Do you want to be a human being? Do you want to be a limited and separated self in a body? Do you want to be an ego? All three are the same question. Or would you rather be something else? Do you want to be a spirit? Do you want to be a pure mind without a body? Do you want to be the holy Son of God? All three of these are also the same question.

You may think you have no choice but to believe you are an ego. You may believe that you are a human being and say, "that is simply the way it is, I can't change that." And if you happen to believe in God, you may believe that God created you as a human being. And so you say, "that's just the way it is - God created me this way and I guess He knew what He was doing." You believe this because you unconsciously want to preserve your ego identity, and deny your Christ Identity. And this wish is unconscious because you are keeping it unconscious. But you can learn to make yourself aware of the choice you are making. This is exactly what the Course is teaching us to do. To become aware of the choice we are making about what we are, and thus about what God is.

As we have seen in Chapter 5, God created you as his perfect Son. He could not create you any other way and still be a perfectly knowing, loving, powerful, and happy Father. And the Course teaches that you can remember your Identity as God created you. So, whether you presently recognize it or not, you do have a choice about whether you are an ego. You are an ego in your perception of you only because you choose to remain one, not recognizing there is another alternative. You are afraid of the other alternative, and have dissociated and repressed it.

But be glad that you will not hold this choice forever, because the ego is an illusion, and ego identity offers you nothing but illusions. Sooner or later you will make another choice; you will decide to accept that you are as God created you. And *you do have this power of decision. You can* dis-identify with the ego, and accept yourself as God created you. You need but recognize your own power and how you are presently using it. And change your mind.

You were once directly aware of what you really are. You were once aware that you are in Heaven. You were once aware of perfect oneness. You were once aware that you are in God. But you have forgotten. How did this happen? How did you forget what you really are, and come to think you are what you are not?

The Request for Special Favor

The Course's answer to the question of how you came to believe you are an ego is that as God's Son you asked for special favor. As the Course puts it:

> "You were at peace until you asked for special favor. And God did not give it, for the request was alien to Him.... Therefore you made of Him an unloving father, demanding what only such a father could give. And the peace of God's Son was shattered, for he no longer understood his Father" (13.3,10:2-5).

When the Course says, "the peace of God's Son was shattered" it means, among other things, that his mind was split. The mind of God's Son was split when he demanded the special favor God did not give. In other words, a part of the mind of God's Son split off from his perfect and whole mind and identified with its miscreation; with what it created on its own apart from its creator. This separated mind, although it is still really a part of the whole mind, mistakenly believes it is a separate whole in itself because it is identified with the form, image, or body it made. It has forgotten its oneness with the whole. It has lost awareness of what it really is. It now seems to have a separate, different, and special identity. To itself it *is* special, different, and separate.

How should we understand this request for special favor? We will discuss this in detail throughout chapter 8 and chapter 9. But here I will say that the request for special favor could be understood in various ways, or from various points of view. It could be a request for special love from God, or special love from a brother. We could understand this request as a request to create something special, to create something different than what you as God's Son always create. We could understand this request for special favor as a request that God give you something that He does not give to everyone else, or that you be able to give to Him something that not everyone gives or could give. Or it could be a request to be a prime creator like God is; or to be a sole creator of something as God is.. As we have seen, God is the only sole Creator of something and the only Prime Creator of everything.

In any case, regardless of how we understand this request, its fulfillment would result in you being singled out, different, alone -- in some way or for some reason. It would result in you having more of something than someone else has.

The Conditions Necessary For Specialness

I already mentioned that the details of how this request for special favor led to the making of the ego, the body, and the world will be discussed in the next two chapters. The remainder of this chapter will be used to discuss what specialness means to us now that the ego-body seems to be our true identity. In other words, we will look carefully at some of the things specialness entails.

Specialness entails that you *have* something that someone else does not have, or that you *be* something that someone else is not. To be special means you have more (or less) than someone else; you are better (or worse) than someone else. And thus it may seem you have something to "give" that someone else does not have to give, or you are entitled to receive something that someone else is not entitled to receive. It means that you can do something which on one else can do, or at least which not everyone can do.

All of this is glaringly apparent in this world. For example, you may have a talent or an ability to do something that most others cannot do. It matters not what it is. This talent makes you special. It is the "something" you have more of. It is the "something" that makes you better than another.

For example, you may be a good singer. And thus you can give a pleasure to others that a person who does not sing well cannot give them. And so you may receive special love and admiration because of your talent, not to mention an especially high monetary reward if you are "really good". You may think your happiness lies in having this talent or in being the special person you are.

There are numerous ways of being special in this world. You may, for example, have a talent for business or investment and know how to make money easily. You may have more money than someone else, or more and better houses, cars, computers, and clothes. You might think your safety and security depend on this wealth, and that your happiness lies in your special ability to make money, and the special person you seem to be as the result of it.

You may have more power and influence, or more fame, status, and "name recognition", than most people have. As a result you may find that your special wishes receive "special consideration" from others. You seem to like this, it may seem that you are happy because of this. You may think your safety, security and happiness lie in having this fame or this power over others. You may think you are happy because of the unique person you seem to be.

You may be more handsome or pretty than someone else and receive "special love and affection". Again you may think your identity lies in this handsome or sexually attractive body. And that your happiness lies in what it offers you and others. You may think the special love you receive makes you happy, as if your happiness lies in having this especially attractive body.

You may have more "knowledge", or more information, skill, intelligence, expertise, and experience in some area than most people. And as a result receive more respect than others do. You may feel good about yourself, have high "self esteem", and think that your happiness lies in being this "exceptionally intelligent" self.

This is what "specialness" means. It doesn't really matter what you have more of, just so *it is more*. It could even be more sickness, more surgeries, tragedies, accidents, or more "close brushes with death". Or perhaps you have survived despite so much more affliction, pain, and suffering than others. It matters not. As long as it is *more of something* (29.8,8:7). It is the more, the being "better than" that singles you out, and makes you different and special. It makes you unique. It makes you "you", and not someone else.

It is surely apparent that specialness entails *inequality*. And this is why the Course says, "Getting more is against God's Will" (29.8,8:13). All God's children are equal. They have been given everything. "What is God's belongs to everyone, and *is* his due" (25.9,10:10). This is Heaven's justice (see 25.9). Everyone must be equal and the same if everyone is perfect.

Again it may be worthwhile to think about this for a moment. How do you feel about this whole idea of having special favor, of being special? Are you disappointed with this negative evaluation or attitude toward specialness? Do you think that to be special is "good"? Do you think specialness brings happiness?

When we protect and defend our specialness we are identified with the ego, and thus with the body, for you (mind) and an illusion of you meet at the body. We think our ego identity is our life, and we want as good a life as we can have. What makes me unique and makes my life better than that of others are the things of this world that I have, and the qualities I have as a person that others do not have. And I like being unique. I like being better. "There is only one me!" So speaks the ego with pride. So speak all who believe their *humanness* is their reality.

If you are identified with the ego you want to protect your specialness. Preserving itself is what the ego is all about. It evaluates everything in terms of threat or non-threat to itself. But specialness is a lonely existence. As the Course puts it: To "single out" is to "make alone", and thus make lonely" (13.3,12:1).

Eventually we all will recognize the treachery of specialness. It is treachery to yourself, and to everyone around you. Specialness holds both you and your brother in hell. It is the source of all war and fear. Your specialness is what others attack and you protect (24.1,9:4). If you are special you cannot be at peace. "Never can there be peace among the different" (24.1,9:7). Nor can there be love.

Each of us has a wish to be special. We would not be here in this world if we didn't. This world was made as a place to seek and maintain a separate, different, and special identity; an identity different than the one God gave us.

The desire for specialness, and the search to have others affirm our specialness, pervades human interactions and relationships. It pervades this world. If you look carefully you can see that this is so. It is, for example, what lies behind all competition, including the game of "one upmanship", and many other games people play. We ask our children: What do you want to be when you grow up, as if it is up to them, and not God, to determine what they are. Everyone wants "to be somebody".

But we can change the purpose for which we walk the earth. Instead of trying to build a self concept that we and others consider special, we can learn instead to accept the Self God created us as. We can learn that the only worthwhile purpose for this world is to heal our mind through forgiving the world and thus forgiving ourselves. We will discuss this glad change in purpose in Part Four.

Because specialness entails inequality it also entails *difference*. For how could I be better than you unless you and I are different? I cannot be better than you if we both have the same perfect nature. Specialness then requires that you and I be different. Inequality and difference imply each other.

Specialness, beside requiring inequality and difference also requires *separation*. To be special and different, we must be separate selves, cut off from one another. You cannot be the same self I am if either one of us is to be special. Somehow, what I am must be something separate from what you are. We cannot be joined and united as one Self and also be special, unequal and different selves.

Furthermore, in order for you and I to be separate from each other, we both must be separate from God. For everyone that is one with God is perfect like God Himself; They are equal, the same, and joined, united with one another in one Self, the Christ.

Finally, specialness, - which requires inequality, difference, and separation - entails *limitation*. In order to be separate from God one must be limited. For all minds that are one with God are limitless like Himself. Thus in order for a mind to even seem separate from another mind, each mind must be limited in at least two senses. First, it must be limited in awareness. It can no longer be aware of reality where everything is one with it, and nothing is separate. Second, it must be limited in the sense that it is a form or a body of some kind which defines it and keeps it separate from others. There must be something with which the mind identifies and can say, "this is me and that is you who are separate and different from me."

The body, which the mind uses to limit its awareness need not be thought of as only a human body - and at first, given what we know about evolution, could not have been. It needs be merely some *form* or image that makes the mind seem separate from other minds. The Course frequently mentions this use of the body as a separation device, for example, when it says, "The body is a fence the Son of God imagines he has built to separate parts of his Self from other parts" (Th5,1:1). Or again, "Only by assigning to the mind the properties of the body does separation seem to be possible" (18.7,3:2).

It is surely apparent from this brief discussion that the conditions necessary for *specialness* are the same conditions necessary for *evil*. In other words, the conditions necessary for specialness and the conditions necessary for attack and suffering are the same; they both require that you be a limited and separated self in a body. This is no coincidence. For, according to the Course, the reason for all our suffering, regardless of its form, is our "tiny mad desire to be separate, different, and special" (25.1,5:5).

Let's summarize what we have learned in this chapter. We have seen that the self that experiences evil must be a limited and separated self in a body. In short, only the ego suffers. This self must be an illusion of your self because God did not create this self. The ego is the mind's false thought of what it is. The ego is an illusion of what you are.

The ultimate explanation of why you seem to be an ego even though you are not, is that, as God's Son, you asked for special favor. But God did not give it. However, you demanded it and thus the mind of God's Son split. The part that split off from the Whole is identified with the ego-body and seems to live in this world, attempting to preserve, protect, and defend itself as a separate, different and special self. It is the task of the next chapter to fill in the details of the psycho-logical steps which led to the making of the ego, the body, and the physical world. In setting forth the origin of the ego, the body, and the world we hope to firmly set the second pillar needed to support the new and radical solution to the logical problem of evil we offered in chapter 3.

8

THE ORIGIN OF THE EGO, THE BODY, AND THE WORLD

You were at peace until you asked for special favor.
ACIM (13.3,10:2)

In the last chapter we examined the nature of the self that suffers. In this chapter we will examine the origin of this self and the world in which it seems to live. We learned that the self that attacks, suffers, and dies must be a limited, separated self in a body. The Course calls this self "the ego". The ego is the mind's false belief about what it is. You as an ego, then, are a mind that is deceived about what you are, and this deception always involves identification with a body of some kind, and thus a belief that you are a separate self. As we learned from the last chapter, only an ego-body can attack and suffer. Only the ego can experience evil. Evil is real only to an ego. Evil is not real to a mind that knows itself as purely mind. Such a mind does not experience evil, for it cannot attack or be attacked; hurt or be hurt, kill or be killed..

In this chapter, then, we will answer the second of the three questions we raised at the end of chapter 3, namely, if God did not create the body or the world, who did? Before we turn our attention to directly answering this question I want to make some preliminary remarks about the importance of this topic for theodicy.

THEODICY AND THE QUESTION OF WHO MADE THE WORLD

The question of who made the world is a central issue for theodicy. Most, if not all, theodicies start with the assumption that God created the world and knows about the evil its inhabitants experience. As I mentioned earlier it may be fair to say that this assumption is crucial in engendering the problem of evil. Without this assumption the logical problem of evil dissolves, and the whole issue of God and evil is seen from a different perspective.

As we have seen, the assumption that God created the world lies behind all previous failures to solve the problem of evil. We have seen as well that Miracle Theodicy's success in solving the problem involves not accepting this assumption. And it is this that makes it radically different from any other theodicy.

Miracle Theodicy denies that God is maker of this world. However, Miracle Theodicy does, like all other theodicies, start with the affirmation: "God is." This affirmation is made with the understanding that the term "God" means a perfect being, one having all the attributes of perfection. The author of the Course not only affirms that God *is*, but that *God* is, i.e., a *Perfect Being* exists or is real. It may be possible some day for some scholar of the Course to show that all its positive teachings are actually nothing more than logical deductions from this starting point, along with a few other axioms and definitions.

The assertion that "God is" is simply a starting point of theodicy. For theodicy is simply the attempt to show that this belief can be consistently held even though humans experience attack and suffering.

It is fair to say, however, that some traditional theists would like to rely on "proofs" for the existence of God. For if one gives a *positive proof* that God exists, then he could use this as a counter argument against the conclusion of the AFE, viz., that there is no God.

For example, the well known argument for the existence of God, called "the argument from contingency", starts with the observation that the existence of everything in this world is contingent, that is, it exists only because something else that exists caused its existence. For example, you exist because your parents caused your existence, and they exist because their parents caused theirs, and so on.

Using this "principle of cause and effect" the thinker infers that there must be a being whose existence is not contingent, but necessary. His existence does not depend on someone else who caused him to be. This being is said to be an uncaused cause and the uncreated creator of the physical universe. Sometimes it is even said that this creator also preserves the existence of everything in the world. If He did not do so the thing would die or go out of existence.

Then, without any real logical justification, the thinker using this argument infers that this creator of the world, whose existence has been inferred to, can properly be called "God".

It has been shown throughout the history of philosophy that such "arguments for the existence of God" possess major flaws. The logical force of cosmological arguments for the existence of God is not such that one can truly say they "prove" God exists. They do, however, sound convincing to those who already believe in a "God" before they give serious consideration to the logical force of the argument. To those who already believe in God, the arguments seem to offer some logical or reasonable support to their belief.

There is a powerful argument against the idea that cosmological arguments prove the existence of God. It runs like this: Even if one were to grant some value to the argument as an argument, it only proves, at best, that *some kind of a mind* or personal being made the world. And it may legitimately be inferred that this mind has power and intelligence, at least enough power and intelligence required to make the world.

However, the argument in no way proves that this mind has *all the attributes of perfection!* Therefore calling this maker of the world "God" is a totally unjustified leap in the reasoning process. In other words, simply because your reasoning leads you to the conclusion that the physical universe must have been made by some mind or personal being, this same reasoning does not justify the conclusion that this mind is the *Mind of God*, or that this personal being is God. It could be some other mind or personal being who made the world, and not the Perfect Being we call God.

Early Christian theologians and philosophers like Augustine and Thomas Aquinas, who did not have the benefit of modern science, accepted the idea that God created the world because the assertion is made in the Bible, and the cosmological proofs for God's existence seemed to add some rational support to the Biblical statement. Thus they seemed convincing as proofs for God's existence. For who else but "God" could this being, whose necessary existence they proved, be? Some readers of this book, of course, are well acquainted with Thomas' *quinque via* or "five ways" of proving the existence of "God". But when

Thomas concludes each of his arguments with the phrase "and this being all men call God" he is making a leap in reasoning that is not justified. For there is nothing in the cosmological arguments which prove that this maker of the world, whose necessary existence has been inferred to, has all the attributes of perfection Thomas ascribes to God in other parts of his *Summa Theologica*.

In Genesis we find not only the well known statement, "In the beginning God created the heavens and the earth" (Gen 1:1), but also the famous formula by which God supposedly made all these things, namely, God said, "let there be, and it was so". For example, God said, "let there be light, and it was so". God said, "let there be firmament, (or the dry land, or vegetation, or fish in the sea, etc.) and it was so."

"Let there be, and it was so." That is the way God created the physical universe, including human beings. All in six "days" according to Genesis.

Much has been written on these passages. Of course, the main point of the story is not so much the exact order of steps, or exactly *how* God, as spirit or pure mind, could create a physical world and human beings. The main point for our purpose here is simply the idea that the world and humans are said to have been created by *God*. God is said to be their Source. The story also contains the point that God created the world simply by willing it. He merely spoke the word, as it were, saying "let it be". And so it was. This, of course, reveals just how powerful the author of Genesis considered God's Will to be.

As far as theodicy is concerned, then, the main point the author of Genesis is making is that the maker of the "heavens" he sees (i.e., the sun, moon, and stars), and of the earth on which he stands -- and of all the human and other bodies he sees around him -- is *God*. It is clear that the writer of Genesis conceives of his God as maker of the world of bodies and personally aware of, and causally involved in, the activities and events of human history.

This is still the official interpretation of the story in Genesis. In other words, the idea that the maker of the physical universe is God is still an idea taught as theological and philosophical truth by most, if not all, Western institutionalized religions, including Judaism, Christianity, and Islam.

Many contemporary theodicists, including Hick and Griffin, who have the benefit of information, theories, and physical laws offered by modern science, say that the evolution of the physical universe, including the stars, the galaxies, the sun, the planets, the earth, animal and human bodies, was initiated, and in some sense directed, by God.

Once a modern theodicist accepts the idea that God is cause and creator of the physical world, he has several issues he must deal with in defending this position. For example, it becomes reasonable to ask whether God's creation of the physical world follows necessarily given the very nature of God, i.e., God could not help but create this kind of world given what God is. An alternative to this position would be that God *freely chose* to create this world, i.e., God could have chosen not to create this world, but for some reason did so anyway. And for this reason, whatever it is, God freely chose to do it, even though he could have chosen not to.

If one does say that God freely chose to create this world then one must answer the question of *why* God would make such a choice. Why did God do such a thing? What was His purpose for creating limited and separated selves in a body who, as such, would inevitably suffer and die? He must have known they would experience evil. Why would a Being Who is perfectly happy create beings who can oppose His Will? One would think that His perfect happiness is due to the fact that His Will is done. So why create beings who have the power and freedom to make you unhappy? It doesn't make sense. Why would God do such a thing? It is easy to see why this debate about why God created the physical world and human beings seems to be never ending. As we have seen, Miracle Theodicy ends all such debates.

Another debate that ensues, once one claims that God created the world, is whether God created the physical world *ex-nihilo* ("from nothing"), as Classical and Person-Making Theodicy maintain, or whether God created it from some "material" or "stuff" which has co-existed along with God for all eternity, as Process Theodicy maintains.

There is no reason for us to enter any of these specific debates here, or to examine the arguments and counter-arguments they involve. For any question that assumes that God created the world has no meaning for Miracle Theodicy. Why did God create a world of finite bodily beings? Miracle Theodicy's "answer" is: He didn't. The question contains a false assumption.

There is another question closely related to this one, and which many consider the central question for theodicy itself: Why does God permit evil? Miracle Theodicy answers this question in the same way it answers the last one: He doesn't.

To say that God permits evil is to say, firstly, that God is aware of evil, and to say, secondly, that God has the power to prevent it, but does not do so for some reason. Miracle Theodicy, as we have seen, says that God is not even aware of evil. He is not aware of beings who attack and suffer and die. He is not aware of this dream world at all. Beings who attack and suffer simply do not exist for God. He did not create them. Such things are illusions and can exist only in minds apart from God. They are not real. They do not exist in His Mind where only His perfectly happy creations exist.

214 God, Self, and Evil

Therefore it does not make sense to say that God permits evil, since God is not even aware of evil. Evil does not exist in reality as He created it, and God knows only reality. Nothing He did not create is real. The question: why does God permit evil? then, is ultimately a meaningless question. It arises from the false assumption that God does permit evil to exist in His creation.

WHO IS THE MAKER OF THE WORLD?

Although Miracle Theodicy can easily dismiss questions that are so meaningful, significant, and crucial for other theodicies, it does, nevertheless, have its own correspondingly difficult questions to answer. The obvious one is, if God did not create the body and the world, who did? And once we answer this question we too, have the "why" question. Why was the world made? Why did the maker of the world, whoever he is, make this world? What was the purpose?

Let's examine the question about "who". As we have seen, according to the teachings in *A Course in Miracles*, reality consists of God and His perfect creations, or God and His Kingdom. So if God did not create the world, then it seems it must have been made by the Sonship, or by God's Son. It seems the Son is the only candidate left to be the maker of the world, given that God did not create it.

The world is said to be a dream. Who is doing the dreaming? Who is making up illusions? Who is deceived that illusions are true? It is clear that it is not God. God is not dreaming. God is not asleep. God is not aware of illusions. Nor is He unaware of reality. The world is not God's dream. Is it not, then, His Son's?

Can we say that it is God's Son who is dreaming, or that it is God's Son who made the world?. You are God's

Son. So, is it you who made the world? Is it you who are dreaming? Is the world your dream?

The Course, in fact, does say that "you" are the maker of the world, yes, you the Son of God made this world. But we must be careful here. We must be very careful! Otherwise we will fall into contradiction, and the whole thought system, the whole theodicy, will collapse. And our solution to the problem of evil will be no more successful than previous "solutions".

It cannot be that the perfect Son of God made the world because a perfect being would not, and could not, make such a world as this! Neither a created perfect being (God the Son), nor an uncreated One (God the Father), could be maker of an imperfect world of time, space, and bodies - or of an imperfect anything.

But if it is not the perfect Son of God, if it is not Christ, if it is not *You as God created you*, then who is the "you" who made the world? And who is the "you" who seems to live in the world you made? In other words, where did the maker of the world come from? If he is not God, nor anyone God created perfect like Himself, then who is he? How did he originate? Where did he come from?

We do, indeed, have an interesting question to answer! And perhaps one of the most difficult. What is the origin of the maker of the world? What led to such a thing as a sleeping mind that is dreaming a dream in which it seems to be body in a world of bodies when it really is not? What mind is dreaming?

The remainder of this chapter is centered around answering this question. And in answering this one we will, of course, have to answer some closely related ones.

We said the maker of the body and the world is you. Who is this "you"? According to the Course, this "you" is *you as the separated mind of God's Son identified with the ego.*

Throughout the Course various terms are used to refer to this mind who is maker of the world. Sometimes the Course uses simply the term *you*, or *the mind*, or *the separated mind*, or *the separated mind of God's Son*, or *the separated Son of God*, or *the Son*, or *you who identify with the ego*, or simply *the ego*, depending on what is appropriate for the context.

To say that *the ego* made the world is meant to be a kind of shorthand. It is always clear when these terms refer to the original maker of the world. Any one of these terms or phrases when used to refer to the maker of the world is meant to refer to the same thing. In all cases the understanding is that the original maker of the world is you, as the separated mind of God's Son identified with the ego. It is not, for example, "You", as Christ, or "You" as the perfect Son of God, or "You" as God created You, since God did not create you as a separated mind, nor did He create you as an ego, or a mind identified with the ego.

Thus we say *the world was made by you*, the Son of God, only in the sense of your separated mind, the separated mind of God's Son identified with the ego. This is why we can just as well say that the world was made by the ego.

The ego is merely a part of your belief about yourself; or a part of the mind's belief about itself, about what it is. The ego is merely a false way of thinking and willing in which the mind is identifying with a false thought of what it is. This thought always includes the idea that it is a separate thing. The ego is you who believe you really are a separate "I", a separate whole in yourself. The ego is a part of your mind that thinks you are something you are not. It is your mind deceived that an illusion of you is really you. The world was made by this mind that is deceived about itself.

The world was not made by the Christ, *God's Son as He created him*. It was not made by You as God created you. Christ is your true and eternally perfect Self, the true

Thought of what you are. Christ is your Mind that co-creates with God His Father, and knows What He really is as God created Him. The ego is a substitute you, a substitute thought of what you are. To the mind that believes it is separate, its separation is real. For "all beliefs are real to the believer" (3.7,3:3).

It may be difficult to accept the idea that the world was made by you. You may believe that it is arrogant to think that you made the world. The Course addresses this concern and would have you consider this:

> Is it not strange that you believe to think you made the world you see is arrogance? God made it not. Of this you can be sure. What can He know of the ephemeral, the sinful and the guilty, the afraid, the suffering and lonely, and the mind that lives within a body that must die? You but accuse Him of insanity, to think He made a world where such things seem to have reality. He is not mad. Yet only madness makes a world like this. (L152,6)

The second question raised by our solution to the problem of evil is: if God did not make the body and the world then who did? We now have an answer: you did! Your mind identified with the ego did. The ego made the world.

This is the Course's teaching on who made the body and the world. You made the body and the world. The more one reads and studies and reflects on this teaching, and uses its implications in one's daily life, the more understandable and acceptable it becomes. The world is but your dream of being separate from your Creator and the creations you created in union with Him. God did not create it. God could not have created it and still be God. And since God did not create the world, the world is not real, it is an illusion.

Reason will tell you that if something is not reality it must be illusion.

Now that we have an answer to the question of who made the world we need to get a better understanding of the Course's explanation of the process by which the mind made the ego. To do this we must answer the question which introduces this section. How did this maker of the world originate? How did a you as *the separated mind of God's Son identified with the ego* come about? In short what is the origin of the ego, a mind that believes it is a separate self? It is to answering this question that we now turn.

"Into Eternity, Where All is One"

There is no one place in the Course that explicitly sets forth a detailed logical sequence of steps which led to the making of the maker of the world. The Course does, however, often make statements related to the origin of the ego, and the world it made, but most often the statements are found within the context of an overall discussion whose main theme is something other than this topic. And very often the statements are brief. Thus from the beginning of the Text, through the Workbook and the Manual, this topic of origins is introduced, related to the topic at hand and then dropped, to be reintroduced and developed further, dropped again to be developed more later - until finally, when the Course is completely written, we have enough material to be able to construct some order of steps which led to the making of the ego and the world. Let me give one example of this approach before I set forth my understanding of the entire logical sequence of steps.

There is a section in the Text (27.8) entitled, *The "Hero" of the Dream*. It is clear that the Course identifies the "hero" as the body, the dreamer as you (the sleeping Son of

God), and the dream as the world of time, space, and bodies. Your body, then, is but a figure in your dream of being a separate self. It represents you in the dream (4:3). (Note: while we are discussing this section in the Text, namely, 27.8, I will reference passages with only the paragraph and sentence numbers without the chapter and section numbers.)

One could say that the main practical point of this section is that the secret of salvation from all pain and suffering is recognizing that "you are doing this unto yourself" (10:1).

In other words, among other things, this section is teaching you that everything you experience is caused by you, because your experience as an ego, is your own dream; you, as mind, are the dreamer of the dream. The body, the "hero" of the dream, represents your separate self in the dream, a self separate from other selves who also seem to be separate minds in separate bodies. Thus you, the mind that is dreaming, are the *cause,* and the dream is the *effect.* But the dream, and the figures and events in the dream (bodies and what they say and do), *seems* to be the cause, and your experience *seems* to be the effect. It seems as if things are being done to you, rather than you doing them to yourself. After all, if the world is your dream, then whatever happens to the figure that represents you in the dream is caused by you the dreaming mind.

This theme of the *reversal of cause and effect* is reiterated over and over in this section, as well as in other parts of the Course. The idea that we, who seem to live in this world, have reversed cause and effect is a central theme in the Course's teachings, and applies to many aspects of our experience in this world. This is one reason the Course says of itself that it is helping to bring about "thought reversal" (L126,1:1).

In the middle of this section we find the passage relevant to our topic here. This passage is perhaps the one

most frequently found in Course literature whenever the
topic is that of origins. It is the passage most likely to be
quoted by a student of the Course in response to the
question: how did our experience of being ego-bodies in a
physical world come about? How did it all start given that
we were all created as eternally one?

The often quoted passage is introduced with this
sentence: "Let us return the dream he gave away unto the
dreamer, who perceives the dream as separate from himself
and done to him" (6:1). And then follows the passage that
has become famous in Course literature:

> Into eternity, where all is one, there crept a
> tiny, mad idea, at which the Son of God
> remembered not to laugh. In his forgetting
> did the thought become a serious idea, and
> possible of both accomplishment and real
> effects. (6:2-3)

Immediately following these two sentences the
author begins his return to the main point of the section,
which we have just discussed. He says nothing here about
what the tiny mad idea is, or exactly what happens after "the
thought becomes a serious idea". However, in the transition
back to the main point a few more things are said about what
seem to be the results of this "tiny mad idea":

> Together, we can laugh them both away, and
> understand that time cannot intrude upon
> eternity. It is a joke to think that time can
> come to circumvent eternity, which *means*
> there is no time. (6:4-5)

So "time" seems to be one of the results of taking this
idea seriously. But obviously if reality is timeless and eternal

it must be "a joke" to think that time is real. This means "there is no time". Time, then, must be an aspect of the dream. It must be illusion; not reality.

Notice the line "we can laugh them both away". Both *of what?* Well, both the idea that it could be accomplished, and the effects of its supposed accomplishment. In other words, we can laugh away any seemingly real effects of the tiny mad idea, and any belief that it has been accomplished in reality. This involves understanding that time cannot intrude upon eternity. Anything that happens in time must be unreal and illusory, and has no effect on reality at all.

The next few lines describe other things that seem to result from taking the tiny mad idea seriously, but the ending of these things "starts at their beginning". In other words, in reality, in eternity, where all is one, these things really ended the instant they began. They cannot exist in reality, but only as part of a dream. Here are the things that are a "joke":

> A timelessness in which is time made real; a part of God that can attack itself; a separate brother as an enemy; a mind within a body; all are forms of circularity whose ending starts at its beginning, ending at its cause. (7:1)

After this brief excursion, which was made for the purpose of "returning the dream unto the dreamer", the author then turns back to discussing the central theme of this section - that what you are doing to yourself seems to be done to you by a world which seems outside your mind because you have reversed cause and effect. But actually the world is in your mind as a dream, and only seems to be outside it:

The world you see depicts exactly what you
thought you did. Except that now you think
that what you did is being done to you. The
guilt for what you thought is being placed
outside yourself, and on a guilty world that
dreams your dreams and thinks your thoughts
instead of you. It brings its vengeance, not
your own. (7:2-5)

And so, after little more than a paragraph, the author
is back to his theme of the secret of salvation. It is a secret
you have kept from yourself. And the secret is: that although
it seems that evil things are being done to you by others
outside you, actually you are doing these things to yourself.
This is true because you are the dreamer of the dream and
the body you identify with is the "hero" of the dream merely
carrying out the intentions of your mind, including intentions
to hurt yourself as a way of punishing yourself for your
imagined sin. This is just one of the many ways the ego
usurps what it believes is God's role. For the ego's purpose is
to replace God.

In a few sentences of this one section, then, we are
given a brief mention of the origin of the dream, which is the
same as saying that we are given a brief statement about the
origin of the ego and the world: "Into eternity, where all is
one, there crept a tiny mad idea." And the Son of God took it
seriously.

This passage appears on pages 586-587 of the 669
page *Text*. And this perhaps is why there is no explicit
mention of what the tiny mad idea is, or what steps led to the
dream when the idea was taken seriously. The author has
good reason to assume that the many questions which might
arise in his student's mind regarding this "tiny mad idea"
have been previously answered by what had already been
said, or by what will be said later.

Although there are many examples like the passage we quoted above, where the Course only briefly refers to things related to the origin of the ego and the world it made, there is one passage which packs in a series of steps which, when reflected upon in light of the Course's entire thought system, can be seen as offering just what we are looking for. This is the passage on the request for special favor which we introduced in the last chapter. This passage consists of three paragraphs. I will use these three paragraphs as the springboard from which I set forth the steps leading to the origin of the ego or the self who made the world.

HOW THE MAKER OF THIS WORLD ORIGINATED

So let us begin. The passage we will use is from a section in the Text entitled "The Fear of Redemption" (13.3). These are the last three paragraphs (10-12) of that section. They are pregnant with ideas which, when explicated and amplified, can be used not only for the task of this chapter, but for that of the next two as well. Thus I quote them in their entirety:

> 10   You who prefer separation to sanity cannot obtain it in your right mind. You were at peace until you asked for special favor. And God did not give it for the request was alien to Him, and you could not ask this of a Father Who truly loved His Son. Therefore you made of Him an unloving father, demanding of Him what only such a father could give. And the peace of God's Son was shattered, for he no longer understood his Father. He feared what he had made, but still

more did he fear his real Father, having attacked his own glorious equality with Him.

11   In peace he needed nothing and asked for nothing. In war he demanded everything and found nothing. For how could the gentleness of love respond to his demands, except by departing in peace and returning to the Father? If the Son did not wish to remain in peace, he could not remain at all. For a darkened mind cannot live in the light, and it must seek a place of darkness where it can believe it is where it is not. God did not allow this to happen. Yet you demanded that it happen, and therefore believed that it was so.

12   To "single out" is to "make alone," and thus make lonely. God did not do this to you. Could He set you apart, knowing that your peace lies in His Oneness? He denied you only your request for pain, for suffering is not of His creation. Having given you creation, He could not take it from you. He could but answer your insane request with a sane answer that would abide with you in your insanity. And this He did. No one who hears His answer but will give up insanity. For His answer is the reference point beyond illusions, from which you can look back on them and see them as insane. But seek this place and you will find it, for Love is in you and will lead you there. (13.3,10-12)

"You were at peace until you asked for special favor" (10:2) What is this request for special favor? I mentioned that there are many ways one could state what this request is. I interpret it as the request to create something special. In other words, the Son is asking His Father to allow him to create something on his own, apart from his Creator. This indeed would constitute a special favor given to any Son Who received permission to do such a thing. We will discuss this first step in great detail in the next chapter. For our purposes here we simply identify what the request is, and that this is "the beginning" step in the making of the ego and the world. It is the Son's wish to create something separate from his Father that is referred to by the phrase "tiny mad idea". This idea "crept" into eternity, where all the minds of God's Son are one, co-creating with one another in union with God, their Father, the Prime Creator.

Let me just mention that the Course is using metaphorical language here. It is no surprise that the Course needs to use metaphorical language since it is trying to convey to us something that does not involve language at all. It simply speaks to us, who have made words, in a language we can understand.

"And God did not give it for the request was alien to Him" (10:3). In other words, God did not allow His Son to create something special or something different from what he always creates. The whole idea is contrary to God's nature. The Father knows His Son only as He created him, and He created him as His co-creator with the function of extending the perfect Self they share. This is the Son's joy, just as it is his Father's. This can never change. The Father and the Son will always and forever be co-creators. Their perfect happiness lies in this. Their nature and their function lie in it. It is impossible that things be otherwise. And so, "God did not give it for the request was alien to Him."

A Father Who truly loved His Son could not give him permission to create something on his own so that he could be special and different from God and all His Sons. God cannot change Himself from being perfectly loving to being unloving. He gave everything to all His Sons. He cannot allow some Sons to create something special and different from what everyone creates. Only an unloving father could give what is being asked for here.

It is at this point that the psycho-logic of the Son takes a crucial step. The Course indicates that at this point the Son distorts the nature of his Creator, his Father, thinking Him something He is not. "Therefore you made of Him an unloving father, demanding of Him what only such a father could give" (10:4). The Son thinks of his Father as unloving because His Father did not give him what he asked for.

Even though the Father did not give it, the Son, nevertheless, still wants it. He has taken seriously the idea of creating separately from his Creator, thus being a sole creator of something, and thereby meriting special favor because he is special, having created something special and different from what anyone else created.

God gave His Son the power to create and He could not take it from him. And the Son, having this power, demands the fulfillment of his wish. But God his Father says, as it were, "You are my Son, and We are one. Everything I have is yours, even the power to create the perfect. We are co-creators always. You cannot create apart from Me, and I cannot create apart from you."

In effect, the Father is saying, "No". (Again, out of necessity, we use analogical or metaphorical language to describe a situation that does not involve language at all.)

At this point, it is as though a fixed, immovable and unchangeable object is faced with an irresistible force. A perfectly knowing, powerful, loving and happy God cannot grant His Son's request. But his perfectly powerful Son demands it! By demanding that his request be fulfilled the Son is, as it were, making a will different and separate from his Father's. In this sense He is denying his Creator -- and his Self.

So what happens? The next line says, "And the peace of God's Son was shattered" (10:5). This means a part of his mind split off from oneness with God's Mind, and from his own Mind as God created It. And why was his peace shattered? "For he no longer understood his Father."

His Father is perfectly loving, but the Son made him unloving. If the Son thinks his Father is unloving, when in truth He is really loving, then he "no longer understands his Father."

I said that the mind of God's Son split when he attempted to accomplish his wish to create something on his own, apart from his Creator. This implies that when his mind and will is wholly one with God's Mind and Will, the Son is at peace. His peace lies in this Oneness. In fact, every aspect of his perfection lies in his oneness with his Father.

Here is an example where one's understanding of the Course's overall teaching - presented in the *Text, Workbook, Manual, Clarification of Terms*, and the two pamphlets - plays a part in interpreting particular passages, and specifically this line about the peace of God's Son being shattered. Based on the Course's overall teachings about the mind, its activity, its thought, and its state, we can say with confidence that in attempting to create on his own, separate from his Creator, the mind of God's Son split. The crucial role that the concept of a split mind plays in the Course's teachings will become obvious as we proceed in the building of our theodicy.

In fact, we will have much to say about the split mind of God's Son from here to the end of this book. I will limit my comments here, however, only to those that are necessary for achieving the purpose of this chapter, which is simply to set forth in a logical sequence the steps that led to the making of the ego, the body, and the world.

Before we continue the order of steps, a few explanatory remarks regarding this step of the splitting of the mind of God's Son are necessary in order to understand the next step.

The part of the mind that is split off from the Whole is called "the separated mind" (L99,4:1). This separated mind is separate only in the sense that it *believes* it is separate. It believes it is separate because it is identifying with the "special creation" that was made in the Son's attempt to create separately from his Father. The "special creation" is the image, or form, or body that was made. At this point the body obviously is not a human body, but simply an image, or form, or figure of some kind. The Course does not get into naming different kinds of bodies (astral, causal, etc.) with which the mind may identify. Any body identification is ultimately a mistaken identification, since reality is formless. Since the mind is identifying with this image or body, it believes it is a separate thing. It believes it is an ego, a separate "I".

At this point we can also mention an important distinction made by the Course. It is the distinction between *creating* and *making*. Only what is created in union with God is a *creation*. What is not created in union with God is called a "miscreation" or a "making". This is one of the reasons I have used the term "make" rather than "create" when talking about the origin of the world. The ego and the world were "made" not "created".

Thus the Course says that the inappropriate use of the power to create is miscreation. In other words, the very attempt to "create" apart from your creator, or to "create" something special, is an inappropriate use of the power to create. The results of this misuse can only be a thing that was miscreated or made. If such an attempt is made, separation results. A part of mind splits off from the Whole. The miscreation can exist only in the part of the mind that is apart from God's Mind. It cannot exist in reality, in God's Creation, in God's Mind, in Christ's Mind, or in any mind that is as God created it. A miscreation can exist only in a mind apart from God's Mind.

I already mentioned that the split off part of the mind is called the separated mind. But only a part of this separated mind identifies with the miscreation, or the ego, or the body.

In the other part of the separated mind of God's Son is God's Answer to the request. We will speak of this Answer, which the Course calls the "Holy Spirit" or "the Voice for God", in much detail in Chapter 10. What needs to be understood at this point is simply that God's Answer, viz., "You are my Son, and We are one," abides in part of the separated mind of God's Son.

This Answer represents the Love of God Who could deny the Son's request only by reminding him of the perfect oneness of reality. Thus God's Answer serves as a reminder. It is an answer to the mind's belief that it is separate. It offers a correction of his error in thinking he really is a separate thing.

So far, then, the split off part of the mind of God's Son thinks it really is a separate self. It thinks it is what it made. Identifying with what it made, it thinks, then, that it is an ego. The term ego refers not only to the mind's belief that it is separate, but also to the thing it believes it is which makes it seem separate. In other words, the mind believes it is a separate thing *because* it believes it is the image or body it made. This image or body serves as "a separation device" (6.5A,2:3). The body, then, is the mind's image of what it is *as* a separate self (24.7,9:5). Just as now your human body is an image of yourself as a separate self different and separate from other selves.

The term *"self"*, as a general term, refers to the mind's thought of what it is. The ego is merely the mind's *false* thought of what it is, namely, that it is a separate whole in itself. The image or body, then, is a thought in the mind. The mind must think it is a form or body of some kind in order to believe it is separate, for as we have quoted several times previously, "only by assigning to the mind the properties of the body does separation seem to be possible" (18.6,3:2). "The body is the symbol of the ego, as the ego is the symbol of the separation" (15.9,2:3).

Having finished our digression to make these remarks about the separated mind of God's Son, let us return now to continue the logical sequence of steps that constitute the origin of the ego, the body, and the world.

Fear and a Wrathful God: Sin, Guilt, and More Fear.

The next sentence in our selected passage provides the next step after the spitting of the mind. It reads: "He feared what he had made, but still more did he fear his real Father, having attacked his own glorious equality with Him" (10:6).

What is it he "feared"? And who is the "he" that feared it? This line says "he feared what he had made". Let's recall that the "he" is the mind. And the mind we are talking about at this point is the separated mind of God's Son. We are not talking about the Mind of God's Son *as God created it*. We are talking about the part that is (or seems to be) separated from the perfect Whole. We are talking about the part split off from the Christ Mind. The Mind of God and the Mind of Christ remain perfect, and perfectly united, the same, and equal. Therefore They could never experience fear.

So what is it that the mind, which thinks it is separate, feared? "He feared what he had made." What did he make? I think there are two things referred to here. First, he feared his own thoughts. The thought he "thinked" (thought) brought fear, rather than maintaining perfect happiness and love. He did make the thought of separation. He did make the ego. He thinks he is separate, he thinks he is the ego, he thinks he is the image of himself that he made on his own. This is fearful. "The ego is quite literally a fearful thought" (5.5,3:7).

There has never been this state or experience of fear before. It is a strange and alien state of mind. It is an unreal and illusory state. Love is absent. Where there is fear, love must be absent. And only love is real. Thus the first fear resulted from the denial of reality, the denial of Love, the denial of God.

Second, he feared the father he had made. This seems to be what the passage is specifically referring to. Earlier in the paragraph we read: "Therefore you made of Him an unloving father" (10:4). It is, then, an unloving father that he feared, a father he made, which is merely a distortion of his real Father. That it is this unloving father that he feared also makes sense in light of the next clause in the sentence: "but still more did he fear his *real* Father".

His real Father is still loving. But if this is so, why did he fear his real Father? The reason given for fearing his real Father is that he had "attacked his own glorious equality with Him" (10:6)

So at this point the mind that thinks it is a separate thing is afraid of God, the Father. But it is afraid of God in two different senses. He is afraid of God *as Love*. God as Love is represented by God's loving Answer in one part of the split mind. But he is also afraid of God as an "unloving father." We need to explore this *fear of God* a little more.

The part of the split mind that identifies with the ego is afraid of God's Loving Answer which abides in the other part of the mind. Thus the mind is split between the ego and the Holy Spirit Who represents God's Love. And representing Love means that it represents the truth of oneness.

To the ego then, this Answer is fearful because it means death to the ego! To the ego, love is death! Unity, sameness, and equality mean the ego is not real, it cannot be real. The ego has no existence in Love. The ego is related to love as darkness is related to light; where one is the other cannot be. Like darkness cannot exist where there is light, so the ego cannot exist where everything is One, the same, equal, and united. When Love is accepted into awareness the ego disappears, just as when the light is turned on in a room darkness disappears. It is gone. It never was anything but the absence of light.

Thus we see that the part of the split mind that is identified with the ego is afraid of Love; it is afraid of God's Answer. It is afraid of God. But it does not recognize that this is the source of its fear. It merely feels threatened by something, it knows not what. But it wants to preserve itself as a separate thing, for its only experience of "life" is as a separate self. This is the only "life" it is aware of having.

The ego feels threatened but does not know the source of threat. The part of the mind identified with the ego, then, interprets its fear as the result of something it has done, and for which it deserves punishment. In other words, it feels guilty. It believes it has attacked God by separating from Him. Now believing in attack, it believes that God is justified in retaliating. Thus Love has been made fearful! As the Course puts it:

> The ego is the part of the mind that believes in division. How could part of God detach itself without believing it is attacking Him? ... If you identify with the ego, you must perceive yourself as guilty. ... and you will fear punishment. (5.5,3:1-2,5-6)

This belief that it has attacked God by separating from Him, (by creating apart from Him, by usurping His place as Prime Creator) is what the Course calls the mind's belief in *sin*. *Fear, guilt, and sin,* then, all come together at this point as aspects of the mind identified with the ego. Guilt is the mind's belief that it has done something wrong for which it deserves punishment. In this case the something wrong is to have attacked God or to have "sinned". The fear is the emotional state brought by the thought of deserving to be attacked, hurt, or killed, rather than loved.

The steps we have just set forth can be summarized this way. The mind identified with its miscreation experiences fear. It interprets the cause of its fear as God threatening it. Why is God threatening it? Because it has attack Him; it has "sinned". This seems to make sense to the mind. It is as if the minds that are separated from God and each other say, "Yes, that explains our experience, we have attacked God, and He is justifiably threatening us in return. He is retaliating."

At this point, then, the separate mind is "justifiably" afraid of God. In his own perception of himself he "understands" why he is afraid that God is going to punish, even kill, him. Once guilt has been accepted into the mind of God's Son, the mind has committed to the idea that it is really a separate self, a self separate from other selves and from God as well. The fear and guilt confirm that his seeming separation and sin are real.

The mind identified with the ego, then, inevitably feels guilty and afraid. It believes it did something wrong for which it deserves punishment, and it fears the punishment it deserves.

This belief in the reality of sin takes many forms and is described throughout the Course in many different ways, including the following: you believe you have opposed the Will of God and succeeded; you believe you have disobeyed

God and made a will of your own separate from His; you believe you have attacked God and offended Him by separating from Him; you believe that you have created something real on your own, apart from God; you believe you have changed God's creation and rendered the perfect imperfect; you believe you have usurped God's throne and taken it for yourself; you believe that you have usurped God's role as Prime Creator of everything, and therefore have usurped God's place as your Creator and Author; you believe that you have created yourself and that the direction of your own creation is up to you. You believe you have violated reality and have succeeded. All of this is what you believe when you believe you have "sinned".

And all of this is really impossible. Sin is impossible. But the separated mind of God's Son identified with the ego is deceived in believing its separation is real; that it really is a separate whole in itself, that it has really sinned, has really attacked God and offended Him. You, as the separated Son of God, believe the unreal is real. You believe the false is true. You believe the impossible is possible and has been accomplished. You believe illusions are the truth. This is why the Course says, "Sin is insanity" (Th4,1:1). The mind that believes it is guilty of sin is sick and needs healing. It is insane, mad with guilt. There is no sin. There is only a belief in sin. Just as there is no death, but there is a belief in death.

Feeling guilty for sin, then, is an essential element in "the decent to separation" (28.2,12:7), which descent the Course also calls, "the descent from Heaven" (23.2,21:6), and the "descent to hell" (L44,5:6), as well as "the detour into fear" (2.1,2:1).

Guilt makes the mind's seeming separation real to itself. For why would it deserve punishment from God if it had not really sinned by separating from Him? Thus, if guilt does not enter in, the apparent separation can easily be undone. The correction of the error can be easily accepted.

The apparently separated mind of God's Son could merely give up the ego, and accept God's Answer instead, realizing that the ego does not increase joy, since it offers nothing real. The seemingly separated part of the mind could return to awareness of the Whole of which it is really a part, by accepting the truth that it *is* a part of the Whole and wants nothing else. He could simply return to the awareness of perfect oneness, and to his function of co-creating with God, thanking his Father for everything He has given him, for He has given him everything.

The crucial role guilt plays in reinforcing the belief in the reality of separation is reflected in the following statement from the Course: "The acceptance of guilt into the mind of God's Son was the *beginning* of the separation, as acceptance of the Atonement is its end" (my emphasis) (13.IN,2:1).

In other words, once guilt has entered into the split off part of the mind, the apparently detached mind has reached the point where it seriously believes its separateness is real. But the mind not only believes that its separateness is real, but that its separation amounts to evidence of its having attacked and offended God. Separation has "begun" in the sense that it is now experienced as being accomplished and as having real effects. In other words, the separation has begun in earnest when the mind believes its fear is due to God's justifiable retaliation for a real attack on Him.

Thus separation, believed as really having occurred, begins here - in the mind's experience of guilt. Separation is no longer a mere jest, or a silly idea. It is sin. The mind, identified with the ego and feeling guilty, believes it really has sinned by separating itself from God. The separated mind now fears the retaliation it believes it deserves for having attacked Him. To the separated mind attacking and being attacked now seem real, for they have "real" effects.

THE MAKING OF THE PHYSICAL WORLD

Once guilt is accepted into the mind, the need to hide is almost inevitable. We are very close now to the making of the physical world. In its fear of God, the mind seeks to escape from God to avoid the punishment it mistakenly believes it deserves. It seeks a place to hide where it can be "safe" from the vengeful God who now is perceived as "deadly enemy" (Q17,5:8). God is now thought to be, not only an unloving father, but one who is positively angry, and intent to punish, and even kill, his sinful son.

The mind, then, seeks a way of escape from the vengeful God it made up and believes will kill it. In other words, the separated mind identified with the ego, thinking it deserves punishment and death for its sin, seeks a way to preserve itself. "It cannot live in the light", and so "it must seek a place of darkness" (11:5).

But where can it go? Nowhere! The mind, then, must *make up* a place to hide in order to preserve and protect itself as an ego, a separate self. It must make "a place of darkness where it can believe it is where it is not" (11:5). And so it does. This place of darkness is the physical universe, a world of bodies, space and time; a place where God can enter not, and where the light of truth is obscured.

At this point the physical world begins. If we accept present day science, and its theories of the origin of the physical universe of space, time, and bodies, we might say that at this point the "big bang" occurs. This is the beginning of the physical universe, which after eons of time, has led to the world as we presently see it. In other words, the physical world had its beginning in our insane desire to escape from God perceived as an enemy intent on punishing us for our sin. Yes, as strange as it may sound at first, the physical world was made by minds terrified with guilt!

This world, as the author of the Course says, was meant to be a place where the Son of God can "live" apart from his Father:

> The world was made as an attack on God. It symbolizes fear. And what is fear except love's absence? Thus the world was meant to be a place where God could enter not, and where His Son could be apart from Him. Here was perception born, for knowledge could not cause such insane thoughts. (Th3,2:1-5)

And this world was made by minds insane with guilt:

> The world you see is the delusional system of those made mad by guilt. Look carefully at this world, and you will realize that this is so. For this world is the symbol of punishment, and the laws that seem to govern it are the laws of death. Children are born into it through pain and in pain. Their growth is attended by suffering, and they learn of sorrow and separation and death. Their minds seem to be trapped in their brain, and its powers to decline if their bodies are hurt. They seem to love, yet they desert and are deserted. They appear to lose what they love, perhaps the most insane belief of all. And their bodies wither and gasp and are laid in the ground, and are no more. Not one of them but has thought that God is cruel.
>   If this were the real world, God *would* be cruel. For no Father could subject His

children to this as the price of salvation and
be loving (13.IN,2-3:2).

It is clear from this last passage, along with
everything we said above, that the Course teaches that this
world was made by its maker out of its own guilt and fear of
punishment from God. It was made by a mind that
mistakenly believed it had offended God and that God
intends to retaliate by killing it. We have identified this mind
as the separated mind of God's Son identified with the ego. It
is also clear that the mind who made this world originated as
a result of a request for special favor made by God's Son.
God did not grant the request, but the Son attempted to fulfill
it anyway, and his mind split. It is the split off part of the
mind that is the maker of this world. This world is its dream.
    The last two lines of the passage quoted above
express a central theme of this book, namely, that we cannot
in our right mind believe that God created this world. In
these lines we are told that if the world of attack and
suffering, of pain and death, were real, *God would be cruel.*
In other words, if God were creator of this world, since this
is the only way it could be real, God *would* be cruel. This
means that God cannot be *both* maker of this world *and*
loving Father. If we believe that humans, or egos, or limited
and separated selves born in bodies, doomed to suffer and to
die, are really God's creations, then it makes no sense to call
God perfectly loving. No Father could be loving and subject
his children to the things that inhabitants of this world are
subjected to. The world we see, then, was not created by
God, but was made by "those made mad by guilt"
(13.IN,2:1).
    Let me make a point here about the use of terms. In
the last long passage quoted, as well as many others, the
Course uses the phrase *the world you see.* Some readers,
including some beginning students of the Course, may be

tempted to interpret this phrase as referring only to *the way* you see this world of bodies, or how you interpret and perceive it. It does refer to this. But it refers to more than this. It is meant to include the entire physical universe, or the entire world of bodies, the entire perceivable world. This is true because "the world you see" is a world of *perception*. It is not the realm of *knowledge* or truth. In reality there is nothing that is "seen" or "seeable" or "perceivable". God does not "see" or "perceive" at all, nor do you as God created you. This is because God does not have or use a body. Nor did he create you as a body. Perception is a function of the body. If there were no body, there would be no perception. Where there is only pure mind there is only knowledge. "Only the body makes the world seem real" (C4,5:9).

Thus when the Course says that you made "the world you see" and God made it not, it is saying that God did not create a seeable world, a world of forms, a world of perception, a world that involves minds using bodies, and which is real only to minds using bodies. Thus the phrase "the world you see" refers to the entire physical world as well as your false perception, or the way you falsely interpret what the body's eyes see..

Only a mind using a body can perceive and experience sights and sounds and touch. In reality, in God's creation, there are no sights, or sounds, or touch. You made a world of sights and sounds and touch, by making a body and identifying with it. You made the body. You made perception. You made the world. And this includes the entire physical universe, the entire world of time, space, and bodies. You made the world you see. "God made it not. Of this you can be sure" (L152,6:2-3).

COMMENTS ON THE ORIGIN, PURPOSE,
AND REALITY STATUS OF THE WORLD

What we said about the making of the world by the separated mind of God's Son should not be taken to imply that the body and the world as we experience them today were made by the ego in one instant of time, any more than the Genesis account is taken to imply that God created the entire physical universe in six 24-hour periods. On the contrary, the Course implies that the process, which in another place it calls "the decent to separation" (28.2,12:7), took millions of years in terms of time. "Just as the separation occurred over millions of years, the Last Judgment will extend over a similarly long period" (2.8,2:5).

The scientific description of the evolution of stars and galaxies, the solar system, and the "life forms" on planet earth, including the human body as it today, can be incorporated into the Course's explanation of the origin of the world, just as theologians have attempted to incorporate it into their thought system which holds that God created the world. From what we have said already, it is obvious that the significant difference for theodicy between the Genesis account and the account found in *A Course In Miracles* lies not in *how* the world was made, but in two other points about the making of the world: namely, *whose mind* is maker of the world, and secondly, what is said to be the *reality status* of this world.

As we have seen already for most contemporary theologians in the Judeo-Christian tradition the creator or maker of this world is *God*. And *because* it is God who is its maker, the world itself must be *real*, a part of reality, a part of God's creation. And, furthermore, according to contemporary Classical theology, God Himself is not only aware of everything that happens in the physical world, but He Himself is personally involved in its evolution, and in the events of human history. God, the Father, or God the Creator, is conceived to be well aware of everything that happens in the daily life of every human being. It is even said that He knows the number of hairs on your head. This awareness of everything in the world, as we have seen, is considered to be part of what it means to say that God is omniscient.

A Course in Miracles, on the other hand, teaches that the maker of this world is not God. And *because* God did not create it, the world itself is not real; it is not part of reality. The maker of this world is said to be the ego, or "you" as the separated mind of God's Son identified with the ego. Thus the process of world making is one of making images, or imagining. And the result is merely illusions. The world then is the Son of God's *dream,* and not reality at all. The dream exists in your mind apart from God's. Since the dream is not God's creation, God, the Creator of all that is real, is not aware of its contents. God, the Creator of a spiritual universe is not personally involved in the evolution of the physical world, nor in the events of human history. Nor does He know the number of hairs on your head. He does not know what occurs in your dream, nor does he see the illusory picture of yourself that is part of your dream. He knows only His creations, for only They are eternal and real and true. God is perfectly aware of everything that is true and real, everything He created, including You as His perfect Son and the creations You co-create with Him, Which are infinite in number, and everyone of Which is perfect like Their Creator. It is this perfect awareness of everything that is real and true which constitutes God's omniscience.

In the process of setting forth the steps in the origin of the ego and the world, we have given the *purpose* for which the physical universe was made. It was made to be a place to live apart from God as a special, different and separate self. The world, then, was made in order to be "safe" from Love which would undo all specialness, difference, and separation. To be safe from Love (God), to be safe from unity, sameness, and equality, is really the underlying purpose for the making of this world!

The information that physical science offers us provides no answer to the question of *why* the physical world was made. Nor could it ever do so. The three theodicies we examined in Chapter 2, however, do offer an answer to the why question. But each one gives us an answer in terms of why *God* created the physical world. And each answer, as we have seen, is different.

It is clear that modern science cannot offer us an answer to the *why* question. Astrophysicists seem to be very close to explaining, in terms of mass-energy and the laws that govern it, *how* the physical universe evolved moments after the "big bang", but they do not pretend to explain *why* the universe exists, or why the big bang occurred, or what conditions led up to the big bang.

Why does the physical universe exist at all? For what purpose? This is a question beyond the capacity of the astrophysicist, as physicist, to answer. Very few even try. At best they can only decide on the purpose of their own life in this world. As a human being, who happens to be a scientist as well, one must enter the realm of meta-physics, if he is to have an answer in terms of *purpose*. By providing an answer to the *why* question, then, we have filled a vacuum that physical science must inevitably leave empty.

And by answering the why question we have also given an alternative answer to the ones offered by traditional theism, which mistakenly gives the name "God" to the maker of the world. And, having done so, proceeds to make a futile attempt to offer a reasonable explanation of why God, Who is a perfect being, would create an imperfect world in which His supposed creatures can oppose His Will and inevitably suffer in doing so.

There is no World!

As we have seen, since God did not create it, the world is not real but an illusion. But it seems real to the mind which made it. The world is a dream which seems real to the dreamer. This world is not reality. It does not really exists. It exists only in your mind as your own imagining.

There is a lesson in the Workbook which powerfully states in no uncertain terms that the world is unreal. You might want to read this lesson right now. For those who do not have the Course available I will quote several of the sixteen paragraphs which constitute this lofty lesson. It is Lesson 132, entitled "I loose the world from all I thought it was." There we read:

There is no world apart from what you wish, and herein lies your ultimate release. Change but your mind on what you want to see, and all the world must change accordingly. Ideas leave not their source. This central theme is often stated in the text, and must be borne in mind if you would understand the lesson for today. It is not pride which tells you that you made the world you see, and that it changes as you change your mind.

But it is pride that argues you have come into a world quite separate from yourself, impervious to what you think, and quite apart from what you chance to think it is. There is no world! This is the central thought the course attempts to teach. Not everyone is ready to accept it, and each one must go as far as he can let himself be led along the road to truth. He will return and go still farther, or perhaps step back a while and then return again.

But healing is the gift of those who are prepared to learn there is no world, and can accept the lesson now. Their readiness will bring the lesson to them in some form which they can understand and recognize. Some see it suddenly on point of death, and rise to teach it. Others find it in experience that is not of this world, which shows them that the world does not exist because what they behold must be the truth, and yet it clearly contradicts the world.

And some will find it in this course, and in the exercises that we do today. Today's idea is true because the world does not exist. And if it is indeed your own imagining, then you can loose it from all things you ever thought it was by merely changing all the thoughts that gave it these appearances. The sick are healed as you let go all thoughts of sickness, and the dead arise when you let thoughts of life replace all thoughts you ever held of death. (L132,5-8)

This idea that you made the world you see, and that you can change your mind about its reality status, realizing that it is not real because it was not created by God, is crucial in the Course's teachings. As it says, "There is no world! This is the central thought the course attempts to teach" (L132,6:2-3).

This idea is a central thought because it pervades every aspect of the Course's teachings. So much of what it teaches is centered around the idea that the world is an illusion, that the world does not really exist, even though it seems real to us. This should not be a surprise if we realize that the world came from nothing, from a tiny mad idea taken seriously. From nothing comes nothing, no matter how much we deceive ourselves into believing that nothing is something.

Incidently, we see here that Miracle Theodicy agrees with many traditional theodicies on the point that the world was made *ex-nihilo*, "from nothing". The difference is in the answer to the question: *who* made it from nothing?

This teaching that the world is illusion is crucial, not only for solving the theoretical problem of evil, but also for understanding the true meaning of forgiveness. For, as we shall discuss in Part Four, we cannot really understand what it means to forgive until we understand that *forgiveness is for illusions,* and not for the truth. You cannot pardon reality. Reality and truth do not need forgiveness. Thus recognizing that the world is an illusion is central for the possibility of attaining true happiness. "Seek not to change the world, but choose to change your mind about the world" (21.IN,1:7).

An attitude that has often been expressed by students in the classes I teach on the Course runs like this: "Personally I can accept the idea that God did not create the physical world. But I find it difficult to accept the idea that I made it, or we made it. It is hard to believe that we have such power."

The Course teaches us that we are denying the power of our own mind. We do have such power. For God shared His own power with us, His Sons. The power to create, which we have been given by God, is the same power He has. But we do not have to keep using it inappropriately by choosing to accept illusions as true. What we want to be true we have the power to make true - in our own perception. If it cannot be done in reality, it will be done in dreams. It is just as meaningful to say that the Son of God has the power to make this world as it is to say that God has the power to create it. The only difference is that God Himself would not create it, and could not make it and remain God, a perfectly loving Father. And we could not make it without splitting our mind. Only a mind that rejected God's Answer of eternal oneness could have ended up making this world of bodies to preserve its identity as a separate self.

The World As Dream

Throughout our discussion I have referred to the world of bodies, the world of perception, as a dream. The Course often uses the metaphor of a dream when it talks about the world of bodies, or the world of separation, as contrasted with the oneness of reality or Heaven. Why does the Course do this? There are several very good reasons. The list of reasons I give below is not intended to be exhaustive, but to indicate some of the more significant points the author wants to make by saying that this world is a "dream".

First, calling this world of bodies a dream is a way of making the point that this world, and the figures and events in it, are *not real*, not part of reality. According to the *reality formula* this world is an illusion, for it does not meet the requirements for saying something is real. Recognizing that this world is not reality but merely a dream helps us to recognize that what happens to everyone and everything in this world has not really occurred. Everything in this world is an illusion. Nothing in this world is the truth. Our entire experience in this world is illusory, both its joys and sorrows. Knowledge is truth. Truth is eternal, changeless, and unalterable. Illusions are temporal and changing. Nothing that happens in this world has reality in truth. The making of this world is nothing more than the mind making a dream. In explaining our experience of being separate selves who attack and suffer while in a world of bodies the

Course says, "Nothing has happened but that you have put yourself to sleep, and dreamed a dream in which you were an alien to yourself" (28.2,4:1).

Second, calling this world a dream points to the idea that the body and the world are *in the mind*. Where else could a dream be but in the mind of a dreamer? The body and the world are not outside your mind, even though they seem to be. Everything that is part of the dream is in the mind. In the mind is where everything in dreams is. Just as everything that happens in your night dreams is entirely *in* your mind, so too are the events, persons, and situations of this world, for this world is your dream of separation. It is the result of your attempt to live apart from God. When you wake from your sleeping dreams at night you simply shift from one kind of dream to another. Calling your waking dreams "reality" does not make them so.

Third, the Course's teaching that the world is a dream points to the idea that the world you see is *made up by your mind*. Just as the night dream that is in your mind is made up by your mind, so too the world in your mind is made up by your mind. You are the dreamer, and as the dreamer you make the dream what it is by you choices. The dream may be happy or terrifying. The forms in the dream seem to come and go as if by magic and beyond your control, but the content of the dream, whether it is happy or fearful, is up to you. Do the forms witness to the love in your mind, or to the fear and hatred?

Nothing that occurs in a dream can be a true witness against the fact that you are God's holy Son. But you can think it is if you chose not to be God's Son, and choose not to learn that the world you see *must be* a dream because it *cannot be* reality. For *the Self God created is the only real you*. In your dream the ego-body seems to be your self, and the world of bodies is an environment that witnesses to the "reality" of this bodily self. But a dream is a dream, and reality is reality. A dream self is a dream self, and a real Self is a real Self - forever, despite dreams.

The dream, then, issues from your insane refusal to accept yourself as God created you. It is a "substitute reality" (see 18.1). "You are at home in God, dreaming of exile but perfectly capable of awakening to reality" (10.1,2:1). Thus although it seems you are in the world, actually the world is in you! You made it up. It is your dream of separation.

You seem to be in the world because you identify with a body which makes you separate from other minds who seem to live within a body. Space is merely a gap you perceive between one body and another. The gap between bodies does not make you separate from your brother. Only your wish to use it as evidence for separation makes you seem separate. Only your wish to identify you and your brother with the body makes your mind seem separate from his. There is no gap between minds. "Minds are joined without the body's interference" (15.11,7:1).

Thus the body, and the world in which it seems to live, is merely a dream in your own mind apart from God's. Your waking dreams have no more reality than your night dreams. They are simply different kinds of dreams. But they are both merely "perceptual temper tantrums" (18.2,4:1). You identify with a figure in your dream, a figure you name, and call yourself, as does everyone in your dream. Your name in the dream is but a body label, a name for the "hero" of the dream. You think you are this hero. You who are the dreamer of a dream are the producer, director, script writer, and the body is the actor. It merely acts out the intentions of its maker. You determine everything that seems to happen to the hero of the dream. The body merely responds to the intentions of your mind. As the Course puts it:

> Dreams   are   perceptual   temper
> tantrums, in which you literally scream, "I

want it thus!" And thus it seems to be. And yet the dream cannot escape its origin. Anger and fear pervade it, and in an instant the illusion of satisfaction is invaded by the illusion of terror. For the dream of your ability to control reality by substituting a world that you prefer *is* terrifying. Your attempts to blot out reality are very fearful, but this you are not willing to accept. And so you substitute the fantasy that reality is fearful, not what you would do to it. And thus is guilt made real. (18.2,4)

Recognizing all this helps us to accept responsibility for everything that seems to happen to us. We need to recognize that "This is not done to me, but I am doing this to myself" (28.2,12:5). This is the secret you have kept hidden from yourself. The Course would have you:

Say only this, but mean it with no reservations, for here the power of salvation lies:

I **am** responsible for what I see.
I choose the feelings I experience,
and I decide upon the goal I would achieve.
And everything that seems to happen to me I
ask for, and receive as I have asked.
(21.2,2:2-5)

There are numerous "self help" books available these days, and all of them address the idea of accepting responsibility for yourself. Is there a better description of accepting responsibility for your own experience than the above passage? This kind of responsibility is the key to happiness! You need but stop wanting to punish yourself and others, and of accusing others of attacking and hurting you. You need but give up your belief in the reality of guilt, sin, and separation and death. Your terrifying dreams can be replaced with happy dreams. And from happy dreams you can awaken to reality. In happy dreams you are willing to give welcome to truth without fear.

Finally, calling the world a dream helps us to understand why, what is actually unreal and illusory, nevertheless, seems real and true. While you are dreaming, you are unaware of reality, so your dream seems to be reality, and what happens in your dream seems real to you. What else but your dream could be real to you, given that you are unaware of what *is* real? "What is seen in dreams seems to be very real" (2.1,3:5). "Where is the ego? In an evil dream that but seemed real while you were dreaming it" (C2,6:12-13). "The body is the symbol of the ego, as the ego is the symbol of the separation" (15.9,2:3). There are no symbols in reality for there is no need of them. Reality is clear and unambiguous. Neither the ego, the body, or the world is real. They are merely symbols made by the mind to deceive itself into believing that what cannot happen has happened.

SUMMARY

This chapter has provided an answer to the second of the three questions raised by our solution to the problem of evil, namely, if God did not create the body and the world, who did? Our answer is that *you* did. You, as the separated mind of God's Son identified with the ego, made the world you see. In short, we say, "you as ego made the world" or "the ego made the world".

In giving this answer I have presented the Course's teachings on the origin of the ego, the body, and the world. We set forth the logical sequence of steps which led from the request for special favor to the making of the world that we as human beings now perceive and experience.

In the process of setting forth these steps we have answered three questions crucial to the development of our theodicy. We have answered the question of 1) *who* made the world, 2) *how* this maker originated, and 3) *why* he made the world. We have also reiterated a crucial point for Miracle Theodicy, viz., the world is not real because it was not created by God. It is an illusion; a dream of separation.

Despite the fact that we have answered our second question, there may be some readers who find our answer not quite satisfying. And this may be so because they have in mind an objection that any thinking person who has followed our argument might have at this point.

One might claim that what I said here in Part Three seems to contradict what was said in Part Two. For if it is true that we were created perfect, which implies we have everything that makes us happy, how could we have ever asked for special favor? How could we have ever asked for *anything*?

The Son's asking for something seems to imply that he lacked something. What could we have "lacked" given that we were created perfect? It seems to make no sense to say that we were created perfect, having everything and lacking nothing, and then to turn around and say that we asked for something from Him Who had already given us all things.

In the next chapter I will respond to this objection. It is perhaps the most powerful objection that could be raised against the consistency of Miracle Theodicy.

9

PERFECTION AND
SEEMING LACK

The inappropriate use of extension, or projection, occurs when you believe that some emptiness or lack exists in you, and that you can fill it with your own ideas instead of truth.
ACIM (2.1,1:7)

In the previous chapter we traced the origin of the ego, the body, and the world back to a request made by God's Son. This request suggests there was something the Son did not have.

But what could the Son not have if he has everything he could possibly have? It is the purpose of this chapter to answer that question. But before we address the question directly, there is need first to discuss in more detail some teachings of the Course we have merely touched upon earlier.

We have seen that the Son's request ultimately led to a part of his mind identifying with the ego or self it made. This identification with the ego-body is a terrible mistake, and is the source of all experience of evil regardless of its form.

I have already mentioned and discussed the idea that the Son's attempt to fulfill his wish on his own had no effect on reality. It cannot and did not change God and His creation. It cannot and did not affect the eternal oneness of reality.

IDEAS LEAVE NOT THEIR SOURCE

The Course teaches that "everything is an idea" (5.1,2:4) and that "ideas leave not their source" (26.7,13:2). This means that thoughts do not leave the mind that thinks them. This principle plays a central role in the Course's teachings about the nature of mind and its thoughts. And it operates at both the spiritual and bodily level of experience.

Some of the implications of this idea are stated in the following passage:

> Ideas leave not their source. The emphasis this course has placed on that idea is due to its centrality in our attempts to change your mind about yourself. It is the reason you can heal. It is the cause of healing. It is why you cannot die. Its truth established you as one with God. (L167,3:6-11)

Let us apply this principle to God and His Thoughts. The principle that ideas leave not their source implies that God's Thoughts do not leave His Mind. They forever remain in His Mind as part of It. Since God's Thoughts are His creations, God's creations cannot leave His Mind. And since we, the Sons of God, are God's creations, we as such cannot leave His Mind. We are forever one with Him and with each other as well. Ideas leave not their source, then, is a law of mind whose truth "established you as one with God" -- forever.

You and I, and everyone God created, then, are still part of God, despite any experience we have to the contrary. "He [God] created you as part of Him, and this must still be true because ideas leave not their source" (26.7,13:2). Thus we, as God created us, can never be separated from Him or from one another.

Your eternal and true Self, the Christ, then, remains where God established him. You and I are forever in Heaven, forever in God's Mind, forever His Son, one with Him, and perfect like Himself. We need but to remember this. And what a happy memory it is!

Any thought you think apart from God is obviously not God's Thought or God's creation, and therefore cannot be real or true, and must be illusion. This is why you who think you are an ego must be deceived, for the ego is a thought you think apart from God. It is a false idea of what you are which serves as the foundation or starting point of an entire thought system in which every idea is false; a thought system which leads the mind away from God and Heaven toward idols (false gods) and hell.

In reality you cannot think apart from God or have true thoughts apart from His. In truth your mind is still one with God's. "My mind is part of God's. I am very holy" (L35).

In introducing the ten lessons of Review Four the Course states:

There is a central theme that unifies each step in the review we undertake, which can be simply stated in these words:

My mind holds only what I think with God.

That is a fact, and represents the truth of What you are and What your Father is. It is this thought by which the Father gave creation to the Son, establishing the Son as co-creator with Himself. It is this thought that fully guarantees salvation to the Son. For in his mind no thoughts can dwell but those his Father shares. Lack of forgiveness blocks this thought from his awareness. Yet it is forever true. (R4,2)

THE PARADOX

If we were created perfect, we were created as having everything that maintains perfect happiness. And thus it seems that there is nothing we need and nothing to ask for. Thus the question arises, if we were created perfect, how could we have asked for something?

It is clear that the Course does teach that the Son of God asked for something. And when his Father did not give it, he demanded to have it. This demand, as we have seen, plays a crucial role in the Course's explanation of the origin of the ego, the body, and the world.

The task of this chapter, then, is to show that the Course, and thus Miracle Theodicy, is not contradicting itself when it says that, on the one hand, the Son of God was created perfect, and on the other hand, the Son of God asked for something he did not have, implying that he was not created perfect.

We must admit there is a paradox here. But a paradox is only a *seeming* contradiction. It may or may not be a real contradiction. We need to show that this paradox is not actually a contradiction. Stated simply and explicitly the contradiction would be this: The Son of God was created perfect and the Son of God was not created perfect.

In other words, we need to show how it is logically possible for the Son, even though he was created perfect, to believe he lacked something, or that there was some emptiness in him. To do this we must discover exactly what the Son does not have in reality, and then show, even though he does not have this thing, it is still true that he was created perfect.

We must also show how it might be possible that this request was made even though reality, God and His creation, are timeless, changeless, and eternal. For if co-creation of the perfect is the only dynamic or activity in reality, and if this process is always the same forever then "when" did this request take place? How could it have taken place? In other words, if it did take place then was this not a change of some sort in reality?

This is perhaps the most difficult intellectual task of this book. And as far as I know, at the time of this writing, no student or teacher of *A Course in Miracles* has yet made an attempt to clearly set forth how the Course actually avoids contradicting itself when it says that the Son was created perfect, and yet this same Son asked for something he did not have.

So at the start I appeal to any student or teacher of the Course who sees another way of showing that the Course is not inconsistent on this point to please share it with us. As one long time student of mine has said more than once, "this seems to be the chink in the armor".

For now, however, I will proceed with my belief that the Course is not inconsistent or contradictory in its teaching that the Son of God was created perfect. It is the purpose of this chapter to show just that.

The Mere Form of a Question

We must be vigilant when we raise questions about our experience of evil, or our experience of being limited, separated selves in a body doomed to suffer and die. We must be careful to insure that the questions we raise are not only sincere and honest, but also meaningful. We must avoid any question which is actually a statement hidden in the mere form of a question to which an answer is impossible.

We do not want to be like the prosecutor who wants to "prove" that the defendant is guilty as charged, and so he puts him in a situation where he must answer either yes or no, and then asks him, "do you still beat your wife?" No matter what answer the defendant gives, whether it be "yes" or whether it be "no", he will have admitted that a beating occurred, it happened to his wife, and that he is the one who did the beating.

In the following passage the Course points to this need for vigilance in asking questions related to our experience of being an ego, a separated self:

> The ego will demand many answers that this course does not give. It does not recognize as questions the mere form of a question to which an answer is impossible. The ego may ask, "How did the impossible occur?", "To what did the impossible happen?", and may ask this in many forms.

Yet there is no answer; only an experience.
Seek only this, and do not let theology delay
you. (C-IN,4)

In this passage each one of the two versions of the
"question", which the ego may ask in many forms, contains
an assumption. The first assumes the impossible occurred,
and the second that the impossible happened to someone.
(Just as the prosecutor's question assumes that a beating has
occurred, and that it happened to this man's wife, and the
husband was the one who did the beating). In other words,
both versions of this ego question presuppose the truth of the
statement "The impossible occurred". But the statement
cannot *be* true. The statement itself is a contradiction. And
that is why it is impossible to give an answer to this
"question". It is a contradictory statement presented in the
mere *form* of a question. If it is taken as a question the only
answer is "it didn't."

The first form of the ego's "question", "how did the
impossible occur?" contains a contradictory statement that
we can explicate and display as follows:

1. x is impossible. This means that
2. x is not able to be; x cannot occur, and thus
3. x did not occur.
4. But x did occur.

The contradiction is obvious when we put statement
4 and 3 together: "x did occur and x did not occur." This is
obviously a contradiction. Thus the questioner (the mind
identified with the ego), who denies that "x did not occur",
would have us admit instead that "x did occur".

We can substitute for "x" one of a number of things
that the Course says has not occurred in reality. When we do

so we will have one of the many forms of the "question" the ego may ask.

For example, the Course teaches that sin is impossible. Sin is merely a false idea. It is your false belief that you have opposed God's Will, and have succeeded in reality. You believe you have separated from God and thus have attacked Him. And, as we have seen, this *is* impossible. Neither sin nor separation has occurred in reality.

If we replace "x" with the word "sin" the ego's question becomes "How did sin occur?" This assumes sin did occur, and thus denies the Course's teaching that sin did not occur in reality, because it cannot occur, since God is perfectly powerful; His Will is done, and cannot be opposed.

Another example: the Course teaches that what God created can never be separate from Him. Separation is impossible. Separation is a false belief that you are really separate from God and His Creations.

You who identify with the ego ask, "How did the separation occur?" This assumes the separation did occur, that God's Thoughts did leave His Mind. Thus it denies the Course's teaching that ideas leave not their source. And it denies that God is perfectly powerful and loving. In other words, it denies that there is a God. For if God is real there is no separation. If separation is real there is no perfect being.

Other terms we could substitute for "x" are: attack, suffering, death, limitation, the body, time, space, the world, and evil. Anything that is unreal, but believed by the mind to be real, can be substituted for "x".

For example, if attack is impossible then how did I get attacked by this man? If suffering and pain are impossible then how did this pain of cancer occur? If death is impossible then why does it seem that my mother died? If a world of evil is impossible then how did a world of evil occur? All these are forms of the ego's "question". It asks these questions as if it itself were real, as if the dream it made were real, and as if its experience in the dreamworld establishes what is real and true, not only for itself but for God as well.

We can see that these "questions" are actually statements which deny what the Course teaches about the nature of reality, of God and His creation. The Course says that separation and sin, attack and suffering, sickness and death, are all impossible in reality. But your mind, identifying with the self it made, unaware of reality, and believing your dream is reality, refuses to accept this. You may say, "Look around you. There is ample empirical evidence that separation has occurred. There is ample evidence that evil has occurred. How can you reasonably say that separation, attack, suffering and death cannot occur? They have occurred! And, obviously, if they have occurred then it is possible for them to occur."

Thus we see it is merely the ego, or more strictly speaking, a mind identified with the ego-body, that says, "I have sinned, you have sinned. Look at this world and you will see that everyone, past, present, and most likely future, is guilty of sin. Don't tell me there is no sin, or suffering, or death."

The question "how did sin occur" is, then, merely the mind proclaiming the reality of the ego and dreamworld it made. It is merely the expression of your continued wish to be special and different; your continued belief that your existence is defined by separation; your continued wish that something unattainable in reality is attainable somewhere, somehow. And in your self-deception your wish has come true, your dream for you *is* reality. What else could be reality for you while you are dreaming and unaware of reality as God created it?

The second version of the ego's "question" is, to what did the impossible happen? This version, like the previous one, is also the statement of a contradiction in the mere form of a question. The contradiction can be displayed as follows:

1. x is impossible. This means that
2. x is unable to be; x cannot happen to anyone, and thus
3. x did not happen to anyone.
4. But x did happen to someone.

Again substitute the word "separation" for "x". The mind identifying with the ego asks, "To what did the separation happen?" With this question it is stating "separation did happen to someone; someone is separate from someone."

And to whom did the separation happen? The ego answers, "To me! To you! And to that other person over there!" It is as if one mind identifying with the ego-body is saying to another that is doing the same, "you and I are separate, so it must be true that, if we were created one with each other and with God as well, then someone must have separated from someone, and from God as well. For obviously, each of us is separate from the other. You are separate from me, and I am separate from you. And we both are separate from God."

So underneath this version of the ego's question the ego whispers, "You are the one to whom the so-called impossible happened" or "I am the one to whom the so-called impossible happened. The so-called impossible is not impossible but possible. I know it is possible because it happened to me and to you, and to everyone I see!"

The Course teaches, however, that all this is a mistake. It is merely the mind deceiving itself that its seemingly separated condition, and its experience of evil, is simply part of the nature of *reality*. We look on evil and say, "Well, that's the way people are sometimes", or "that's just the way the world is" - as if the world we see were reality.

Or we say, "Well, that's the way life is" - as if this parody of life, this travesty on God's creation (24.7,10:9), were really life. It is not life at all. At best it seems like life, at worst like death.

You can never really be something God created you not. You can never really be something separate from your Source. The ego is merely your false belief that you are. And how can the false be part of truth? The ego-body is an illusion of what you are. And illusions are not true, they are merely substitutes for truth. And who made these substitutes? You did. You, as a mind. You see what is not real as if it were. You mis-take illusion for truth. And you think the truth of oneness and perfection is illusion.

If you identify with the ego you will believe that the notion of the perfection and oneness of all reality is an illusion, a false idea. It may be advocated by so-called mystics, you say, and now by the apparently deluded author of *A Course in Miracles*, but to me, as a human being who experiences evil, it is merely a false doctrine.

There Is No Answer, Only An Experience

Notice the last line of the passage we quoted above. The author states that "there is no answer" to these forms of the ego's question. There is only "an experience". "Seek only this, and do not let theology delay you."

What is the "experience" referred to here? As I mentioned earlier,[7] he Course uses a variety of words to describe this experience because it can be described from different perspectives. Some words I have already introduced to describe this experience are: "the peace of God", "the awareness of oneness", "love", and "happiness".

The *experience* of being one with God and everyone is the only convincing answer to this question, and it is this experience we should seek. It is the Course's purpose to train us in the way to attaining and keeping this state of feeling the love of God within us.. The way to this peace and joy is forgiveness. Through forgiveness we experience the peace of God. We experience salvation, healing, and happiness. Forgiveness ends all sense of separation and sin. Through forgiveness all evil disappears from the world we see.

Another term sometimes used to refer to this experience is *Atonement*. Atonement is the state of being "at-one" with everything, resulting from the undoing of the belief in the reality of separation. The mind in this state can be nothing but wholly joyous. It can suffer no pain, no attack or fear, no doubt or loneliness, no loss or grief, no sickness or death. In short, it cannot experience evil.

We see, then, that the ego's "question" is meaningless to one who experiences his oneness with all his brothers and with his Father, God.. Sin is meaningless to one who experiences his eternal innocence. The sinless, guiltless, and fearless respond to such a question with a smile and a gentle laugh. To the holy, evil is silliness, foolishness.

Only this experience, then, will thoroughly convince you that you remain one with your Father, and have not really separated from Him.

It is faith, *supported by reason*, however, that will tell you *why* this is true. It is true because it *must be* true. And it must be true because God is God; *a perfect being*.

This experience of oneness with God, attained through forgiveness of your brother and yourself, is the Course's goal for us. When you have accepted Atonement for yourself you no longer take the question "how did the separation occur?" as if it refers to something real. The question is wholly meaningless. You are no longer deceived that separation is real. Your forgiven mind has recognized the falsity of the idea, and therefore has let it go.

In another passage the Course beautifully describes how the experience of oneness is the final convincing answer to the ego's "question". It involves the experience that you are not the ego, that there is no ego, that there is no separate "I".

And thus the ego's questions are ultimately meaningless. The ego is gone because it never really was. The ego is nothing, it but seemed to be something. As the darkness is gone when the light has come, so the ego is gone when the truth has come:

> Where there was darkness now we see the light. What is the ego? What the darkness was. Where is the ego? Where the darkness was. What is it now and where can it be found? Nothing and nowhere. Now the light has come: its opposite has gone without a trace. Where evil was there now is holiness. What is the ego? What the evil was. Where is the ego? In an evil dream that but seemed real while you were dreaming it. Where there was crucifixion stands God's Son. What is the ego? Who has need to ask? Where is the ego? Who has need to seek for an illusion now that dreams are gone? (C2,6)

The Best Question You Could Ask

Are there any questions related to our apparent separateness which are not simply statements in the mere form of a question to which an answer is impossible? Are there any honest questions to which there are answers? Yes, there are.

The questions I raised in chapter 7 and in chapter 8 are examples of such questions. In chapter 7, for example, the question was not so much, how did the impossible occur, but why do we *seem* to be separate even though in reality it is impossible that we be separate from God or from each other? Why do we *seem* to be egos, or human beings, or minds with bodies, even though in reality we are the perfect Son of God; spirit, the Christ, pure minds?

In chapter 8 we did not so much claim that the world we see is real, but asked rather, how does the Course *account for our experience* of an illusory world and the evil we see in it? Why do we, who were created as pure and perfect minds co-creating in heaven, seem to be imperfect minds within a body living in a world of space, time, and bodies?

All of this can be put another way. We are asking for an explanation of our *experience of evil*, an experience which is obviously contrary to the experience we should be having, based on the conclusions of reason which logically follow from the premise that there exists a God Who is a perfect being.

These questions are not proclaiming that the separation, or the ego, or the world of bodies, or evil are real. No, we simply want to accept the Course's teaching that God created us perfect. But we seem to have encountered a problem in accepting this. For we do not understand how a mind that was created perfect could ask for something.

The Course clearly teaches that we as the perfect Son of God asked for "something". And it also teaches that the attempt to obtain this something is the reason why we now seem to be in an impossible situation, a situation that even involves asking questions! There are no questions in reality, for everyone knows everything. There is no need for learning, and thus none for teaching.

Fortunately, we have the Course to provide the answers once we, as minds identified with the ego, raise the questions.

So, we simply want to examine the Course's answers to see if they are consistent with one another. And so, when we think we see an inconsistency, instead of coming to the conclusion that the Course's theory is untenable because contradictory, we first try to see if we can resolve the apparent contradiction. Our hope is that there is no real contradiction here, for if there is, our theodicy will collapse.

The process of resolving an apparent contradiction can, in fact, lead us to a better understanding of the Course's teachings. This in turn could make us more willing to practice the exercises in the Workbook and thus attain the experience that is its goal for us. Otherwise, we justify not doing the exercises on the ground that the theory, which provides the framework for the exercises, cannot be true because it includes something contradictory. We can easily feel justified in saying, "why should I do exercises that are meaningful only within a framework which is built upon a false theoretical foundation?

My conviction that this question about the Son's perfection is indeed an honest one, is strengthened by the fact that the author himself raises a very similar question. Furthermore, he says that it is not only reasonable to ask this question, but that it is "the best question you could ask":

> It is reasonable to ask how the mind could ever have made the ego. In fact, it is the best question you could ask. There is, however, no point in giving an answer in terms of the past because the past does not matter, and history would not exist if the same errors were not being repeated in the present. (4.2,1:1-3)

Your own state of mind is a good example of how the ego was made. When you threw knowledge away it is as if you never had it. This is so apparent that one need only recognize it to see that it does happen. If this occurs in the present, why is it surprising that it occurred in the past? Surprise is a reasonable response to the unfamiliar, though hardly to something that occurs with such persistence. But do not forget that the mind need not work that way, even though it does work that way now. (4.2,3)

Some comments on this passage are in order. From the first paragraph quoted, the last sentence, we take note of the clause, "history would not exist if the same errors were not being repeated in the present". This is an interesting thought in itself, but here is not the place to discuss the Course's view of human history. I simply want to note that the mind's making of the ego involves *errors*, and that we, as minds, are repeatedly making the same errors. We need but look at our present state of mind to see how the ego is and was made. In fact, this is what many of the lessons in the Workbook have us do.

Furthermore, we notice that history exists only because we are repeatedly making the same errors. This is the same as saying that the dream, or the world you see, exists or seems real to you only because you are repeatedly making the same errors. What are the errors? Well, they all involve mis-taking illusion for truth, wanting specialness instead of equality, difference instead of sameness, and separation instead of oneness.

From the second paragraph we take note of the sentence, "When you threw knowledge away it is as if you never had it." This is our situation now; our state of mind is *as if we never had knowledge.* It is as if we never were aware of our perfect oneness with each other and with God as well. It is as if we never were a perfect Self, the Christ, the Son of God as He created him. We have so denied and dissociated the truth that it is almost impossible for us to become aware of it again. In fact, it *is* impossible for us to do so alone. We need help. And Help is available, as we shall see.

Thus the mind's making of the ego involved "throwing knowledge away" or dissociating the truth. In this sense the making of the ego involved "leaving Heaven"; for Heaven is simply "the awareness of perfect oneness, and the knowledge that there is nothing else; nothing outside this oneness, and nothing else within" (18.6,1:6).

Also from the second paragraph quoted above, the last line, we take notice of the sentence, "But do not forget that the mind need not work that way, even though it does work that way now." In other words, we do not have to keep making the same errors which make the ego seem real, nor do we have to continue to remain unaware of our perfect oneness. You are presently mistaken about yourself, but you need not be. You can change your mind about yourself. You can accept the Christ as your Self. He is always here to be acknowledged as yourself. "Deep in your mind the holy Christ in you is waiting your acknowledgment as you" (L110,9:4). So just as Jesus acknowledged Christ as his Self, so can we. In fact, Jesus says in the Course, "If you want to be like me I will help you, knowing that we are alike. If you want to be different, I will wait until you change your mind" (8.4,6:3-4). And in another place he says,

> There is nothing about me that you cannot
> attain. I have nothing that does not come
> from God. The difference between us now is
> that I have nothing else. This leaves me in a

state which is only potential in you.
(1.2,3:10-13)

Split Minds

I want to digress just a little at this point, and say something about the Course's concept of minds and thoughts. The Course implies that a part of mind can split off from a mind without affecting the condition of the mind it split off from. And a part *will* split off if there is an attempt on the part of the mind to hold contradictory or opposing thoughts.

Opposites cannot coexist in a united or integrated mind. In fact, a mind is integrated *because* it does not hold opposites. And so a mind that would hold opposite thoughts must split. The mind must deny one thought if it accepts its opposite. The thought of being special, different, and separate is the opposite of being equal, the same, and joined (united).

Miscreations are thoughts different from those the mind thinks with God and the entire Sonship. They are not real or true thoughts because they are not "thinked" (thought) with or by God. These untrue thoughts cannot coexist in the same mind that has only true thoughts. Thus the mind that would hold thoughts apart from God must be split off from the mind that thinks with God. The part which thinks with God holds only true thoughts, the other part of the mind holds only illusions.

Perhaps the use of an analogy may help in understanding this concept. Consider the process biologists call *mitosis*. A cell divides, and the result is two cells, one exactly the same as the other. As the original cell divides, we could see this as a process whereby a part of the original cell splits off from the whole. We could say that the second cell is split off from the original first cell. In mitosis, the result of this splitting is two cells that are exactly alike. The one that split off has the same nature as the one it split off from. So in a sense we can say that the split did not affect the nature of the original cell. We could say that the process by which a part split off from the whole did not affect the nature of the whole. Its nature remains as it was before the split, completely unaffected by the part that is split off from it.

There is both a similarity and a difference with regard to the splitting off from the perfect Mind of Christ, God's Son. The similarity is that the Whole from which a part splits off remains perfect as it always was and is. It has not changed; its original nature has not been affected. It remains as it always was before the split. As far as it is concerned nothing at all has happened.

The difference from mitosis, however, is that the part that splits off from the perfect Christ Mind contains thoughts the *opposite* of those contained in the Mind it split off from. Instead of being exactly the same, as in the case of mitosis, the split off part contains thoughts that are the *exact opposite* of those in the Mind it split off from. In fact, the wishing to have different thoughts is what led to the split in the first place, because opposite thoughts cannot exist in a unified mind. Now one part of the mind, the perfect part, still has only the truth. It is the only part of the mind that is real. The other part of the mind has nothing but the false. Actually it has nothing. It contains only illusions - nothing, that seems like something. Its thoughts are not only the opposite of the truth, but were made up to be substitutes for it. And that is what illusions are; the untrue seeming to be true, the unreal seeming to be real. Illusions are things made up as substitutes for reality and truth.

And the two parts of the mind shall never meet as long as one part holds onto illusions. Yet if illusions are brought into the presence of truth, the truth shines them away, and the mind becomes reintegrated. For the truth is like light, and illusions like darkness. Illusions are nothing, but seem like something. But when the light has come it is clear the darkness is gone, for it was nothing but the absence of light. When this happens the split mind is returned to its state of wholeness. It reunites with the whole of which it is really a part; for all its false thoughts have been given up; they have been undone. And they are gone.

This reintegration is the healing of the mind. When this occurs there is no mind that thinks it is separate. All illusions have disappeared, are gone, completely forgotten. The mind simply recognizes its oneness with all minds including the Mind of God.

In the last chapter we set forth the sequence of further mistakes made by the separated mind once it split from the whole and identified with it miscreation, the self it made. These mistakes ultimately led to the making of the physical world, and finally to a world with human bodies as we now perceive them.

DOES THE SON'S REQUEST IMPLY
THAT HE WAS NOT CREATED PERFECT?

Having made this digression let us now return to dealing with the paradox. Throughout the Course we find many passages which help us answer "the best question you could ask", namely, how could the mind ever have made the ego? And in every case the answer involves the idea that "you threw knowledge away". And you are still avoiding the knowledge you threw away. You are constantly, with great effort, trying to keep it dissociated, which you must do if you are to believe that the self you made is real.

In other words, the answer to this question always involves the idea that the mind put itself to sleep, or made itself unaware of reality. The mind is now attending to a dream instead. And while the mind is dreaming, and wants to continue dreaming, what happens in its dreams seems real to it. This, as I have so often mentioned, is something that in no way affects reality, or God Himself, or the perfect Self God created you as. Despite your dreams you still remain at home in God. "You are at home in God dreaming of exile, but perfectly capable of awakening to reality" (10.1,2:1).

Given, then, that we are vigilant to ask only honest questions and not make statements that imply the separation is real, -- or that the impossible occurred, or that a Thought of God left His Mind, or that the ego is real, or that the dream is reality, -- what kind of questions do we have before us in this chapter?

We said before that they are questions which address the apparent contradiction between the Course's teaching that God created His Son perfect, and its teaching that this same Son asked for something. This request seems to imply that he did not have everything, and therefore that he was not created perfect.

The Course does teach that the Son asked for something, as if he believed he lacked something. This, as we have seen, is how the author of the Course ultimately explains the origin of the ego, the body, and the world.

In the last chapter we learned that the origin of this illusory world of bodies traces back to a "tiny mad idea" that "crept into eternity", where all the minds that God created are one. The idea entered the mind of God's Son, and the Son "remembered not to laugh". We have also seen that once the idea was taken seriously, and considered possible of accomplishment and real effects, an error was made. And once the original error was made each subsequent mistake inevitably led to the next, ultimately resulting in the illusory world we see. For once a part of the mind of God's Son identified with its miscreation, and guilt was accepted into the mind, the stage was set for making a place of darkness in which to hide from God, a god now thought to be intent on getting revenge for the attack on him. The physical world of bodies is that place of darkness.

After discussing all of this in the last chapter we now proceed to resolve the paradox mentioned above by first asking what, exactly, did the Son ask for, and does his asking imply that he was not created perfect?

Resolving the Paradox

At first glance it does seem that the author of the Course contradicts himself in teaching, on the one hand, the Son of God was created perfect, yet, on the other hand, he asked for something. The apparent contradiction can be stated in another way besides our statement above: The Son of God both *has* everything and does *not have* everything.

In order to resolve this paradox, and see that it is only an apparent and not a real contradiction, we need to recall the Course's teaching about creation. The Course's concept of the nature of perfect creation can be represented as follows:

Father - Son - S - S - S - S ...

We notice that the Father is Sole Creator of something, namely, the first Son. We also notice that the Father is Prime Creator of all Sons. He is First Cause of all His effects; Prime Creator of all creations; First Father of all Sons, First Thinker of all His Thoughts, and First Extender of all His extensions. Thus the Father is the Creator of everything and everyone that exists in reality, in creation.

Every Son, in creating his first Son, creates him *with the Father*, as well as with all the Sons created "before" him.

The term "before" as applied to God and His creations is not a time concept. One Son was created "before" the Son he himself created in the sense that this is a logical priority not a temporal priority. It is a conceptual necessity. Creation does not take place in time but in eternity. However, it is always true that the creator creates his creation, but it is equally true that a creation does not create his creator. The relationship of "created" is not reciprocal or commutative.

We also notice that God the Father has no Father. And thus, in His activity of creating, He creates not with a creator, because He has no creator. However, once He created His first creation (His first Son), *He always co-creates,* that is, He creates His second Son *with the first Son.* And He creates the third Son with the first and second Son, and the fourth Son with the first, second, and third, and so on; endlessly, changelessly.

This is how God's Kingdom increases. Creation causes it to grow in number, and as more minds share the perfect Self, the joy of the Kingdom is increased. In other words, all creations were created to create, all minds were created to create. Thus every Son of God is both Father and Son because he has both Father and Son (11.2,1:3)

Next we notice that all Sons are co-creators with the Father. And each Son has an immediate creator (the Son that is created immediately before him), and an immediate creation (the first creation that he creates with his creator). Along with having an immediate creator and an immediate creation, each Son also has mediate creators and mediate creations.

Notice also that no Son is sole creator of anything. Nor is he the prime or first creator of anything. Anything that any Son creates is created with his creator(s). And, except for his immediate creation, is also created with his creation(s).

Only the Father, then, is Sole Creator of something, and Prime Creator of everything. He is the Creator of all created creators. Only He is Creator of all His co-creators. It is only God the Father who does not create with a creator, for only He has no creator. No one created Him. He is and has always been without a creator of Himself. The Son, however, is a creator who has been created, and as such must create with his creator(s), including the Prime Creator, God the Father. Only the first Son, the immediate Son of the Father, was not created by a created creator. All other Sons were created by a created creator creating in union with the uncreated Creator. But this does not make the first Son any more perfect than any other Son.

Every Son, then, is perfect like His Father because He is the extension of the Father's Thought of what He is. Every Son shares the same Self. Among other things, all of which we have already mentioned, this means that every Son of God has everything. He lacks nothing. There is no emptiness in him.

And here is where our paradox arises. The Son asks for something! And it is this that we must explain. How can the Son ask for something if he already has everything? If he really lacks something then it would not be true that he was created perfect. And if that is the case then our whole theodicy collapses! For the foundation of the system, namely, that what God creates is perfect like Himself, would be shown false.

We must acknowledge that if the Son asks for something then he must believe he "lacks" the something he asks for. The Son's request, then, involves at least three things: a) he thinks there is something he *does not have*, b) he believes it *is possible* to have the thing he does not have, and c) he *wants* it. This is what it means to say he believes that some "lack" or emptiness exists in him. He thinks there is something he wants and does not have.

Let us briefly consider each of these three points further:

a. It does seem that there is something the Son does not have. Specifically, he does not have prime creatorship of everything, nor does he have sole creatorship or first creatorship of anything. Only God has prime creatorship, sole creatorship, and first creatorship. The Son is not sole creator of anything; everything he creates he creates with someone who created him. He does not create without a creator co-creating with him. Nor is he first creator of anything in the sense that what he creates has never before been created by some other creator. In fact, the Son he creates (causes to be) has the same nature as himself and his creator.

b. It also seems that the Son could have the idea, momentarily at least, that it may *be possible for him to have* the thing he does not have. Why does this seem understandable? Because there is already Someone in reality Who does have it. The Father has it. What the Son is asking for, then, is not in itself something impossible for someone to have.

In other words, if it is inherently impossible for the Son to have sole creatorship, or for him to create apart from his Creator, it is not impossible in exactly the same sense that making a round square is impossible. No one, not even God can make a round square, for this is a contradiction in terms, and represents a contradictory concept. A round square simply cannot exist. The idea is wholly meaningless. But this is not true for the concept of "sole or first creator of something". Such a thing does exist. And in *reality*.

c. Given that the Son believes it possible he be sole creator of something, it seems reasonable he might wish to be so.

The Son having this, however, would require that he create something on his own, apart from his Creator. This, he thinks, would fill the lack or emptiness he believes exists in him.

And so the Son asks for it. He asks for the one thing he "lacks"; the one thing he *does not* have, but thinks he *could* have, and now *wishes* to have.

And his Father does not give it. From the last chapter you know the rest of the story. When the Father did not give it the Son made of Him an unloving father, demanding of Him that He allow him to create something on his own, as the way of getting the special favor that would follow from being the creator of something that he alone created. And in his attempt to create apart from his creator, his mind split. One part of his mind remains co-creator with his Father, for it cannot change or be changed. The other part of his mind is aware only of what it "created" (miscreated or made) on its own. This miscreation exists only in a dream because it cannot exist in reality. Only what God creates exists in reality. Only what God creates is creative, eternal and real.

At this point in our attempt to resolve the paradox we have at least shown that it is indeed possible to say without contradiction that the Son was created having everything, and yet there is a sense in which he does not have everything. There was something he did not have. But we have seen that the "something" is not really something, because it is *something he cannot have if reality is to remain perfect*, and it must remain perfect, for this is the Will of God. And so in that sense the Son actually lacks nothing. In other words, the Son does not really lack the thing he asked for because he cannot really have the thing he asked for, at least not in reality.

In dreams anything is possible. And it is indeed in a dream that the mind has what it thought it lacked. It has its own makings. It is sole maker of something and prime maker of everything it experiences in its dream.

The Son cannot really have the thing he asked for because, having been created perfect, and imbued with God's own loving will to create, he must create as he had been created. This is the law of creation that God established by creating by it, namely, what you create (or extend) you are. So the Son must create the perfect in order for all God's creation, all reality, to be perfect. And this is what he was created to do. In fact, the Son's free will was given him for his joy in creating the perfect.

Creating the perfect is the Son's function in heaven as a perfectly created being. If he does not wish to create the perfect he cannot really create at all. If he attempts to use his power to create inappropriately he merely puts himself to sleep and dreams a dream in which his miscreations seem real, but are not real because the dream is not reality. A part of the mind is merely dreaming it is what it is not, for it identifies with the thing it "created" (made) on its own.

It is easy enough to see that in order for all reality to be perfect, like God Himself is perfect, all God's creations, who are also creators like Him, must create creations who are like Him. And to do this they must co-create with God, the perfect Creator. They cannot create alone, on their own, apart from their creator. It is this law of mind and its creative activity that keeps everyone united, equal, and the same, maintaining the perfect oneness of everything real. If one of God's creations really created something on his own apart from his creator then there would be something God has not and is not. And thus God would not be perfect, having and being everything that is.

Thus in explaining that the Son asked for something, even though he has everything, the Course says that the Son does in truth have everything he could possibly have as a perfect being that *had been created* (versus uncreated), but that he, momentarily at least, believed he lacked something he did not really lack. And in asking for it he mistakenly took God's Answer as an unloving response to his request.

We have now answered the question of what the Son could possibly have asked for, given that he has everything. And thus we have resolved this paradox, and have shown that it is only a *seeming* contradiction, and not an actual one. In short, we can say that although the Son was created perfect he does not have sole creatorship. But since he cannot have sole creatorship he does not *really lack* anything. He has everything a *created* perfect being can possibly have.

The Son could not create something on his own without it being *imperfect*, and without making God, his Father, imperfect. He must create with his Creator in order for his own creations to be perfect like himself and his Father. Doing so maintains the perfection of all reality, both God's perfection, His Son's perfection, and His Son's Sons' perfection.

Does the Son's Asking and the Father's Answering Imply that Reality is not Timeless and Changeless?

There remains, however, another question that must be answered before we can say that our theodicy is not inconsistent. The question relates to the Course's teaching on the timelessness and changelessness of reality. We now turn to that question.

It seems that the concept of the Son's request and the Father's answer implies "time" or "change" in some sense. It seems that some time must have passed in this exchange, for "at the time" the Son is making his request he must not have been changelessly co-creating in union with his perfect Father, for he was asking to do the opposite. And the Father had to give answer.

So did time enter timelessness? Did change enter changelessness? Did a beginning and an ending take place within eternity? Did the "tiny mad idea" change what is always and forever the same? Did reality, which is timeless, changeless, and eternal, experience a moment of time, a moment of change, a moment of "something" with a beginning and ending? All these questions are one question.

And they all sound like the ego's question: "How did the impossible happen?" We must be careful here, to be sure our question is meaningful. Yet we realize we must acknowledge that the Course is telling us that "something" happened in Heaven, in "eternity, where all is one". And the Course also tells us that this "something" involved the Son requesting special favor, God not giving it, the Son making Him an unloving father, and demanding of Him what He did not give because He could not give and still remain Himself.

In the Course's marvelous consistency it does admit that in some sense a "tiny instant", a "brief interval", a "tiny tick of time" passed in Heaven while the request and answer were made:

> "Merely a tiny instant has elapsed between eternity and timelessness. So brief the interval there was no lapse in continuity, nor break in thoughts which are forever unified as one. Nothing has ever happened to disturb the peace of God the Father and the Son" (L234,1:2-4).

In other words, the Son's request had no effect on the endless co-creation of the Kingdom, because God gave answer in the same instant the request was made. "The instant the idea of separation entered the mind of God's Son, in that same instant was God's Answer given" (Q2,2:6). The request was answered, the error corrected so quickly as it were that there was "no lapse in continuity, nor break in thoughts". Co-creation continued unabated.

In a passage I will quote below, the author of the Course tells us that even though there was a tiny instant, a tiny tick of time, this brief interval "passed away in Heaven too soon for anything to notice it had come." The tiny tick of time "disappeared too quickly to affect the knowledge of the Son of God." In other words, the tiny instant had no effect on reality, no effect on God or on His Son as He created him. Everything is exactly as it was "before" the mistake was made and immediately corrected.

In the passage below we will also read that the tiny tick of time "in which the first mistake was made, held also the Correction for that one mistake." "What God gave answer to is answered and is gone." Metaphorically speaking, "Not one note of Heaven's song was missed".

This teaching on "the tiny tick of time" is crucial. For it is this teaching that actually maintains the consistency of the Course's metaphysics, and thus, in turn, the consistency of Miracle Theodicy, inspired by this metaphysics.

As I already mentioned, we who seem to live in this world have need for the Course to explain to us, in terms we can understand, why we experience evil, even though evil is not real. It must explain the sleep and the dream, the appearances we perceive, the illusory world of separation in which we seem to live. It must explain the origin of ego-bodies, of forms and limits, of change, and of the beginnings and endings we perceive. Yet it must at the same time be able to consistently claim that reality is, and forever remains, formless, limitless, timeless, changeless, and eternal. In short, perfect.

And so the Course explains all this by saying that the Son made a request that God could not grant, but to which He did give a loving response which the Son mis-took as not loving. Yet because the mistake was corrected in reality the same instant it occurred, the mistake had no affect on reality. It had no effect in Heaven. And in this sense it never happened at all. For having no effect, it is not a cause. And not being a cause it does not exist. It "passed away in Heaven too soon for anything to notice it had come."

Nothing happened but that you have put yourself to sleep and dreamed a dream. Dreams do not affect reality. They affect only the dreamer who thinks his dream is reality. This is the situation of the split mind; it contains dreams that it believes are reality. It contains illusions it thinks are true. Yet it is making it all up. It still remains one with its Self Which remains one with Its Creator, but mistakenly believes it is not Itself, but something else -- a separate self in a body, separate and different from other selves in bodies.

And it uses the dream world it made to "prove" that it is right, and thus keep itself in the illusion of separation. For only in time can the untrue seem true. But the mind for whom the untrue seems true must be split off from the Mind that knows only truth. It must be unaware of reality while it is dreaming a substitute reality. But this dreaming in no way has an effect on reality as it is, nor does it "establish reality" for anyone but the dreamer while he is dreaming. But a dream is still but a dream. And God is not aware of your dreams or anything that seems to happen to "you" in them. He has no knowledge of your dream of evil.

Notice how the following passage, while speaking of the "tiny instant", combines Level I and Level II. We find this combination in many passages in the Course. This passage is speaking to "you" (the separated mind of God's Son - Level II of mind and experience) who are using time to keep yourself in the illusion of separation. Yet it is speaking to you about Heaven (One-Mindedness - Level I of mind and experience). Yet, we notice that in speaking of Heaven, the author does so in terms of things you made and experience, in terms that can be understood by a mind that made time and thinks it real -- even though in reality there is no time:

> Time lasted but an instant in your mind, with no effect upon eternity. And so is all time past, and everything exactly as it was before the way to nothingness was made. The tiny tick of time in which the first mistake was made, and all of them within that one mistake, held also the Correction for that one, and all of them that came within the first. And in that tiny instant time was gone, for that was all it ever was. What God gave answer to is answered and is gone. (26.5,3:3-7)
>
> The tiny instant you would keep and make eternal, passed away in Heaven too soon for anything to notice it had come. What disappeared too quickly to affect the simple knowledge of the Son of God can hardly still be there, for you to choose to be your teacher. Only in the past, - an ancient past, too short to make a world in answer to creation, - did this world appear to rise. So very long ago, for such a tiny interval of time, that not one note in Heaven's song was missed. Yet in each unforgiving act or thought, in every judgment and in all belief in sin, is that one instant still called back, as if it could be made again in time. You keep an ancient memory before your eyes. And he who lives in memories alone is unaware of where he is. (26.5,5)

The Course's teaching on "the tiny tick of time", then, serves to maintain the consistency between its teaching that all reality is perfect on the one hand, and its teaching on the origin of the imperfect self and the illusory world of evil it sees, on the other.

This can be put another way. The notion of the tiny tick of time allows the author of the Course to say without contradiction that something other than perfect creation occurred in Heaven, and yet this occurrence in no way affected Heaven. And thus reality remains always and forever the same.

And thus the Course ultimately remains consistent even when it says that the Son of God was created perfect, and yet there was a tiny instant in which the Son asked for something. It solves this paradox by saying that in the same instant the request was made the answer was given. In other words, the one mistake was corrected and answered by the Perfect Creator in a way that rendered the mistake ineffective in reality. In this sense we could say that God prevented any evil from occurring in reality. This is what we would expect from an all-loving and all-powerful being.

And this is why the Son still remains perfect as the Father created him. He is still perfectly knowing, still perfectly powerful, still perfectly loving, still perfectly happy - and he is still timelessly, changelessly, and eternally so. Reality remains perfect as it always is despite the dream in a mind split off from it, asleep to it, and unaware of it.

And this sleeping mind is perfectly capable of awakening to reality, and of being once again aware of perfect oneness. And this awakening is guaranteed, as we shall see in the next chapter. In other words, all sleeping Sons of God will ultimately awaken. It is merely a matter of time. The Course, in fact, is training us to use time for this very purpose; to awaken to reality, after first attaining the happy dreams that learning its lessons are intended to bring.

It is difficult for us, who seem to live in time, to understand and appreciate that time is not real, that there is no time. Yet the Course clearly teaches that time is an illusion. "Time is a trick, a sleight of hand, a vast illusion in which figures come and go as if by magic" (L158,4:1). Apparently, Albert Einstein, who is considered to be one of the greatest experts on time and space, would agree with the Course on this point. For he himself once said, "time is an illusion, although a stubborn one."

Contradiction, Time, and the Split Mind

I want to say something about what the Course teaches on the relation between contradiction, time, and a split mind. It is, of course, beyond the scope of this book to set forth every aspect of the concept of time that the Course sets forth.[1]

In the first part of this book we made clear the centrality of the law of non-contradiction to our reasoning process. Recall the statement of the law: "A thing cannot both be and not be at the same time and in the same sense." There I explained why the phrase *at the same time* needs to be part of the statement of this law.

It is obvious that it *is* possible for a thing to both *be* and *not be*, if we allow for time. For a thing can be at one time, and not be at another time. A statement can be true at one time, and be not true at another time. But a thing cannot be both true and false *at the same time*; it cannot be true and false timelessly and changelessly, or eternally and always.

Time, then, plays a crucial role in making it possible for a mind to have and hold false ideas. In other words, time is necessary for a mind to believe in illusions. Only in time can a mind perceive something that seems real and true but is not.

The Course teaches, then, that time is merely a device the separated mind uses to keep itself in the illusion of separation. Time makes it possible for the mind to hold thoughts which contradict the truth of oneness. A mind holding such thoughts would have to be split from the Mind that knows the eternal oneness of reality and truth.

The mind, however, does not have to use time for the purpose of maintaining separation. It can change the purpose for which it uses time. Instead of using time to reinforce separation, to hold onto ideas that contradict truth, it can use time for welcoming the truth. It can learn to accept Atonement for itself. In this lies the disappearance of evil and the coming of the peace of God.

In other words, the mind can learn to use time for healing, for salvation, for forgiveness, for miracles, for letting its belief in the reality of separation be undone. This undoing reintegrates the apparently separated mind with the Whole Mind of which it is really a part. It then recognizes its own oneness and perfection.

The Course calls the instant of time in which you experience your oneness with God and your Self, "the holy instant". The holy instant is the time in which you experience the peace and joy of God. It is the time of true happiness. It is the time in which you are joined in the holy relationship with your brother. It is the time in which you see the face of Christ in one another, because you both share the goal of truth and see one another as sinless. It is the time you experience the love of God, the only love there is: "There is no love but God's" (L127).

The Course trains us to extend the holy instant throughout the day. As we progress in our learning there is less and less time that we do not experience the love of God. There is less and less time in which we perceive attack and experience suffering and pain, fear and anger. A day in which the holy instant has been extended throughout is a day without evil. It is a happy day.

Indeed there is no evil, and now, in the holy instant, your experience and perception tell you so. They tell you that God was right about you. You are still his holy Son, forever innocent, forever loving and forever loved. Your dream is happy now. And from the happy dream you will ultimately awaken to reality, and to your eternal Self, the Christ, God's Son as He created him.

A BRIEF REVIEW

In this chapter we have examined a paradox in the Course's teachings, viz., the Son of God was created perfect yet the Son of God asked for something he did not have. We have shown that this is not a real contradiction even though at first glance it seems to be.

Let me put the resolution of this paradox into the context of the new theodicy we are developing. In Part One we refuted the argument from evil (AFE).

This solution raised three questions: First, if God did not create the world what did He create? We raised and answered this question in Part Two. There we saw that God created a Son perfect like Himself, and that what you are as God created you is part of this perfect Son.

The second question raised was: if God did not create the world, who did? We raised and answered this question in chapter 8. The world was made by you, the separated mind of God's Son identified with the ego.

Finally, we used this chapter to resolve the paradox raised by our explanation in Chapter 8 of the origin of the ego, the body, and the world. We needed to resolve this paradox so that our refutation of the AFE cannot be rejected on the grounds that it includes something contradictory.

Now that we have resolved this paradox we can continue with the further development of our theodicy. We have yet to deal with our third question: if God Himself, God the Father, is not aware of us as human beings, and thus not aware of the evil we experience, then in what sense is Divine Help available to us?

In the upcoming Part Four, we will answer this all-important question.

Note

1. See Kenneth Wapnick's book on this topic, *Time: A Vast Illusion,* listed in the bibliography.

PART FOUR

FORGIVENESS:
THE WAY TO REMEMBER GOD
AND YOUR PERFECT SELF

PART FOUR

FORGIVENESS:
THE WAY TO REMEMBER GOD

The way to God is through forgiveness here.
There is no other way.
ACIM (L256,1:1-2)

Introduction

The last part of this book deals with two closely related issues. The first is the link that keeps us one with God despite our apparent separation. The second is forgiveness as the answer to the *practical* problem of evil.

Chapter 10 deals with the first issue. It involves a problem that philosophers of religion have recognized for centuries. Briefly stated the problem is this: if we acknowledge that God is a perfect being, and if we infer from the attributes He possesses as a perfect being that God could not be Creator of this imperfect world, then it seems to

294 *God, Self, and Evil*

follow that we human beings are alone in this world without any direct help from God Himself.

For if God Himself is not aware of this world, and not aware of us and our suffering, then it seems that there is no Divine Help available to us. What, then, is the basis for religion? Religion has to do with our relationship with God. But it seems we have no relationship with God, given that God is not aware of us as humans.

To whom, then, can we turn to save us from attack and suffering and death? Where can we turn for protection, safety and security? How can we experience the love of God if God does not know about the world in which we (seem to) live? What Divine Help in the form of guidance, counsel and strength is available to us while we walk the earth?

These and other questions all arise from our solution to the problem of evil. It is the task of chapter 10 to answer these kinds of questions all of which are contained in the third question we raised at the end of Chapter 3, namely, if God is not aware of us as humans, nor of our suffering in this world, then what Divine Help is available to us?

Once we understand the sense in which Divine Help *is* available to us we begin to understand what we need do to avail ourselves of It. And having It, we begin to experience the love of God in us; we experience His power and glory, and His peace and joy, and we recognize it as our own.

Chapter 11 fulfills the promise we made in chapter one. There we said that we would offer a solution to the *practical* problem of evil and would show how it relates to our solution to the *theoretical* one. And this we shall do.

According to *A Course in Miracles* only forgiveness is the solution to the practical problem of evil. Through forgiveness evil disappears. And by means of forgiveness you recognize the Christ in your brother and yourself, and thus remember God.

It is the task of chapter 11, then, to set forth the Course's radical teaching on forgiveness. When we fully understand what forgiveness really is, we easily see why "forgiveness is the key to happiness" (L121).

Chapter 12, the final chapter, offers a brief summary of the new theodicy we have constructed. I have also included brief remarks on some issues that Miracle theodicy directly impacts, but which could not be fully discussed in this book. My hope is to deal with some of these issues more fully in another book.

Let us turn now to describing and explaining how Divine Help is available to us even though God Himself is not aware of this world nor the evil we experience and perceive while using a body.

10

THE MEMORY OF GOD

God's memory is in our holy minds, which
know their oneness and their unity with their
Creator.   ACIM (Th11,4:5)

From Part Three we learned that in the Son's attempt
to create something apart from his Creator, a part of mind
split off from the perfect Mind he shares with his Father. The
part that is split off from the Whole is separated in the sense
that it identifies with the form it made in the act of
miscreating. This form or body is the mind's thought or
image of what it is. And it is unreal and false because it was
not created by God. It is the mind's illusion of what it is. It is
a figure in a dream the mind is dreaming.
   Because of its identification with a false thought of
what it is the mind believes it is really separate from God. It
believes it is in a body and is separate from other minds that
are also in bodies separate from its own. The mind, in fact,
has a strong tendency to believe it really *is* the ego-body. But

the mind is simply deceived, thinking that an illusion is true. It believes it is what it is not, and is not what it is.

THE MEMORY OF GOD

God's Answer Which corrects this mistake, however, abides in the mind where it was placed by God. It remains there as a *Memory.* And although the mind exerts great effort in denying and dissociating It, the true Thought of what it is and Who created it remains within it.

In other words, the memory of God is dissociated and buried deep in your mind beneath layers of fear, defenses, and denial which keep this Memory from arising to your awareness.

Although the mind can deny its true nature, and deceive itself into believing it is what it is not, it is perfectly capable of giving up its self deception. In doing so, it remembers the Self That God created it as.

As the Course says, "Truth can be unrecognized, but it cannot be changed" (Pf3,1:5). And the truth is that you are as God created you. You are still the Self That God created. And although this truth is temporarily unrecognized by you, it is possible for you to remember it. In fact, it is inevitable. In the end, everyone will choose to accept the Atonement for himself. It is simply a matter of time and of willingness before we all return to our home in Heaven with God, our most loving Father.

We said that this Memory of God is in one part of the split mind. It is the sane answer God gave to your insane request for specialness. It stands for the eternally true Thought of what you really are. Yet the other part of your split mind, which is identified with the ego, is afraid of it. It feels threatened by God's Answer. God's Answer stands for the truth of God's Love, Which is still in you. But Love, whose meaning lies in oneness, entails that the ego, a separate self, is unreal. In Love's presence the ego would disappear into the nothingness it is, as darkness disappears when the light has come.

The "Dynamics" of the Ego

To the mind identified with the ego, then, love is fearful. For love would undo the ego. The ego does not understand undoing. To the ego love is death. Love would kill it. So the ego defends itself against love to keep itself "safe". The ego literally lives on fear.

We said before that the experience of fear was the first effect of miscreating. The real cause of the fear is simply the denial of reality, and thus the unawareness of Love. For the absence of love is fear. Just as the absence of light is darkness.

But instead of realizing this and giving up its attempt to deny reality, the split off part of mind interprets the source of its fear as God retaliating for its attack on Him. This makes sense to the mind that believes it has attacked God by separating from Him. And so it believes it actually deserves God's attack in return for its attack on Him. Having accepted guilt the separation seems real indeed. For if he has not really separated why is he being attacked?

To the mind identified with the ego, then, God's Answer is perceived as threatening, for such a mind cannot believe that God loves it. Such a mind perceives God as an enemy, an angry father intent on killing his guilty son. Such a mind perceives its own situation as one of "kill or be killed" (See Q17).

As we have seen in chapter eight once guilt has been accepted into the mind it becomes terrified at the immensity of its "enemy". For the powerful and vengeful father he believes he has offended can and will destroy him! And so the mind attempts to escape the "wrath of God", a god made up of its own projections. The mind now is insane, made mad by guilt.

As we have seen, to escape from the vengeful and fearful God the mind identified with the ego makes a place to hide. It makes a physical world, a world of time, space, and bodies, where it can believe it is where it is not. Here it can seem to live apart from God.

And now the mind seems to have forgotten the immensity of its "enemy" and merely accepts its separation, forgetting how it attained it. It still feels guilty but has forgotten why. It is still afraid, but does not recognize its own guilt as the source.

The guilt is still in the mind, but now unconscious, since it has been repressed and covered over. The guilt now gets displaced, projected onto whatever is available. The source of fear seems to be something else and somewhere else. The mind perceives the attack as coming from a world outside itself. The mind's ego-body identity, then, is continually supported by the "sinful, guilty and fearful" world it sees around it. It does not realize it made this world, and that all the attack it perceives is merely its own attack upon itself.

It is important to realize that all the ego's defenses merely defend illusions against the truth. They do nothing more than "protect" sin, guilt, and fear from correction and undoing. If sin, guilt, and fear were not real to you, neither would be the ego, the body, and the world. Nor would separation. If you released guilt and accepted forgiveness for yourself, instead of projecting the guilt in an attempt to get rid of it by seeing it outside, the truth of what you are would dawn upon your mind of Itself.

Your mind, then, is constantly preoccupied with defending the ego. This is your insanity. A mind that does not know itself is sick and in need of healing, in need of Atonement. And "the means of the Atonement is forgiveness" (C-IN,1:2).

The ego "dynamics" I have just described are a small part of what the Course has to say about the devious ways we go about protecting and defending the concept of the self we made as replacement for the truth of what we are.

For our purposes in completing our theodicy we need not present everything the Course has to say about the split mind and ego dynamics. What I have said above can serve to make clear why we are unaware of the presence of God's Answer which still abides within. Our lack of awareness is due to our unwillingness to look within and acknowledge the Presence. We choose not to be aware because we mistakenly think the ego-body is our life, and we want to preserve our "life". And so we use our time to preserve, protect, and defend it at all costs.

Yet we must realize it is not worth defending by recognizing that it is not worth keeping. We do not really want it. It is nothing more than an illusion of what we are. It offers us nothing of real value. It never has and it never will.

How God's Answer Functions in Our Minds

To complete our theodicy, then, we must concern ourselves with "God's Answer". God's Answer to your request for special favor abides with you even in your seeming separation. It is in a part of your apparently separated mind. As we read in the long passage we quoted in the last chapter: "He could but answer your insane request with a sane answer that would abide with you in your insanity. And this He did" (13.3,12:6-7).

God's answer to your original request can be stated in many ways. One way, which I have used quite frequently up to this point, is: "You are my Son, and we are One." God's Answer constitutes a reminder to the Son who he is. It corrects any contrary thought.

In the mind that believes it has separated and sinned this sane answer is available in whatever form it may be needed and is meaningful. But regardless of its form it always implies that you are not guilty of sin. For the separation has not really occurred. You cannot really attack God. For God is wholly unassailable. His will is wholly without opposite.

In other words, in one part of the separated mind is the problem, the belief in the reality of separation. In the other part is the solution, the correction of this belief, the Atonement. In one part is the thought "I am a guilty ego", and in another part is the answer, "you are not a guilty ego, you are still God's holy Son, a part of Him, and one with Him."

Stated in the same terms that your specific false beliefs are stated in, this Answer is a correction of each specific false belief. Thus, for example, this One Answer translates into specific answers which answer specific forms of your one error. Some specific corrections are: you are not a body, you are not an ego, you are not sinful and guilty, you do not deserve punishment, there is nothing to fear, you cannot attack or be attacked, you cannot suffer, be in pain, or die.

In other words, God's Answer that you are His holy Son, forever one with Him, still abides in your mind. This Answer serves to undo your denial of the truth. It undoes the false. The truth is that you are the holy Son of God. This is true eternally. And thus it is true *now*. You have denied the truth. You say, "I am not the holy Son of God. I am a guilty ego. I am a body. I am a human being". God's Answer, then, *denies your denial*, it denies that your substitute for truth is true. It says, you are *not* an ego. You are *not* a body. You are *not* really a *human* being. You merely seem to be.

In the most general terms, then, God's Answer stands for the truth in terms of your false belief in the reality of separation. It teaches you that the separation is *not* real; it has not really occurred. Thus in its most general form it teaches *Atonement*. Atonement is the only lesson you need learn. "Atonement is the one need in this world that is universal" (6.2,5:5). "Atonement is for you. But learn this Course and it is yours" (Q13,8:7,10).

Your apparent separation is just that - *apparent*. It is appearance. And like all appearances it is illusion. You need but recognize it as such. When you do, you are freed from all pain and suffering. You have the peace of God. You are happy again. For "illusion recognized must disappear" (L187,7:1).

Another way to put all of this is to say that in one part of your mind is the false thought of what you are, namely, a sinful and guilty ego; and in the other part of your mind is a Memory, the true Thought of what you are, namely, the holy Son of God, the Christ.

This true Thought, however, is available to you mainly in the *form* of an answer to all the false thoughts. It denies their truth. So just as in one part of your mind is an entire thought system based on a false premise of what you are, so too in another part of your mind there is an entire thought system based on the true premise of what you are. This true thought system consists of thoughts *in the form of* a denial of the false thoughts. The *content* of these thoughts is truth and love, but the thoughts as form, as specific, are not the Truth Itself Which is formless. The thoughts in the true thought system stand for the truth, *reflect* the truth, are in accord with the truth, but are not formless Truth Itself. Thus this true thought system contains only thoughts that stand for the truth *in a mind that made and is aware of forms*. In other words, they are an answer to your insanity. They heal the sick mind. They stand for the truth within the mind that believes it is separated.

For example, "I am not a body" or "I am not sinful and guilty" is true in the sense that it is a correction of the false. It is the correction of the idea "I am a body" or "I am sinful and guilty". In reality, in truth, there is no body; there is no sin or guilt that needs to be forgiven or denied or undone. Thus neither the idea "I am a body" nor the idea "I am not a body" is meaningful in reality. For in Heaven the idea of a body is not even thinked (thought).

Thus the Memory in your *right mind* serves as the foundation for a thought system which corrects the entire false thought system in your *wrong mind*. Illusions are always *forms* of some kind and are always perceived, never known. Reality is formless and is only known, never perceived. Thus God's Answer in your mind serves to translate the truth, which is formless and known, into a correction of the false, which is always form and perceived. This corrective function ultimately lies in the truth of what you really are. This Memory of God, then, keeps you linked to God regardless of what you mistakenly believe about yourself.

Think of the story of the prodigal son. Just as the memory of his father brought him back to himself and his father's house, so too will the Memory of your Father bring you back to your Self and your Father's Home. Even though you have temporarily denied and forgotten your oneness with God, it is guaranteed that you will ultimately accept and remember it again.

The Structure of the Mind

It seems worth while to offer a diagram that models the structure of the split mind as we have been and will continue to discuss it.

God: Mind - Thought (Christ Mind)

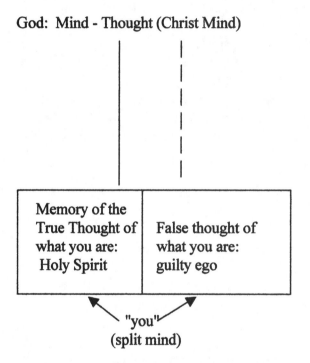

| Memory of the True Thought of what you are: Holy Spirit | False thought of what you are: guilty ego |

"you"
(split mind)

The top line of the diagram represents God and His Creation. God is Mind, and His creation is His Thought. His Thought, being His creation, being an extension of Himself, is perfect like Himself. His creation is His Son. His Son is You. You are the Christ Which is also a Mind like God's. We have already discussed this in Parts Two and Three.

The broken line represents the split that occurred when the Son of God attempted to create on his own apart from his Creator. The Course refers to this split off part of the mind as "the separated mind" (L99,3:4). Thus it refers to us who believe we are separated as "the separated Sons of God" (2.2,7:2), or "the separated ones" (L41,1:1). In any case the separated mind is the mind that believes it is separated. It seems to be really separated from the Mind of God and Christ only because it holds a false idea of what it is.

Since the separated mind consists of two parts there are many contexts in which the Course refers to the separated mind as "the split mind". It is a mind that not only seems split off from the Christ Mind, but is also split within itself. It is uncertain and conflicted about what it is. Since it identifies with the body it also thinks it is a self different from other selves who are in bodies and separate and different from it.

This split mind is the "you", the student to whom the author of the Course is speaking. It is the mind that is reading this book. Your mind is the dreamer of the dream, and this book, or any book, is part of the dream. The Course, because of the change of mind it brings about, may be the most helpful book you find in this dreamworld, for it will help you awaken from the dream to reality, and to your Self Which is perfectly happy co-creating with God, your loving Father.

One part of the split mind is constituted by the ego thought system whose starting point or foundation is the self "created" (made) separately from God. It is the self you made. This part of the mind is called the wrong mind. You, who are really the Son of God, are wrong-minded when you think you are an ego-body. This false idea of you leads to mistaken choices about what you want to have and be, think and feel, do and see, and happen to you.

Another way to say this is that an entire thought system is built up from this mistaken starting point about what you are. Since the thought system rests on a false foundation not one thought in the ego thought system is true.

They all are illusions, thoughts that seem true but are not. And this thought system leads the mind to hell, to misery; to war, fear and pain. This movement of the mind in the direction of hell (fear) is automatic, for the mind cannot but be dictated by the thought system to which it adheres.

The solid line in the diagram represents the unbroken connection between you and God. It represents the fact that in your mind is something that links you with God. This Memory is the remaining communication link between God and His separated Sons.

The solid line also represents the fact that God's Answer "came with you" when a part of your mind split off from the Whole. "The light came with you from your native home, and stayed with you because it is your own" (L188,1:6).

Your communication with God, then, is not completely broken, even though God Himself is not aware of any of the forms you made as witness to your separation from Him and from all your brothers.

This means that you are not alone and abandoned in the miserable world of separation you made. Awareness of your oneness with God is possible because the true Thought of what you are, which is what God is, remains in your mind as a Memory. The Thought of what you really are is still in your mind and can never leave it. It is "God's Answer to the separation" (5.2,2:5). This Answer abides with you, even in your insanity. It reminds you of spirit, of your Self, and of your oneness with God and His creations as well as yours.

When you accept Atonement for yourself, when you accept that the separation has not really occurred, when you accept the true Thought of what you are, when you accept your Identity as spirit, in short, when you accept Christ as you, you experience your oneness with all your brothers, and with God as well. And you are truly happy. All evil is gone.

Attack, fear, pain, suffering and death are wholly meaningless.

The Course's training, then, can be seen as helping us to remember God. To remember God is to remember your Self, just as to know God is to know your Self. Any thought of God that does not include you is incomplete. "Whenever you question your value, say: *God is incomplete without me.* Remember this when the ego speaks, and you will not hear it."(9.7,8:1-2)

The part of your mind in which this Memory of God exists is called your right mind. You are right-minded when you accept the right Thought of what you really are. And when you accept the truth of what you are, you recognize your true innocence, and that of all your brothers who temporarily have forgotten their Father and their Self. Like you, your brother has misunderstood his Father. But you both can remember.

Remembering God is possible only by being willing to give up the false thought of what you are for the true one. As we shall see later, this is done on a very practical level by forgiving your brother for what you mistakenly think he has done to hurt you. In this way you forgive yourself as well. Through forgiveness you recognize that minds are joined, and thus remember your oneness with all minds and with God's as well. In this remembrance lies your happiness.

You mistakenly believe you have sinned, for you mistakenly believe that you have separated from God and from your brothers. But you *cannot* sin, for you cannot really be separate from God and His creations. You can only dream that you are. But your fantasies, dreams, and false ideas about yourself do not change your reality. By giving them up you realize this. "What is sin, except a false idea about God's Son? Forgiveness merely sees its falsity, and therefore lets it go" (Th1,1:5-6).

You can give up the false for the true. You can change your mind. And there is good reason to do so. Your happiness depends on it. In other words, by letting go of your perception of your brother as a body, you see the face of Christ and recognize the Christ in you. And to remember this Self is to remember God. To remember God is to be aware of Love's presence. It is to be at peace, to be happy, and to experience pure joy -- a joy that no one can take from you, nor would they want to, for your joy is theirs, and they would increase your joy by sharing it.

The author of the Course says he wants to teach you "to associate misery with the ego and joy with the spirit. You have taught yourself the opposite" (4.6,5:6-7). And what you have taught yourself has cost you dearly. You do not recognize your confusion of pain and joy (7.10,3:4). But you will increasingly learn to distinguish them as you read and study his Course, and practice and apply the exercises as he directs in the Workbook.

In the process of commenting on this diagram we have answered our third question. It is this: the Divine Help available to us abides in our mind as the Memory of God and of our Self. This Memory serves as God's Answer to our false belief in the reality of sin and separation, of attack and suffering. This Answer reflects our knowledge and awareness of our oneness with God. It serves as God's Word to us when we forget who we are:

> God's memory is in our holy minds, which know their oneness and their unity with their Creator. (Th11,4:5)
> His awareness is in everyone's memory, and His Word is written on everyone's heart. Yet this awareness and this memory can arise across the threshold of

recognition only where all barriers to truth have been removed. (Q26,1:2-3)

Our problem is of our own making. It is we who have buried God's Answer under layers of defenses against it. All our defenses merely function as barriers to our remembering God and our Self. They are obstacles to true peace and happiness. The final obstacle to peace is the fear of God, the fear of true Love. For to experience true love is to be egoless. And as long as you identify with the ego you will be afraid of God; you will be afraid to be like God. God is egoless, and so are you as He created you. As long as you think you are an ego, however, love will be perceived as fearful. But love is not fearful, for it is reality and reality is not fearful. Everything in reality maintains your perfect happiness and increases joy. To be aware of Love is to be aware of God. To be aware of Love is to be aware of your true Self, for what He is *is* what you are. "Only Love creates and only like Itself" (Th11,1:2). And Love created you. "God is but love, and therefore, so am I" (R5,4:3).

To conclude our commentary on the diagram, then, we can say that in one part of your mind is the entire ego thought system, or what the Course also calls "the voice of the ego". The thought system this voice speaks for consists of nothing but illusions which support the false premise of your specialness, difference, and separation. It tells you that you are sinful, guilty, and deserve punishment and death.

In the other part of your mind is the Memory of God and of your Self as He created you. This Memory serves as God's Answer to your false beliefs. It stands for the truth in answer to all illusions of what you are. It represents your Self and your Creator Who are one. The Course also calls this Answer "The Voice for God". The thought system this Voice speaks for is one that is a correction of the ego thought system, for these two thought systems are opposite in every respect -- in foundation, nature, and outcome.

THE HOLY SPIRIT

The most common phrase the Course uses to refer to this Memory of God in our separated minds is: the *Holy Spirit*. This may seem strange at first. Why is the memory of God and of your true Self called "the Holy Spirit"? There are several reasons for this, two of which I will mention here.

The first has to do with one of the purposes for which the Course has come into the world. Many students and teachers rightly view the Course as a correction of errors found in traditional Christianity, and that is why it is filled with Christian terminology, even though the Course deals with spiritual themes that have meaning to all humans regardless of their religious background. In other words, with respect to Christianity the Course offers correction of the mistakes made in passing on Jesus' message from generation to generation in the two thousand years since he walked the earth.

Thus, Jesus, as author of the Course, uses terms and concepts that have been traditionally used in Christianity in order to speak to those who see him as the clearest manifestation of God's Love for us, and who want and claim to be his followers. Some aspects of the meaning of these terms as they have been traditionally used are acceptable. But other aspects are not. Thus the author evicts the false meanings these terms have acquired at the hands of the ego and replaces them with correct meanings. The terms, with newly acquired meanings, can now serve to transform our thinking. In fact, changing concepts (which, of course, is what these terms represent) can be understood as one of the main tasks of salvation! As the Course puts it, "Concepts are needed while perception lasts, and *changing concepts is salvation's task."* (31.7,1:3) (my emphasis).

We can appreciate this task of salvation even though in reality there are no concepts. The mind that knows, or has knowledge, experiences reality directly. It has no need of learning. Nor is there need for symbols. But since we made a world of symbols to support the self we made, and since we made learning and concepts and words and voices, the author of the Course, if he is to help us at all, must communicate in language we can understand. And so he has. Would it not be strange that an author who speaks in the name of Jesus would have nothing to say about "the Holy Spirit", since he is reputed to have said that he would send the Holy Spirit Who would guide us into all truth? (Jn16:3)

But there is a substantive and logical reason for which Jesus, as author of the Course, uses the term "Holy Spirit". Recall that "spirit is the Thought of God which He created like Himself" (C1,1:3). Thus we could very well view the Holy Spirit as the "Holy Thought". He is the Thought of God. And He is the Thought of Your true Self, the Christ. He represents both your Father and your Self, the Christ.

Thus the Holy Spirit is the Correction of the false thought of what you are. This correction is based on His knowledge of what He is, what God is, and what you are, which are one. This Holy Thought abides in your right mind. It is the mind's thought of itself as holy, as being part of God. "The Holy Spirit is part of you. He is both God and you, as you are God and Him together" (16.3,5:1,3).

The term "holy" carries with it many connotations. In the Course's usage, to be "holy" is to be innocent, to be sinless. It is to be like God. It is to come from and belong to God. It is to be a part of God. "My mind is part of God's. I am very holy" (L35).

The thought of yourself as holy is also the thought of yourself as whole or complete, lacking nothing. It is the thought of being at one with the Whole, Which is God and Christ. The thought of you as holy, then, is a correction of the thought of you as unholy or sinful, separate from God, and incomplete.

The terms "holy" and "holiness" are also used as opposites of "special" and "specialness". The Course uses the term this way when it speaks of the "holy relationship" versus the "special relationship", or when it speaks of your brother's holiness versus his specialness, or your holiness versus your specialness.

Thus in your split mind is both the holy thought of what you are and the unholy thought of what you are. The Holy Spirit, then, is the Thought of you as holy; the ego is the thought of you as unholy or guilty. The Holy Spirit is the Thought of you as spirit, as pure mind. The ego is the thought of you as a body. The thought of being unholy always involves the idea of being a body of some kind.

The Course teaches that the body itself is neither holy nor unholy. It is neither good nor evil, neither sinful nor sinless. In itself it is neutral. "My body is a wholly neutral thing" (L294). Ultimately it is nothing. It is an illusion. But unlike some illusions which have positive value (forgiveness, correction, healing, the happy dream) or negative value (sin, guilt, fear, the nightmare) the body is neutral in itself. The only meaning the body has is that given it by the mind that made it and is using it. This, in fact, is true of anything that enters awareness through the body's senses, for they see only form. And the meaning the mind gives the body depends on the purposes for which it uses it. "Purpose is meaning" (L25,1:1).

There are only two possible purposes or meanings: ego purposes or Holy Spirit purposes -- meaning given by the ego, or meaning given by the Holy Spirit. Thus what the body means to you depends entirely on whether you use it for the purposes of the ego or the Holy Spirit.

When you follow the voice of the ego, you use the body "for attack, for pleasure, and for pride" (6.5A,5:3). When you do this you believe you are guilty of sin. And you will fear punishment. When you follow the Voice of the Holy Spirit, you use the body as a communication device. Thus the body is seen as a "serviceable instrument through which the mind can operate until its usefulness is over" (L135,8:2). The Holy Spirit interprets the body as a means for communicating the Word of God and the Love of God to everyone you meet (8.8,2:1). In this sense the body becomes holy because it is used for a holy purpose (Th5,4:4).

> When you meet anyone, remember it is a holy encounter. As you see him you will see yourself. As you treat him you will treat yourself. As you think of him you will think of yourself. Never forget this, for in him you will find yourself or lose yourself. Whenever two Sons of God meet, they are given another chance at salvation. Do not leave anyone without giving salvation to him and receiving it yourself. For I am always there with you, in remembrance of you. (8.3,4)

Other Descriptions of the Holy Spirit

The Holy Spirit is described in various ways, depending on what aspect of His nature or function is being pointed to in a particular context. Most often the Holy Spirit is referred to as the "Voice for God" (see, 5.2 and C6). We will have more to say about the Holy Spirit as the Voice for God a bit later.

Besides being called the Voice for God, the Holy Spirit is also referred to as "the communication link between God and His separated Sons" (C6,3:1), "your remaining communication with God" (5.2,8:3), "God's remaining communication link with all His children" (10.3,2:6), "the great Correction Principle; the bringer of true perception" (C6,3:4), "God's Answer to the separation" (5.2,2:5), "a Teacher other than yourself Who represents the other Self in you" (L121,6:3), "the Mind of the Atonement" (5.1,6:3), and finally, to complete just a small list of the descriptions found in the Course: "the Christ Mind Which is aware of the knowledge that lies beyond perception" (5.1,5:1).

Essential to understanding the Holy Spirit is the idea that He has a dual function, "He *knows* because He is part of God; He *perceives* because He was sent to save humanity" (C6,3:2-3). The Holy Spirit Who is in your right mind, then, recognizes and perceives the illusions you made, but He does not believe in them. He knows they are not true, because He knows what you really are. This is in contrast to *you* when you are wrong-minded and believe the illusions you made are true. Thus "the Holy Spirit mediates between illusions and the truth" (Th7,1:1). He does this by offering you a correction of your mistakes, allowing your illusions to disappear.

Based on His knowledge, He teaches that illusion is not true. He knows you are spirit, the holy Son of God, so He teaches you that you are not a body, not sinful, not guilty. He knows God is real, so He teaches you evil is unreal. Thus He teaches you to recognize illusions for what they are.

When you share perception with the Holy Spirit, evil is no longer real in your perception, for your perception is His. And He perceives truly. Your perception, then, is in accord with truth, in accord with God's Will for happiness for you. You are thus right-minded and therefore miracle-minded (3.4,4). You can then give the miracles you have received (L159) expressing the Love of God you feel within you.

"You who prefer separation to sanity cannot attain it in your right mind" (13.3,10:1). Only wrong-minded thinking and perception accepts sin and separation as real. And this is insanity! Let us be thankful that One Who knows walks with us, and offers us the means whereby all evil disappears from the world we see (L195,1:7).

Yes, we as humans have been insane for millennia. Perhaps this new millennium will see us return to sanity, to the healing of our mind, the mind of God's Son. For that is the only purpose the Holy Spirit has for the world, for time, and for all appearances (24.6,4).

The Holy Spirit offers you the correction for all your mistaken purposes, thoughts and perceptions. Alone you cannot correct your mistakes, for you are the one who wants them true. Thus you need help, from a Teacher other than yourself, to realize that you do not want them. You need help to recognize that your illusions are illusions, for this is the only way you will let them go. As long as you believe they are true and real you will hold onto them. You need help in seeing how insane it is to believe them true. They are the source of your pain and suffering. And it is this you must recognize. You need the help of the Voice that speaks God's Word to you to save you from your terrible mistake about yourself, your brother, and your Father, God.

This Teacher and Helper is available to you for the asking. The Holy Spirit is in you. He is your inner Teacher. He is God's Word to you. He offers you the principle of Atonement to use on your behalf. He is God's Answer to your mistakes. This Answer offers you salvation from your illusions. God's Answer is His Love in the form you need it. God's Answer is the love that saves you:

"No one who hears His answer but will give
up insanity. For His answer is the reference
point beyond illusions, from which you can
look back on them and see them as insane.
But seek this place and you will find it, for
Love is in you and will lead you there"
(13.3,12:8-10)

Listen to God's Answer and you will escape all
suffering, regardless of its form. You will find love,
certainty, and strength, and you will find joy. The Holy
Spirit is the call to joy (5.2,3:1), He is the call to awaken and
be glad (5.2,10:5). It is through the Holy Spirit, the Voice for
God, that you have all the Help you need to remember God
your Father and His holy Son, for He speaks for both.

I have said that the Holy Spirit is the bringer of true
perception (C6,3:4). The Holy Spirit corrects false
perception by offering you another way of interpreting
whatever enters your awareness. When you share perception
with the Holy Spirit you perceive illusions for what they are.
And when you recognize illusions *as* illusions they
disappear. They have no effect. In terms of the dream
metaphor the Holy Spirit offers happy dreams in
replacement for your fearful ones. In short, when you share
perception with the Holy Spirit, instead of with the ego, you
have an entirely different perception of everyone and
everything in the world. Sights and sounds are translated
"from witnesses of fear to those of love" (Th7,2:2). This is
why the Holy Spirit is sometimes referred to as "the
Translator" (L157,8:2).

The Holy Spirit is also described as your Teacher
(26.5,3:1), He is referred to as "the Healer, the Comforter,
and the Guide" (5.1,4:2). He is called your Helper (25.3,7:2)
and Friend (14.3,13:5), your Savior and Protector (Th1,5:1).
"He brings the Love of your Father to you" (C6,3:9).

"One Who knows goes with you" (L155,10:5) is another description of the Holy Spirit. The Holy Spirit is also the Teacher of forgiveness (L121,6). He represents the truth to you who have tried to hide from it, but which is still in part of your mind, dissociated from the illusions you cherish still.

In the following passage we see that correction and forgiveness are the same thing and that through forgiveness you can recognize that the Holy Spirit's Mind and your mind are the same.

> Correction *you* would do must separate, because that is the function given it *by* you. When you perceive correction is the same as pardon, then you also know the Holy Spirit's Mind and yours are one. And so your own Identity is found. (27.2,12:1-3)

The Holy Spirit, then, is in your right mind and serves as a correction of the illusions in your wrong mind. Both your right mind and wrong mind are part of the perceiving mind and thus are not the One-Mindedness of the Christ Mind. Once you fully reject everything in your wrong mind, having no use for it, and accept only what is in your right mind, your mind then reconnects or reintegrates with your Christ Mind and "your own Identity is found". For "the Holy Spirit's Mind and yours are one."

Your part in all this is to bring your illusions to the Holy Spirit for His gentle correction. Let Him undo them. You have brought truth to illusions (14.9,1:4), but you are now asked to bring illusions to the truth (L140,7:4). By accepting what the Holy Spirit offers in exchange for your illusions you will no longer experience separation as real, nor will sin and guilt and fear be real to you. When you share perception with the Holy Spirit neither attack, suffering nor death; neither lack, loss nor grief will seem real to you. All evil will disappear from your perception. You will look upon a world of mercy and of love, because you feel the love of God within you (L189,5:5).

THE HOLY SPIRIT IS THE DIVINE HELP
AVAILABLE TO US ALL

As one might guess the Course has much to say about the Holy Spirit, as it does about the ego. For our purposes here there is no need to present every teaching about the Holy Spirit that one can find in *A Course in Miracles*.

What needs to be recognized for our purpose in this book is that *the answer to our third question is provided by the Course's teachings on the Holy Spirit*. It is the Holy Spirit Who is the Divine Help available to us while we walk the earth. Even though God Himself does not know of minds within a body, or of any evil such minds experience, He has provided an Answer that abides with us in our insanity. This answer is the only help we need, and the only Help we have to be saved from our illusions. The Holy Spirit is our link to truth, and to the reality that is Heaven.

The Course's teachings on the Holy Spirit, then, fill out the final part of the theodicy we have developed in this book. With the teachings on the Holy Spirit, we can begin to understand that although God Himself is not aware of this world, He has nevertheless provided us with Help; a way of escape from all forms of suffering. His Answer, "you are My Holy Son, and We are one", still abides with us, always reminding us of the truth.

What the author of *A Course in Miracles* teaches about the Holy Spirit not only provides an answer to the third question raised by our solution to the logical problem of evil, but also provides the answer to our personal experience of evil. But we must want the answer. We must want to remember God.

To truly want to remember God means that we are sincerely willing to give up ego-body identity, and accept Christ identity. This is easier said than done. But it must *be* said. If we cannot say it, and be willing to repeat it, how can we even begin to accept it as the truth? If you cannot tell yourself, "I am the holy Son of God Himself; I cannot suffer, I cannot be in pain," then how are you ever going to personally experience the truth in these words?

The Course is simple. But to achieve its aim seems difficult for us. Why? Because we are so invested in our separate self identity that we believe that if we gave it up we would cease to exist. We are afraid that giving up the ego is death. The Course's teaching helps us to realize it is not. And its lessons help us to experience the truth that our life does not consist of being an ego-body, but lies in the Life we share with God. "There is one life, and that I share with God" (L167). "God is my life. I have no life but His" (L223).

To enter and appreciate the training the Course provides we must begin to understand *why it is true* that we cannot be both an ego-body and the holy Son of God. God, Who is a perfect Father, did not and can not create a Son who is limited, separated and in a body, and thus doomed to suffer and to end its life in death. He did not create us as we presently perceive ourselves. He could not have. It is contrary to His very nature. He did not create us as perceiving minds, as minds with bodies in a physical world. He created us as spirit, as an extension of Himself. He created us as pure minds who know Him and love Him, and who are happy co-creating the perfect with Him.

"You cannot behold the world and know God. Only one is true" (8.6,2:2-3). Hopefully what we have said in this book, in the process of solving the logical problem of evil, has made it clear why this *must be* so.

Let us state our answer to the third question again: Divine Help is available to us while we walk the earth with these human bodies. That Divine Help is the Holy Spirit. The Holy Spirit is within our minds serving as the "Voice for God". He reminds us of our Father's Love, and of Christ, our true Self as He created us. Through listening to the Voice of the Holy Spirit we learn to give up the evil self we made (L303,2:2) and return our mind to identity with the Self God created us as.

When we turn to the Holy Spirit, our Friend and Teacher within, and put Him in charge, all evil disappears. God's love becomes real to us again, and all fear vanishes. No attack, pain, suffering or death is real to us. When we are tempted to see the evil in the world as real we remember that "God still is love, and this is not His will" (L99,5:4-5). And what is not His will is not real, and so must be illusion. And illusion recognized must disappear. Thus, with the Holy Spirit's help, we learn to forgive the world we made, overlook its evil, and look upon a happy world through forgiving eyes.

There is another way of putting this in terms of our third question. We can say that Divine Help is available to each of us because the Holy Spirit abides in each seemingly separate mind as a reminder of its oneness with all minds. Thus He functions as the link that makes all minds one with each other and with God. He is our remaining communication link with God and with Christ, the Self we share.

The role of the Holy Spirit is beautifully expressed in the following passage intended to clarify the nature and function of the Holy Spirit:

The Holy Spirit abides in the part of your mind that is part of the Christ Mind. He represents your Self and your Creator, Who are one. He speaks for God and also for you, being joined with both. And therefore it is He Who proves them one. He seems to be a Voice, for in that form He speaks God's Word to you. He seems to be a Guide through a far country, for you need that form of help. He seems to be whatever meets the needs you think you have. But He is not deceived when you perceive your self entrapped in needs you do not have. It is from these He would deliver you. It is from these that He would make you safe. (C6,4)

Hearing God's Voice

Because the Holy Spirit is in your mind He is an ever present Help. The Voice of the Holy Spirit is always available to you. "God's Voice speaks to me all through the day" (L49). Do you have difficulty hearing His Voice? Do you want to hear it? You *can* hear His Voice. Nothing is required but a little willingness. "The Holy Spirit's Voice is as loud as your willingness to listen" (8.8,8:7).

In fact, one of the many ways to describe the Course's learning goal is to say that it teaches you how to listen to, and clearly hear, the Voice for God within you and in your brother. Jesus, as the author of the Course, asks you and me to put the Holy Spirit in charge. The last lesson in the Workbook, which we are asked to do five days in a row -- the only lesson with this requirement -- reads as follows:

> This holy instant would I give to You. Be You in charge. For I would follow You, certain that Your direction gives me peace. (L365)

> And if I need a word to help me, He will give it to me. If I need a thought, that will He also give. And if I need but stillness and a tranquil, open mind, these are the gifts I will receive of Him. He is in charge by my request. And He will hear and answer me, because He speaks for God my Father and His holy Son. (L365,1)

Again, referring to the idea of hearing the Voice of the Holy Spirit Jesus says,

> It is possible even in this world to hear only that Voice and no other. It takes effort and great willingness to learn. It is the final lesson that I learned, and God's Sons are as equal as learners as they are as sons. (5.2,3:9-11)

The sentences preceding this remark actually provide a good summary of several of the points discussed in this chapter:

> The principle of Atonement and the separation began at the same time. When the ego was made, God placed in the mind the call to joy. This call is so strong that the ego always dissolves at its sound. That is why you must choose to hear one of two voices within you. One you made yourself, and that one is not of God. But the other is given you

by God, Who asks you only to listen to it.
The Holy Spirit is in you in a very literal
sense. His is the Voice That calls you back to
where you were before and will be again. It is
possible even in this world to hear only that
Voice and no other. (5.2,3:1-9)

To conclude our discussion on the Holy Spirit as the
Divine Help available to you while you seem to be separate
from your Creator, we can say that in your mind are two
voices, the voice of the ego and the Voice of the Holy Spirit.
You made the one, and God gave you the other (5.2,3:5-6).

The Holy Spirit, as the Voice for God, asks you to
give up all forms of your belief in the reality of sin and
separation. In exchange for your false identity as a guilty
ego, He offers you your true Identity as God's holy Son.

You are free to listen to one voice or the other. One
will lead you to love and the joy of heaven. The other will
lead you to fear and the misery of hell. Who can fail to make
the right choice when he clearly sees the alternatives?

You are Free to Choose
to which Voice you Listen

I said that you are free to choose which voice you
listen to, and herein lies the real meaning of freedom of
choice. As long as your mind is split you have the freedom
to choose between the voice of the ego and the Voice of
Holy Spirit. These two choices or voices are the only real
alternatives for choice. You are free to choose one or the
other, but you are not free to establish the alternatives. There
are only two. One voice speaks for illusions, the Other for
the truth. Illusion is nothing, truth is everything. Illusion is
darkness, truth is light. Illusion is misery, truth happiness.

You can continue following the ego's teaching, or you can change your mind about what you want to be, and listen to the teachings of the Holy Spirit. Let Him tell you what to think, and you will be thinking with God. When you think with God (5.5,4:5) you are certain about yourself. When you think with God you are at peace, you are loving, happy, and wholly joyful. And you share this peace and joy with all your brothers, for that is how you keep it.

"The power of decision is my own" (L152). This means that we can continue to obstruct our awareness of love's presence, or we can choose to let the blocks be removed and thereby remember God and our true Self. "Heaven is the decision I must make" (L138).

Do you want to continue being a guilty ego, or do you want to be the guiltless Son of God? In your perception of yourself, you *are* one or the other. These two are the only alternatives. And you cannot be both, for they are opposites. One is an illusion of what you are, the other is the truth. Truth and illusion are opposites and they cannot be reconciled. It is futile to attempt to do so. Truth and illusion cannot coexist, anymore than can everything and nothing, or light and darkness. You cannot reconcile the two by vacillating between them.

The choice between illusion and truth, the voice of the ego and the Voice of the Holy Spirit, is the only real choice we have. Most often, however, we think we are making a real choice when we are not. Often we are simply choosing between illusions, various alternatives offered by the voice of the ego. This is not a real choice at all. This "choice" merely asks which illusion is true? Which illusion is valuable? Which illusion do I prefer? We merely waste time in making such "choices". One of the purposes of the Course is to save time, by teaching us what the real alternatives for choice are.

To want to remember God and your Self is a change in motivation. And thus it is a change of mind, from the wrong mind to the right mind. "Change in motivation is a change of mind, and this will inevitably produce fundamental change because the mind *is* fundamental" (6.5B,2:5).

Recall that our experience in this world of perception is the result of wanting to create something special, something apart from what we co-create with our Father. That was a mistaken motivation. It led to our forgetting God and our Self as He created us. But we are free to change our mind, to give up the desire to be special, different and separate. When we are willing to do this, the truth of what we are will come of Itself, for It is still in our minds, merely covered up with the defenses we employ to preserve the different and separate self we made. When you allow what blocks the light to be removed, light automatically enters of itself. The Course aims at the removal of these blocks. The first step is making you aware of what they are. The fear of Love and of Truth takes many forms, and that is why there are so many lessons to help completely eliminate this fear from our minds - 365 of them, one for each day of the year.

FREEDOM OF CHOICE
AND FREEDOM TO CREATE

"Freedom of choice is the same power as the freedom to create but its application is different" (5.2,6:5). In other words, when you apply the power of your mind to *choosing* you are using it in a way different than the original purpose for which God shared His power with you. Since you made illusions, you have put yourself in a position whereby you must now choose whether the illusions you made are true or not. And if you want them true you will believe them true. And if you believe them true you will see them all about you, for "projection makes perception" (21.In,1:1). But you merely deceive yourself. And make yourself afraid. "The Son of God can deceive himself" (19.2,3:1).

On the other hand, if you want only the truth true, illusions will no longer seem true for you. You will receive correction of them from the Holy Spirit simply because you are willing to ask for it. Ask for the truth and it will be given you. But be sure you ask truly. "Truth can come only where it is welcomed without fear" (Q12,3:7). The Holy Spirit always hears and answers your requests. It is His function, and He can never fail. Your part is simply to ask and be willing to listen.

> Salvation is not theoretical. Behold the problem, ask for the answer, and then accept it when it comes. Nor will its coming be long delayed. All the help you can accept will be provided, and not one need you have will not be met. (Q26,4:5-8)

I already mentioned that in His creation of you God shared His own loving will to create. This means that in God's very act of creating, you received God's Will as your very own, since He created you perfect like Himself. This means that in reality there is only one will. There are no separate wills. "There is no will but God's" (L74). Creation is a dynamic of the extension of the joint Will of the Father and of the Son. And creation is all there is, a perfect creator creating perfect creations.

Since God's will is that everyone have everything, and thus everyone be perfectly happy, this is your will too. "Your will is His" (L74,1:3). And true freedom is the freedom to do your will. It is the freedom to give everything to everyone of your creations. Thus your true freedom is the freedom to create, to share everything with everyone. It is the freedom to extend God's Will, to extend your Self. True freedom is the freedom to create the perfect. It is the freedom to love perfectly, the freedom to unendingly increase the joy of heaven, and thus maintain the perfect happiness of everyone including yourself.

Thus, in the creation, God gave you "free will" in the sense that He gave you a will that is free to create as He does. Thus your will *is* God's Will. In fact, *you* are God's Will (7.10,8:2). He created you and you co-create with Him as long as you remain as He created you, which is always and forever. Thus you have made time merely as a way of forgetting your will, forgetting yourself as God created you.

Even though your loving will to create seems to be imprisoned while your mind is split, and not unified, creation continues unabated (C1,4:2-3). Your real creations merely wait for your acknowledgement you are their creator, as Christ waits for your acknowledgment that you are He.

The following are some passages from the Course which speak of the free will, the power to create, or the true freedom God gave His creations:

> Child of God, you were created to create the good, the beautiful and the holy. Do not forget this. (1.7,2:1-2).
>
> In the creation, God extended Himself to His creations and imbued them with the same loving Will to create (2.1,1:2).
>
> This requires God's endowment of the Son with free will, because all loving creation is freely given in one continuous line, in which all aspects are of the same order (2.1,2:8).

It still remains within you, however,
to extend as God extended His Spirit to you.
In reality this is your only choice because
your free will was given you for your joy in
creating the perfect (2.1,3:9-10).

In the holy state the will is free, so
that its creative power is unlimited and
choice is meaningless (5.2,6:6).

God asks you do your will. He joins
with you. He did not set His Kingdom up
alone. And Heaven itself but represents your
will, where everything created is for you
(30.2,1:5-8).

How wonderful it is to do your will!
For that is freedom. There is nothing else that
ever should be called by freedom's name.
Unless you do your will you are not free.
(30.2,2:1-4)
Your will is His. (L74,1:3)

I already mentioned that the Son inappropriately
used his power to create. When he uses his power
inappropriately, however, what he miscreates is not part of
creation and therefore is not eternal or real, for it is not of
God. This makes sense because by definition what you do
not create *with* God is not a creation *of* God, and therefore is
not a creation at all. Everything God creates is creative. But
what you miscreate cannot be creative (4.2,8:10-11).

You miscreated when you made the means for
attaining the special favor you requested, and God did not
give. You miscreated when you made forms or bodies. This
split your mind making it a perceiver rather than a creator,
thereby limiting your awareness. Your entire world of
perception is a miscreated and therefore unreal world. By
forgetting to laugh at the idea of creating something on your

330 *God, Self, and Evil*

own, apart from your Creator, and taking it seriously instead, you erred. And from that one error "a world of total unreality *had* to emerge" (18.1,5:3). You now use your perceived world as "proof" you have accomplished what you wished.

By believing your miscreations are real you made yourself unaware of reality, and your loving will to create seems to be imprisoned. Now your mind is split and your only remaining freedom is freedom of choice. "In this world the only remaining freedom is the freedom of choice; always between two choices or two voices" (C1,7:1).

It follows, then, contrary to some of the theodicies we considered in chapter 2, that it is not true that God gave us "freedom of choice". In His creation of us, God gave us freedom to create, not freedom of choice. Choice is meaningless in reality. "In the holy state the will is free, so that its creative power is unlimited and *choice is meaningless"* (5.2,6:6). (my emphasis)

This means that freedom of choice must be a post separation condition. It is a remnant of our true freedom, the freedom to create. In this world it is impossible to create. In this world we are using the power of our mind in a way different than we use it in reality. This is the result of the Son having turned the power of his mind against himself.

Freedom of choice by its very nature presupposes a split mind. There is no freedom of choice unless the mind is split between illusion and truth. "Choosing depends on a split mind" (5.2,6:6). God did not create you with a split mind. If He did He would be split Himself. God can neither deceive nor be deceived. He cannot think He is something He is not.

We see then that God did not create us with freedom of choice, or put us in a situation where we had to choose between good and evil. God did not create us with that intention. Choice is meaningless in Heaven, for there is nothing to choose. There is only the good, the beautiful and the holy. There is only truth, and there is only a loving will free to extend the truth. In co-creating with our Father, in sharing everything we have with our creations, as He shares everything with His, we increase the joy of Heaven. This is true freedom. "Your free will was given you for your joy in creating the perfect" (2.1,3:10).

In summation, true freedom is the freedom to do your own will which *is* God's Will. It is the freedom to create. Freedom of choice is not true freedom. Freedom of choice is a remnant of our true freedom. It is the only remaining freedom we have while our mind is split. It is the only remaining freedom we have in this world. And it is "always between two choices or two voices" (C1,7:1).

In this world, then, we can benefit from our "only remaining freedom" by using it to choose between the only real alternatives. In this world we appreciate our freedom of choice because it is the power by which we can be saved from our illusions. We need but use it to hear the Voice for God instead of listening to the voice of the ego. When you choose to listen to the Holy Spirit's Voice you gradually learn to give up the valueless, let go of the false, and welcome the truth. You do not really want an illusion of what you are. It is the source of all your suffering and pain regardless of its form. "You want salvation. You want to be happy. You want peace. You do not have them now" (L20,2:3-6). Accept what you really are and your happiness is guaranteed. The power of decision is your own.

Summary

In this chapter we answered the third question raised at the end of Chapter 3, namely, if God is not aware of us and our suffering in this world, then in what sense is Divine Help available to us? We have seen that Divine Help is available to us as the Holy Spirit. He functions in our mind as the Voice for God speaking God's Word, and reminding us that we are God's holy Son; that we cannot suffer, cannot be in pain, and cannot die. We need but choose to listen to this Voice, and be willing to give up all false ideas about what we are.

We have now answered all three questions raised by our solution to the logical problem of evil. The 3 pillars needed to support this solution are in place. Our solution is now complete!

We have successfully refuted the argument from evil by denying a premise that contains an implication of God's omniscience that we find is not true, but false. The AFE no longer stands as a powerful proof against the existence of a God Whose happiness, love, power, and knowledge are perfect.

Hopefully the reader can now agree that our solution to the logical problem of evil is intellectually satisfying, and that we have indeed provided an effective response to "the most powerful objection ever raised against belief in God".

Let us now turn to some practical implications of our solution to the theoretical problem of evil; implications that provide a solution to the *practical* one.

11

WHAT FORGIVENESS
REALLY IS

The major difficulty that you find in genuine
forgiveness on your part is that you still
believe you must forgive the truth, and not
illusions. ACIM (L134,3:1)

We have seen that our solution to the logical problem
of evil entails that evil *cannot be* real. And so it must be
illusion. God is a perfect being, and as such He gives His
creations only happiness. God gives no evil, and knows no
evil. Evil is not real to God, and therefore is not real at all.

The atheist claims that if God is real there is no evil,
and if evil is real there is no God. We agree with the atheist
on this point. We do not agree, however, with the atheist's
affirmation that evil is real. Nor do we agree, then, with the
conclusion he rightly draws from these premises, namely,
that there is no God.

Rather, unlike the atheist, we affirm that God is real,
and therefore we accept the logical conclusion that evil

cannot be real. And thus we remain consistent. And we must be consistent to have peace of mind. An inconsistent and irrational mind is doubtful, conflicted and chaotic. It is not at peace, and not really happy.

The recognition that evil is illusion makes forgiveness the only sane response. It gives pardon a sure foundation. *Because evil is illusion forgiveness is always justified.* If attack and suffering *were* real, it could not be forgiven. Forgiveness is for illusions, not for the truth.

As the author of *A Course in Miracles* says, reality and truth are God's creation. They need no forgiveness:

> All truth belongs to Him, reflects His laws
> and radiates His Love. Does this need
> pardon? How can you forgive the sinless and
> eternally benign? (L134,2:5-7).

It is here, then, that we find the most significant relationship between our solution to the logical problem of evil and our solution to the practical one. It is through forgiveness that we can escape all evil; all attack, suffering and death. Evil is undone and eliminated from your experience through forgiveness of yourself and your brother. "Forgiveness is the key to happiness" (L121). And forgiveness is always justified.

We see, then, that *A Course in Miracles* has its own definition of what forgiveness really is. The principle that forgiveness is for illusions and not for the truth is a crucial teaching in the Course. This can be seen in the following passages, taken from Lesson 134, entitled "Let me perceive forgiveness as it is."

> ...pardon is not asked for what is true. It must
> be limited to what is false. It is irrelevant to
> everything except illusions. Truth is God's

creation, and to pardon that is meaningless (2:1-4).
For it is impossible to think of sin as true and not believe forgiveness is a lie (4:2).
It is sin's unreality that makes forgiveness natural and wholly sane (6:1).

TO FORGIVE IS
TO GIVE UP ILLUSION FOR TRUTH

In the last chapter we saw that there are only two alternatives for choice: the ego and the Holy Spirit. There are other ways of describing these same two alternatives. We can say, for example, that the only alternatives for choice are: holding on to the belief in separation or accepting Atonement; holding onto illusions or accepting the truth; holding onto the belief that attack can be justified or accepting that only forgiveness is justified. When we give up illusions, truth comes of itself.

It is not hard to understand that "to forgive" means "to give up for." We either give up illusions for the truth or we do not. We either give up sin for innocence -- guilt for guiltlessness, war for peace, sickness for health, fear for love, pain for joy, separation for oneness, misery for happiness -- or we do not. That is our only real choice in this world.

When we hold the illusion of separation as true, all our choices merely become choices between illusions. This is no real choice at all. It is an illusion of choice. Our "choice" merely indicates what illusion we prefer to be true. This is a wasted use of our power of decision. And a waste of time. For we are not using it for the Holy Spirit's purpose, which is the only meaningful use of time there is.

We have said, and many times, that you cannot believe you are a limited and separated self without believing you have attacked God, and that He will attack you in return (5.5,3). One way we keep this fearful belief hidden from our awareness is to repress it, and tell ourselves that our state of separation is simply the nature of reality and of our existence. And so we "do not remember how it came about" (Q17,6:9).

We can see, then, how forgiveness of sin is related to giving up separate self identity. To give up belief that you or your brother deserve punishment for "sin" is the same thing as giving up all false ideas of what you and your brother really are. It is the same choice.

In other words, the willingness to give up your belief in guilt, and accept guiltlessness for yourself, is the same thing as the willingness to give up ego identity for Christ identity. To do one is to do the other. The Course teaches that everyone must, and ultimately will, make this correct choice. We all shall return to sanity, and finally to the knowledge of where we are always, and what we are forever (8.6,9:6).

Another way the Course describes how you give up your belief in the reality of sin is to say that you "accept Atonement for yourself". In fact, the Course says this is your sole responsibility (2.5,5:1). And to accept Atonement for yourself entails accepting Atonement for everyone. It is to see everyone as sinless and guiltless, worthy of love, and not deserving of attack and suffering and death.

OTHER ASPECTS OF WHAT FORGIVENESS IS

Let us look at the common and traditional meaning of the term "forgive" and note how the Course agrees with it, while at the same time adds one crucial note that gives forgiveness a significantly different meaning than usual.

Webster's New World Dictionary defines the word "forgive" as follows: 1. to give up resentment against or the desire to punish; stop being angry with; pardon 2. to give up all claim to punish or exact penalty for (an offense); overlook 3. to cancel or remit (a debt).

All these ideas are indeed part of the concept of forgiveness found in *A Course in Miracles.* The major shift in meaning involves the Course's teaching about *why* you forgive. Why do you pardon or overlook all apparent attack? The Course's answer: because it is not true! We do not pardon or overlook an evil because we are being "good" or "charitable" or "Christian". We overlook it because it is not true. It is an illusion! We see its falsity, and therefore let it go.

Attack is impossible in reality. The Son of God, as God created him, cannot attack or be attacked. Therefore if I perceive myself as attacked I am misperceiving myself and my supposed attacker or enemy. I am deceived. I overlook attack because attack is an illusion. It is a misperception of reality, myself, and my brother. I need to turn to the Holy Spirit for a correction of my perception. I ask Him to give me another way of looking at this.

In the Course's terms, then, you give up all anger, all claim to punish, all resentment or right to attack, because you realize you have no "right" to attack, or "claim" to punish, or "justification" for anger or resentment.

Nor does anyone else really have a right to attack you. Their attack is merely a mistake, as yours would be. They have forgotten who they are and who you are; they have forgotten God. They have misidentified themselves and their Father.

You have need of no defenses, save one. Atonement is the only defense you need against attack and fear, and all the seeming effects of sin. It is a defense that cannot be used for attack (2.2,4:7-9). Any other defense is a two-edged sword that can be used against its user.

The reason you have no need or "right" to attack is because you do not perceive yourself as an ego-body. You see yourself as the holy Son of God. And thus perceive your brother as he really is. For he is what you are. Thus you teach that only love is real. And so you remember what you have forgotten. Therefore, you teach that no attack or fear is justified. And in demonstrating this, you experience forgiveness and love. All evil is then seen for what it is - nothing that once seemed like "something".

Thus when you identify with the Christ you overlook your brother's error, and perceive the Christ in him. You have no desire to punish or attack him, or cause him suffering in any way. You perceive him truly. You perceive him with "the eyes of Christ" (L161,11:8), and have "Christ's vision" (L158,7). And you perceive a world in which you "have no enemies and cannot sin" (21.7,5:13). As the Bible puts it, you have "let the mind that was in Christ Jesus be in you" (Ph 2:5).

> The Bible says, "May the mind be in you that was also in Christ Jesus," and uses this as a blessing. It is the blessing of miracle-mindedness. It asks that you may think as I thought, joining with me in Christ thinking. (5.1,3:4-6)

When you, on the other hand, identify with the ego, you perceive your brother guilty, for you always perceive him as you perceive yourself. If you identity with the ego you will believe that your brother is an ego too, and that you and he are different and separate and so you can attack him and he can attack you. For "what would have effects through you must also have effects on you" (L26,1:4). Part of recognizing that you cannot be attacked or hurt, then, is to recognize that you cannot attack or hurt.

You cannot see yourself as attacked and hurt unless you believe that you are the kind of thing which can *be* attacked and hurt. And when you do this, your hurt proclaims your brother's guilt. And his guilt activates your right to attack in your own perception of you and of him. Attack is the ego's plan of salvation (L72,1:1). Forgiveness is the Holy Spirit's. Attack is the plan of salvation you established to preserve the self you made.

According to the Course, then, unforgiveness is the cause of all suffering in any form (L193,4:1-2). Not to forgive is to attack. And since only attack produces fear, the only way you can escape from fear is to give up attack thoughts -- both thoughts of attacking and of being attacked. My brother, Son of our Father, if you but realized that attack is never justified you would realize that it is impossible that peace be absent here! For peace would be all that you could see.

You can never make attack right. It has no foundation in truth. But forgiveness is always justified. It has a sure foundation in truth. It is based on the recognition of you and your brother's true Identity.

In any situation, if we asked the author of the Course, "what is the right thing to do? or what decision should I make in this situation?" his response, in effect, will always be: "forgive".

> Forgive and you will see this differently (L193,3:7).
> Forgive, and this (evil) will disappear (L193,13:3).
> Forgiveness is the key to happiness (L121).

> Forgiveness offers everything [you] want
> (L122).

We saw in chapter 8 that once guilt was accepted into the mind of God's Son the original error was made real to him. It became his "sin", and he feared the punishment he believed he deserved. Now in your fear you try to get rid of the guilt by projecting the sin onto another, justifying your attack on him. "He is guilty not me", you think and say. You are actually trying to blame your brother for your separation and unhappiness.

But the sin and guilt remain in you, regardless of your efforts to save yourself by seeing them outside in another body. You cannot be innocent and your brother guilty, nor he innocent and you guilty. You both are either sinful or sinless, guilty or guiltless. You cannot be different. As you see him you will see yourself. Seeing another as guilty is to attack him and thus attack yourself. He who attacks another feels guilty himself, and sees himself as unworthy of love for his own attack. If fact, he expects attack in return. Instead he should learn to forgive himself by forgiving the other.

In this world the attack and the "justified" counterattack continues in a seeming unending cycle. And, as long as it does, we remain blind to the truth of what we are and what our Creator is. As Gandhi once put it, "An eye for an eye makes the whole world blind." And one of the exercises in the Course would have us say to ourselves: "Without forgiveness I will still be blind" (L247).

All the evil in the world takes place in defending an illusory self and the illusory world it made in order to "live" apart from God. All the attack and suffering merely supports the dreamer's wish that his dream of separation be reality. Thus the illusory self underlies our dreams of evil. The "reality" of the world rests on our belief in it. There is no evil except in its dreams. The world you see rests on your mind's belief that the self it made apart from God is real.

But the good news, as we have seen, is that there is a way out of hell; out of all this evil, destruction, malice, envy and despair. All we need do is want a way out. And if we sincerely want the goal of heaven's peace, the means will be provided. We will have all the help we need in learning how to forgive. Our part is but to accept forgiveness as our only function here, because forgiveness is the only means to salvation, the only means to healing our mind. As the Course says, the healing of the mind of God's Son is the only purpose we should see for this world:

> Until you see the healing of the Son as all
> you wish to be accomplished by the world,
> by time and all appearances, you will not
> know the Father nor yourself. (24.6,4:3)

Seeing Attack As A Call For Love

In training us to be "teachers of God", and saviors to one another, the Course trains our mind to perceive everyone and everything in the world differently than we do when we identify with the ego. Thus it trains us to perceive attack differently. It would have us perceive attack as a call for love, an appeal for help, a request for healing. And thus to respond to it by giving love, help and healing (12.1).

As I already mentioned, this response of love is what the Course means by the term "miracle". "Miracles are expressions of love" (1.1,35:1). The Course is called a course in *miracles* because it is training us to give and receive miracles. We give the miracles we have received from the Holy Spirit, the Voice for God.

One aspect of this training is learning to perceive attack as a call for love, a request for a miracle. All through the day everyone is either giving a miracle or asking for one. We simply do not recognize this. And that is why we need the training the Course offers.

To help us understand that attack is a call for love, the Course's reasoning moves like this: There are only two emotions, love and fear. Only love is real (13.5,1:1,10:1). God gave us the one emotion, we made the other. Fear, then, is an absence of love resulting from the denial of reality. Only the fearful attack. Thus attack is a fearful mind's call for love in unconscious recognition of what has been denied (see 12.1).

In the Holy Spirit's judgment, then, there are only two sources of motivation: love and a call for love (14.10,7:1). The only true interpretation of attack, then, is that it is a call for love. As miracle workers we respond to these calls by giving love, by giving a miracle, an expression of love in the form in which both giver and receiver benefit.

When we recognize that our brother's call is our own call for love, we are willing to step back and let the Holy Spirit lead the way (L155). From Him we receive the miracle which we allow to be extended to our brother. The Holy Spirit extends the miracle to your brother through you.

This can be put another way. A call for love is the only meaning the Holy Spirit gives to what appears to you as ego to be attack. And the meaning the Holy Spirit gives it is the only real meaning it has. Identifying with the ego you see it as attack because you want to see it as attack. It represents the punishment you believe you deserve; it also justifies your counterattack giving your brother the punishment you believe he deserves. All of this keeps both guilty, and reinforces identity as an ego-body. To both is evil real. And happiness seems unattainable.

In your readiness to forgive, however, you can step back and receive the Holy Spirit's interpretation of the attack. And in sharing perception with the Holy Spirit you respond with a miracle, answering your brothers call for love, which is also your own. Thus you regain the peace of God you may have momentarily lost.

Forgiveness is Learned

We need to learn how to forgive. In Heaven there is no need for learning. In reality we know everything that is true since God created us like Himself. But since we threw knowledge away by miscreating, and taught ourselves that the false is true, we now have a need for learning, or better, unlearning. All true learning in this world is unlearning (Q4.10,3:7).

Learning to forgive can be seen as unlearning. We "unlearn" what we have taught ourselves. We have taught ourselves sin. And now we need to unlearn sin; to learn forgiveness:

> Forgiveness is acquired. It is not inherent in the mind, which cannot sin. As sin is an idea you taught yourself, forgiveness must be learned by you as well, but from a Teacher [Holy Spirit] other than yourself, Who represents the other Self [Christ] in you. Through Him you learn how to forgive the self [ego] you think you made, and let it disappear. Thus you return your mind as one to Him Who is your Self [Christ], and Who can never sin. (L121,6)

I already mentioned that there are various ways of stating *what* you give up when you forgive. And what you give it up *for*. The above passage from the Course points to what you give up, namely, "the self you think you made"; and what you give it up for, namely, "Him Who is your Self, and Who can never sin".

We have also mentioned that the words and phrases the Course uses to describe the Holy Spirit depend on the context. This paragraph is one example of this. Here the Holy Spirit is described as "a Teacher" and one from Whom you learn forgiveness. He is also said to be a Teacher "other than yourself", and one "Who represents the other Self in you". Hopefully our chart in Chapter 10 helps us in understanding these phrases and the sentences in which they appear.

The Holy Spirit, Who represents both God and You, is experienced in your mind as "a Voice". He appears in the form of a Voice, and thus in the form of words. It is your mind that made words as a way of communicating with others while using a body. Thus the Holy Spirit uses the words you made to communicate to you in a form you can understand. This is how He is "the Word" of God to you. He stands for what God would say if God Himself had a voice and could speak words in response to your errors.

Since God Himself has no body, and thus no larynx and lungs, and because He does not perceive at all, it is the Holy Spirit in your right mind which "speaks" for God. But He speaks to you in terms of your language and symbols, using the body you made, and in terms of what you perceive and experience.

This is one way of describing how the Holy Spirit is "the communication link" between God and His separated Sons. In other words, the Holy Spirit mediates between the part of your mind that thinks it is a separate whole in itself, and the other part that knows all minds, including your own, are still one with God's.

Thus the Holy Spirit mediates between the illusions in one part of your split mind and the truth that still remains in the other part. The Holy Spirit offers you a replacement for every illusion of yourself that you are willing to bring to Him. And as you accept each replacement, you learn through your experience that giving up illusions is the key to your happiness.

The Holy Spirit's replacement for your illusion can be called the truth, if this is properly understood. It is important to keep in mind that His replacement is the truth in the sense that it is a *reflection* of the truth; it is in accord with truth in that it does not contradict God's Will. His replacement is also in accord with the truth because it is a denial of the false with which *you* have replaced the truth. It itself is a replacement of the illusion you once thought was true. It is not the direct truth which can only be known, not perceived.

Let us examine more closely this idea of forgiving as a process of denying illusions and having them replaced by the truth in your mind.

To Forgive is to Deny the Denial of Truth

We have seen that the process of forgiving involves bringing our illusions to the Holy Spirit in our mind to receive the truth in the form of a correction of the error. And this correction is always a form of the thought of oneness which undoes the illusion which is a form of the thought of separation. All illusions are forms, and all forms are illusions. This is because reality is formless.

Forgiveness is for illusions (L134,2:2-3). And ultimately forgiveness itself is an illusion, because there is no forgiveness in reality. In this sense, then, forgiveness could be called "a happy fiction".

> Forgiveness is unknown in Heaven where the need for it would be inconceivable. However, in this world forgiveness is a necessary correction for all the mistakes that we have made. (Pf.3,12:1-2)

Although forgiveness itself is illusion, it is the only one that stops the multiplication of illusions. "Illusion makes illusion. Except one. Forgiveness is illusion that is answer to the rest" (L198,2:8-10).

Forgiveness, then, is not itself the truth, but rather the *denial of the false*. The false is the denial of truth. To forgive, then, is *to deny the denial of Truth*. "The task of the miracle worker thus becomes to deny the denial of truth" (12.2,1:5).

The idea that we are called to "deny the denial of truth" is crucial to our understanding of why our experience in this world can only *reflect* the truth of heaven. It also, however, explains why the Course can still promise that its training in forgiveness will bring us to the perception of a world without evil, a world it calls "the real world". Although the real world is not itself *reality, it is called the real world because it reflects reality*, that is, it has elements in common with reality, for example, the happy state of mind that exists in reality.

Let's examine more closely this process of denying the denial of truth by using an example. The truth of what I am can be stated as "I am spirit" (L97). Thus the denial of truth is "I am not spirit". The thought "I am not spirit" must, however, be symbolized for the mind. That is, since it is not the truth it cannot be directly known. In other words, *as* spirit, I cannot know or even believe that "I am not spirit". A symbol must be made to stand for this denial of truth. "Something" must be made up to *substitute* for the truth of what I am, and to take its place.

The body was made for this purpose. Thus "I am not spirit" is symbolized and represented by the belief and perception that "I am a body". The idea that I am a body replaces the idea that I am spirit. It replaces the truth of what I am. This false idea of myself as a body is a denial of truth. It is also a replacement of it.

Now that I have lost awareness of the truth by replacing it with the false, the idea that I am a body seems true in my perception of myself. And that is what illusions are. They are the false seeming to be true, the unreal seeming to be real. Illusions are substitutes for reality.

When I forgive, then, what I do is to deny that "I am a body". I say, "I am not a body". Thus when I forgive I deny the illusion; I deny the false; I deny *the denial of truth.*

When I am tempted to believe I am a body, I forgive myself by recognizing that I am not a body. Thus forgiveness says "no" to the illusion; it says "no" to the false; it says "no" to the denial of truth. It accepts that only the truth is true, only reality is real. It recognizes the falsity of a false idea and therefore lets it go, no longer holding the false as true.

All this could be represented in the language of symbolic logic. Let "T" stand for truth, and "~T" stand for not truth, or the denial of truth, or the false. To forgive would be to deny ~T. Thus the idea that results from the act of "forgiving" is symbolized as $\sim(\sim T)$.

To the extent that $\sim(\sim T)$ is equivalent to T, the result of forgiving is equivalent to truth. It is not directly the truth because it is not yet knowledge but still perception. Nevertheless, is *in accord with* the truth because it denies the false, and does not contradict the truth, as the false does. In terms of our dream metaphor, forgiveness stands for the truth in the face of all the illusions in the dream. "Forgiveness is the only thing that *stands for* truth in the illusions of the world" (L134,7:1) (emphasis mine)

In the same sense that forgiveness reflects the truth, true perception -- the correction of false perception -- reflects knowledge. And healing, our function in this world, reflects creation -- our function in Heaven. And right-mindedness, the opposite of wrong-mindedness, reflects One-Mindedness.

Along with denying that I am a body, forgiveness involves the denial of any and all thoughts which are part of the ego thought system, the thought system that has as its starting point the self you made. For all the ideas in this system are the denial of truth. They include the following thoughts: I can attack and be attacked; fear, anger and attack are justified; I am sinful, guilty, and deserve punishment; God is fearful for he is a wrathful God who will punish me for my sins; I have what I take, and another's loss is my gain; I can harm and be harmed, suffer and cause suffering, kill and be killed.

To forgive is to recognize these ideas as false, even though at first some of them seem to be true. Forgiveness, then, simply recognizes the falsity of these beliefs, and therefore lets them go.

This, then, is the logic of forgiveness. And this logic is based on the truth of what we are -- the perfect creations of a perfect Creator, the perfect Son of a perfect Father. This truth remains in a part of our mind and rises to our awareness in a form we can understand given the limitations we have imposed on our awareness.

Through the Holy Spirit "you learn to forgive the self you think you made and let it disappear". When you forgive this self you begin to easily recognize an idea as one that belongs to the thought system that rests upon this made up self as its foundation. When we let go of ego identity, all evil disappears from our perception. This means evil has no effect on us. It does not take away our peace and joy. It is not a cause of our experience. And if it is not a cause, it does not exist. For nothing without effect is real.

Thus we can live without fear even while we abide where we are not at home. For we recognize illusions for what they are. How can the sinless be afraid? (23.IN,1:3). "Walk you in glory, with your head held high, and fear no evil" (23.IN,3:1)

The moment of awareness of your innocence, and the peace and joy it brings, is what the Course calls the "holy instant". Our goal is to make the entire day an extended Holy Instant. Our experience during the holy instant reflects eternal reality where there is no evil, and where no attack and suffering can touch the holy Son of God. Our experience, then, is accurately described by these words: "Heaven is here. There is nowhere else. Heaven is now. There is no other time" (Q24,6:4-7).

Forgiveness Is The Means By Which We Will Awaken to Our Perfect Self

We said that the Holy Spirit is the remaining communication link between God and us, His separated Sons. Because of God's gift of the Holy Spirit we have hope for salvation and return to God Whom we have never really left.

This hope lies in the fact that the Thought of God remains in our mind as a memory which serves as the Divine Source to Whom we all can turn for guidance, strength, love and comfort.

It is because of the Holy Spirit, as the Voice for God, that we are not left abandoned and alone in the world we made. God has not abandoned us, nor has His Son really abandoned Him. We are merely mistaken in believing we are separate from Him.

By means of the one remaining freedom we have in this world, the freedom of choice, we can become aware of our oneness with God, our Father. We can experience His love even while we seem to live in this dream world. We become aware of Love's presence by allowing the Holy Spirit to teach us how to forgive. Forgiveness is the Holy Spirit's one lesson. We *must* learn it. Forgiveness is the only way to God, and to the perfect Self we share with Him.

The way to God is through forgiveness here. There is no other way. If sin had not been cherished by the mind, what need would there have been to find the way to where you are? Who would still be uncertain? Who could be unsure of who he is? And who would yet remain asleep, in heavy clouds of doubt about the holiness of him whom God created sinless? Here we can but dream. But we can dream we have forgiven him in whom all sin remains impossible, and it is this we choose to dream today. God is our goal; forgiveness is the means by which our minds return to Him at last. (L256,1)

We have said, and many times, that the peace of God is the one goal we have while we seem to live in this world. We *must* attain this peace and retain it before we can awaken to our perfect Self. We must not only say that we want the peace of God, we must mean these words (L185,1:1-2). We mean them by giving up all ego goals and accepting the peace of God as our only goal.

> The peace of God is everything I want. The peace of God is my one goal; the aim of all my living here, the end I seek, my purpose and my function and my life, while I abide where I am not at home. (L205,2)

That is the only way we will attain the peace of God. It must be the only thing we want. And when we have it, we have *everything*. It witnesses to the fact that we are fulfilling our function here. And when we are fulfilling our function we are happy. Our dream is happy. It is no longer a dream of attack and suffering. Our evil and fearful dream has been changed to a loving and happy one.

To attain the peace of God requires but "a little willingness". This tiny willingness is the only part in salvation that is yours. When you are willing to do your part, the Holy Spirit "will offer His strength to every little effort you make" (L97,4:3). With His help you cannot fail (L80,4:2). You are the Holy Son of God Himself, and you cannot fail to do all that salvation asks (L191,7:4). You will succeed, not only because of who you are -- and because the Holy Spirit will remind you of who you are -- but also because of "how little salvation asks of you" (30.4,8:4).

The Holy Spirit, however, cannot take from you any illusion you would cherish still. Love does not attack. It is up to you not to value the valueless any longer. You must bring all illusory goals to Him, and He will replace them with the single goal of holiness.

The Holy Spirit does not force us to give up our illusions, because he cannot violate our freedom of choice. Letting go of our illusions is a decision we must make, but

He will help us, if we ask. We want to ask because we are weary of all the attack, pain and suffering brought upon us by our belief in the reality of sin, guilt and death. "Tolerance for pain may be high, but it is not without limit" (2.3,3:5).

The Holy Spirit simply reminds us of Who we really are. He does not force us to accept it. But who, recognizing the only real choice, can refuse to make it? As the Course says of the Holy Spirit in relation to our freedom of choice:

> The Voice of the Holy Spirit does not command, because it is incapable of arrogance. It does not demand, because it does not seek control. It does not overcome, because it does not attack. It merely reminds. It is compelling only because of what it reminds you *of.* It brings to your mind the other way, remaining quiet even in the midst of the turmoil you may make. The Voice for God is always quiet, because it speaks of peace. (5.2,7:1-7)

With the Holy Spirit as our Teacher and Guide we learn "the other way", the way to peace through forgiveness. The Holy Spirit teaches us how to give up the evil selves we made, and accept our true identity as Christ. And this is why forgiveness is the key to happiness. For it is the means by which we will awaken to the knowledge of the perfect Self That God created as us:

> Forgiveness is the key to happiness. I will awaken from the dream that I am mortal, fallible, and full of sin, and know that I am the perfect Son of God. (L121,13:6-7).

The Forgiven Mind Perceives
A World Without Evil

As I have said often already, while we are still dreaming, the process of awakening involves letting our dreams of evil be replaced by the happy dreams offered by the Holy Spirit. The happy dream is the forgiving dream, for it is one in which we are saviors. We save the world from all belief in sin, suffering, and death. Through forgiving eyes we see the real world, a world from which all evil has disappeared because we have forgiven it. The world, once evil, ugly and sinful, now reflects the goodness, beauty and holiness of heaven. It is free from fear, and filled with blessing and with happiness:

> How lovely is the world whose purpose is forgiveness of God's Son! How free from fear, how filled with blessing and with happiness! And what a joyous thing it is to dwell a little while in such a happy place! Nor can it be forgot, in such a world, that it *is* a little while till timelessness comes quietly to take the place of time. (29.6,6)

In light of the purpose of this book, it is helpful to express the purpose of the Course's training in terms of the practical problem of evil. For example, a passage we have already quoted, regarding the purpose of the Workbook, can be paraphrased this way: "The purpose of the Workbook is to train your mind in a systematic way to *the perception of a world without evil*" (W-IN,4:1).

In other words, the Course's training brings us to the point where our mind not only understands and accepts that "there is no evil because God is real," but actually experiences this as true. The statement "there is no evil" is seen, not only as an accurate metaphysical statement, but an accurate description of our experience as well.

Thus, in our perception there is no evil because we recognize that evil is illusion. And when illusions are recognized for what they are, they disappear. "Illusion recognized must disappear" (L187,7:1).

And so evil has disappeared from our perception. For the forgiven mind perceives no evil. The forgiven mind no longer perceives itself as attacked, and thus it suffers not. All forms of suffering have disappeared. "No one can suffer if he does not see himself attacked, and losing by attack" (28.6,4:5).

The world seen through the eyes of forgiveness is called the *real world* because it is a world that reflects the happiness of reality. There is no evil in reality, and there is no evil in the world forgiveness sees.

The real world is a symbol, as is everything perception offers. What the Course calls the real world, then, is this world of bodies and perception seen with a mind at peace because it has forgiven itself. It is a world where the happiness of heaven is reflected. It is a world where attack and suffering, sin and guilt, pain and death are no longer seen as meaningful.. It is a world in which there is nothing to fear, for you have accepted the love of God as all there is. You are in a state of grace. Your perception has been corrected; you share perception with the Holy Spirit. No evil is real to you for no evil is real to Him. No evil affects your quiet mind; no evil takes away your peace and joy. There is no evil for you. You see a happy world. You experience heaven on earth. God's Kingdom has come, for you have earnestly sought and found it; you have asked for it and have received as you have asked. It is a friendly world because you have chosen to be friend to it. As the Course puts it:

The real world holds a counterpart for each unhappy thought reflected in your world; a sure correction for the sights of fear and sounds of battle which your world contains. The real world shows a world seen differently, through quiet eyes and with a mind at peace. Nothing but rest is there. There are no cries of pain and sorrow heard, for nothing there remains outside forgiveness. And the sights are gentle. Only happy sights and sounds can reach the mind that has forgiven itself. (Th8,2)

And again:

The grace of God rests gently on forgiving eyes, and everything they look on speaks of Him to the beholder. *He can see no evil;* nothing in the world to fear, and no one who is different from himself. And as he loves them, so he looks upon himself with love and gentleness. He would no more condemn himself for his mistakes than damn another. He is not an arbiter of vengeance, nor a punisher of sin. The kindness of his sight rests on himself with all the tenderness it offers others. For he would only heal and only bless. And being in accord with what God wills, he has the power to heal and bless all those he looks on with the grace of God upon his sight. (25.6,1) (my emphasis)

Forgiveness Offers Everything You Want

You want to be happy. You want peace. You want salvation. You do not have them now. But you can. To have these things you need but truly forgive yourself by forgiving your brother. Forgiveness is the answer to all your problems, because it is the answer to *your only problem*. Your only problem is you believe the separate self you made is real, and thus believe fear, anger, and attack are justified and meaningful.

Forgiveness is the way back to your Father, for Whose love you yearn. It brings you the love and happiness, peace and joy for which you have so long searched and not found. Yet it is your natural inheritance. Forgiveness is the only way you will return to your perfect Self, a Self you once knew and will surely know again. Forgiveness offers everything you want:

> What could you want forgiveness cannot give? Do you want peace? Forgiveness offers it. Do you want happiness, a quiet mind, a certainty of purpose, and a sense of worth and beauty that transcends the world? Do you want care and safety, and the warmth of sure protection always? Do you want a quietness that cannot be disturbed, a gentleness that never can be hurt, a deep, abiding comfort, and a rest so perfect it can never be upset?
>
> All this forgiveness offers you, and more. (L122,1-2:1)

This lesson continues for two more paragraphs describing the "more" that forgiveness offers you! And then it continues:

Why would you seek an answer other than the answer that will answer everything? Here is the perfect answer....Here is the answer! Seek for it no more. You will not find another one instead. (L122,4)

12

SUMMARY AND
CONCLUDING REMARKS

Nothing real can be threatened.
Nothing unreal exists.
Herein lies the peace of God.
ACIM (T-IN,2:2-4)

A SUMMARY OF MIRACLE THEODICY

Miracle Theodicy escapes the conclusion of the argument from evil (AFE) by denying the premise on God's omniscience. This premise, affirmed by all previous theodicies, states that if God is perfectly knowing then God knows about the evil in the world. And if God knows about the evil in the world, the evil must be real, and not illusion.

Miracle Theodicy accepts that God is perfectly knowing, but at the same time teaches that God does not know about the evil in the world. This position follows from its concept of God as a perfect being.

According to the Theodicy we have presented in this book, God, as a perfect being, could not have created this world or any other world of time, space, and bodies. And since only what God created is real, such a world cannot be real, and thus cannot be known by God. Therefore the evil -- the attack, suffering and death -- experienced by the inhabitants of this physical world is also unknown to God. It is not part of His experience or His perfect knowledge. God knows no evil. He knows of no beings who attack, suffer, and die. Everyone and Everything God knows is eternally happy, for He knows only what He created. And what He created is perfect like Himself.

It follows, then, that the evil in this world does not constitute proof that God is either not perfectly loving or not perfectly powerful. Only if one claims that God is aware of the evil in the world does the AFE become a valid and convincing argument against the existence of a God Who is perfectly loving and perfectly powerful. If God *did* know about the evil in the world, the evil *would* be real. And thus God could not be consistently conceived as *both* perfectly loving and perfectly powerful.

According to *A Course in Miracles,* and the theodicy we have constructed based on its teachings, God's perfect love lies in the fact that He wills to share everything He has and is with all His creations. And His perfect power lies in the fact that His Will is done, and cannot be changed or opposed. Thus God, being timeless and changeless, *has* already shared everything He has and is with His creations in the very act of creating them. His act of creating is an act of extending His Self, the Thought of What He is. Therefore all His creations are perfect like Himself, since all are extensions of Himself. All God's Sons, then, are perfectly knowing, loving, powerful, and happy. And they are also formless, limitless, timeless, changeless, and eternal -- all qualities of God Himself as a perfect being. God and all His creations, then, are perfectly happy forever, extending the perfect Self they share. And by so doing, They increase the joy of the Kingdom of God, the Kingdom of Heaven.

How can we say, without contradiction, that God is perfectly knowing even though He does not know about the evil in the world? Well, because God is perfectly aware of everything He created, and only what He created is real. Thus God knows everything that is real and true. And since only the real can *be* known, God knows everything knowable. And to know everything knowable is what it means to be omniscient or perfectly knowing. Thus God is indeed perfectly knowing.

We cannot legitimately say that God lacks perfect knowledge because He does not know about "something" that is unreal and does not exist, or because He does not perceive illusions, or because He is not aware of something He did not create, or because He is not aware of what happens in the dreams that are made up by and exist only in minds apart from His.

Although evil cannot be known by God, or by any mind as He created it, it can be perceived. And only by a mind apart from His. Perception is a function of the body. Only minds using bodies perceive. God has no body, and so God does not perceive evil, because God does not perceive at all. Evil is not part of reality, but part of a perceiving mind's dreams.

We are the dreamers of a world of separation and limitation. We experience evil because we mistakenly believe our dream is reality. And thus we think a reality of perfect oneness is an illusion. We not only believe reality is something it is not, but also that *we* are something we are not, namely ego-bodies, humans. How did this happen? How did we put ourselves to sleep and dream a dream in which we are aliens to our Self?

The answer to this question is long and involved. But given what we said in chapter eight and nine, we can briefly say that we as God's Son were at peace until we asked for special favor. And "God did not give it for the request was alien to Him" (13.3,10:3). But we demanded it, and in our attempt to accomplish the impossible -- to create on our own, apart from our Creator -- a part of mind split off from the perfect Self we all share with each other and with God as well. In this sense we seemed to have left Heaven. Yet we are still at home in God, merely dreaming of exile. However, we are perfectly capable of awakening to reality.

While we seem to live in this world evil seems as real to us as does the world we made. But the "you" who attacks and suffers is an illusory you, a figure in your dream. All that is happening is that a part of your split mind is identified with its "special creation", the ego -- a limited and separated self born in a body. And this ego is merely a false idea of what you as a mind are. It is a false self we as the Son of God made for ourselves to replace the Self God created us as. It is an illusion of what we are. It was not created by God, and thus not really created at all, but miscreated or made.

The body is merely a figure in the dream that represents the self or the "you" who is the dreamer of the dream. And it is only this ego-body that can attack and suffer and believe in death. Attack, suffering, and death exists only in dreams, only in illusions; not in reality, not in truth, not in God's creation, not in heaven. And heaven is all there is. There is no life outside heaven.

The good news, then, is that we are not really the ego-body. We are not really "humans". We are not really inhabitants of a physical environment. We are not really the guilty sinners we believe we are. All this is but a dream. Being a human in a world of bodies is not the natural state in which God created us. Our other life continues as it always was and is, even though we are temporarily unaware of it. We still remain the perfect Son of God as our Father created us -- pure minds co-creating the perfect with Him. This is true despite our illusion of being something else, for what God created is timeless, changeless, and eternal; it is always the same forever.

You will continue to experience evil as long as you identify with the ego. The ego does not know what true happiness is because it does not know anything. And neither do you as long as you think you are the ego and listen to the voice you made to drown out the Voice for God in you.

You are free to choose to listen to the Holy Spirit, the Voice for God, instead of the voice of the ego. The freedom to choose between the ego and the Holy Spirit, the anti-Christ and the Christ, between idols and God, is the only remaining freedom in this world. It is the same power as the freedom to create, but this power is applied differently in this world where choice is meaningful. Choice is meaningless in Heaven where the only activity of the Mind is creating, or Self extension.

The Holy Spirit, as the Memory in our mind of our oneness with God, represents our true Self and our Creator, Who are one. The Holy Spirit, then, is the communication link between God's Mind and your mind. He is the mediator between the world of perception and the realm of knowledge, between the dream and reality. He is the Divine Help available to us while we are using bodies and perceiving attack, suffering, and death as real. Through His gift of Christ's vision we can see a different world and escape all forms of pain and suffering. The Holy Spirit offers us happy dreams, happy perceptions to replace the fearful ones we have made. It is only from the happy dream, the perception of the real world, that we can awaken to the knowledge of our real and perfect Self.

Knowing the truth of what we are, the Holy Spirit teaches us to forgive the illusory self we made, and let it disappear. Through forgiveness we experience our innocence and give the miracles we have received. We recognize that we are not really separate from our brothers or from God but still remain forever one.

As teachers, healers, and saviors to one another we see the world with but one purpose: the healing of our minds. The forgiven mind is the healed mind, for it recognizes illusions for what they are. And illusions recognized must disappear. The forgiven mind perceives a world without evil, the real world, a lovely and happy world, for "only happy sights and sounds can reach the mind that has forgiven itself" (Th8,2:6). The forgiven mind has but happy dreams.

From the happy dream we will waken to reality. And all dreams will be unremembered, for we shall know our own glorious equality with God, our perfect Father.

CONCLUDING REMARKS

It has no doubt occurred to the reader that this solution to the problem of evil has far reaching implications for other areas of theology, the philosophy of religion, and spiritual psychology. I want, therefore, to mention a few of these areas, and to make the point that the interested reader can find a discussion of all these issues in the Course itself, as well as in other books published on the Course's teachings, many of which are listed in the Bibliography.

Here I will simply state, without much discussion or argument, that the Course's teachings on all the following topics are consistent with the teachings used to construct the theodicy in this book.

First, there is the whole issue of Jesus. How is he the same and how is he different from us? What is the meaning of Jesus' crucifixion and resurrection, and the relation of these to Jesus' part in the Atonement and in the salvation of the world? And there is the issue of Jesus as the source or author of the Course itself.

I have already said a few things on these topics in the process of presenting our solution to the problem of evil. As mentioned much more is said in the Course itself, and in the books listed in the Bibliography. Interested readers are encouraged to check these sources.

Second, there is the topic of our relationships with one another in this world. The Course has much to say about the role of relationships in our journey back to God. Some good books based on the Course's teachings have been written on this topic as well.

Let me simply say that the Course asks us to invite the Holy Spirit into our relationships so that our "special relationships" may be transformed to "holy relationships". Included in the discussion of this topic is the whole issue of ego dynamics as they operate in special relationships, including the idea that the special relationship is the ego's answer to God's Answer, the Holy Spirit. Instead of God's Love, the ego would have the "love" found in the special love relationship. But special love is not love at all. It is an illusion of love; it is guilt and hate and vengeance disguised as love (see 16.7,5). The special relationship is "the renunciation of the Love of God, and the attempt to secure for the self the specialness that He denied" (16.5,4:2).

As a personal note I would like to share the fact that included in the publicly stated marriage vows, which Janet and I made to one another in our wedding ceremony in 1987, was the following: "Janet (Robert), I invite the Holy Spirit into our relationship to make it holy, that I may look upon you and see the face of Christ and remember God." This is still the common purpose of our relationship. And it is one we share with all those who enter it.

From the perspective of relationships with others this is one way we could describe the goal of the Course for us - that we look upon everyone and see the face of Christ and remember God. If we can look upon one brother and see the face of Christ, we can look upon all brothers this way. And this is necessary. The Course teaches us that we cannot remember God until we look upon our brother and see the face of Christ. Seeing the face of Christ is a symbolic way of saying that we see our brother sinless rather than sinful, guiltless rather than guilty, worthy of love rather than deserving of punishment. "My sinless brother is my guide to peace. My sinful brother is my guide to pain. And which I choose to see I will behold" (L351).

Third, there is the whole theological issue of how to conceive "the Holy Trinity": God the Father, God the Son, and God the Holy Spirit. The author of the Course says that the Holy Spirit is the only part of the Holy Trinity that has a symbolic function, and because of this He is difficult to understand (5.1,4).

Chapter ten of this book focused on the function of the Holy Spirit. There I emphasized the idea that the Holy Spirit is the Divine Help available to us even though God the Father is not aware of us as "suffering humans" or "suffering sinners". The role of the Holy Spirit has great significance in light of the fact that God Himself is not aware of our suffering in this world. The Course has much more to say about the Holy Spirit than I have included in this book.

I do believe, however, that I have presented enough of the Course's teaching on the Holy Spirit to make it clear that the Holy Spirit, as the Voice for God in your right mind, provides all the Divine Help you need in order to be saved from the illusion of yourself and all the evil it experiences. By learning from the Holy Spirit how to forgive, you will return to your true identification with spirit, and experience the perfect love and happiness that is your natural inheritance. No evil will be remembered by anyone. All dreams, all perception, all space, time, and bodies are gone.

The Course says that the final step of this return is taken by God Himself once all of us have reached complete forgiveness and have no further use for illusions or dreams.

Fourth, there is the issue of the role that freedom of choice plays in our salvation. I have emphasized that we have the choice to listen to either the voice of the ego or the Voice of the Holy Spirit, and that these are the only two alternatives for choice. Listening to and following the Voice for God is the way to escape from all the fear, suffering, and pain that comes from following the ego's voice. Much more could have been said about freedom of choice versus freedom to create, and more is said in the Course itself. We kept our focus only on that part of the issue which directly relates to our solution to the problem of evil.

Fifth, there is the topic of prayer. How does the Course conceive of prayer since it is obvious that God the Father does not hear our words? As part of the Course material there is available a separate pamphlet on the topic of prayer entitled *The Song of Prayer: Prayer, Forgiveness, and Healing.* Discussions of prayer are also scattered throughout the Course itself. And, again, there are several books listed in the bibliography containing sections on the Course's definition of prayer and its role in the healing of our mind. Those readers interested in the topic of prayer are encouraged to consult these sources.

Let me here at least quote one paragraph from the Course itself which will give the reader an idea of how the Course views prayer and its relation to forgiveness and miracles, which is the central practical theme of the Course.

> Prayer is a way of asking for something. It is the medium of miracles. But the only meaningful prayer is for forgiveness, because those who have been forgiven have everything. Once forgiveness has been accepted, prayer in the usual sense becomes utterly meaningless. The prayer for forgiveness is nothing more than a request that you may be able to recognize what you already have. (3.5,6:1-5)

Sixth, there is the question of what the Course has to say about religious experiences. I am referring to things such as visions of God, spiritual or psychic powers, miraculous "physical healings", experiences of religious conversion -- like being "born again" -- or the mystical experience of oneness with God. All of these are interesting topics, and the Course has something to say on each one. An adequate discussion of these topics, however, is simply beyond the purpose and scope of a book on theodicy.

I will, however, quote a paragraph from the *Manual for Teachers* which is but one of four long paragraphs that make up the Course's response to the question: Can God be reached directly?

> Sometimes a teacher of God may have a brief experience of direct union with God. In this world, it is almost impossible that this endure. It can, perhaps, be won after much devotion and dedication, and then be maintained for much of the time on earth. But this is so rare that it cannot be considered a realistic goal. If it happens, so be it. If it does not happen, so be it as well. All worldly states must be illusory. If God were reached

directly in sustained awareness, the body would not be long maintained. Those who have laid the body down merely to extend their helpfulness to those remaining behind are few indeed. And they need helpers who are still in bondage and still asleep, so that by their awakening can God's Voice be heard. (Q26,3)

Seventh, and finally, there is the whole issue of "final things" -- what theologians call *eschatology*. This area of discussion deals with questions about death, life after the body stops functioning, reincarnation, the end of the world, the Second Coming of Christ, the Last Judgment, and finally, the question of who will merit eternal happiness in heaven -- or unending suffering in hell (assuming that this concept of "hell" is part of one's theology).

I have discussed some of these issues in this book, and said little or nothing about others. I do hope, however, that it is clear from what I said before that the Course teaches that everyone in the end will return to God and our heavenly home, to the awareness of our eternal Self, the Christ, Which is perfectly one with His Father, God. This is inevitable. It is the only thing that is consistent with God's perfect love, power, knowledge, and happiness, and the fact that He is always the same forever.

On this point of "universal salvation", we have seen that Miracle Theodicy and Person-Making Theodicy are in agreement. They both teach universal salvation; everyone will be saved in the end. "Salvation is a promise made by God that you will find your way to Him at last" (Th2,1:1).

In this regard, then, we can see that listening to the voice of the ego is merely a maneuver for delaying the inevitable. It is an insane decision to continue to tolerate the pain of living as an ego in a world of separation and bodies.

This is actually the only purpose for which the ego uses time; to delay the inevitable acceptance of God's Answer to the separation.

Sooner or later each of us will recognize that there must be a better way of life than one of trying to tolerate the pain inherent in ego-body identity. "The tolerance for pain may be high, but it is not without limit. Eventually everyone begins to recognize, however dimly, that there *must* be another way" (2.3,3:5-6).

One could, perhaps, include in a book on theodicy a sustained discussion of all seven topics just mentioned. This would be so because the problem of evil can easily enter discussion as soon one raises any question about the nature of God and our experience in this world. However, an adequate treatment of the Course's teachings on every one of these seven topics, along with an adequate presentation of the solution to the problem of evil found therein, would, without doubt, make for a much too lengthy book.

And so, the simple objective of this book has been to provide a solution to the theoretical problem of evil. And as an added dimension to a book on theodicy, to show how this theoretical solution provides the basis for solving the practical problem of evil. This simple purpose led us to focus on specific elements of the Course's teachings, those which helped us demonstrate that we can satisfactorily escape the conclusion of the argument from evil.

I feel confident that we have accomplished that objective. It is not an insignificant accomplishment when one realizes that the argument from evil has for centuries been the most powerful argument ever raised against belief in God, and that this argument has never before been refuted to the satisfaction of a rational mind which cannot accept the idea that contradictions are true.

Here in this book is an intellectually satisfying refutation of the argument from evil. For me it is a great joy to have such a gift. And with great joy I offer it to you. I can only hope it will be as personally meaningful and rewarding for you as it has been for me.

And now, if you have other questions that this book did not raise and answer, I urge you to pick up *A Course in Miracles*. It contains the answers to all your truly meaningful questions. In fact, it is likely to offer answers to questions that you have not yet even raised!

But most of all you will find in your hands a beautiful and profound and effective mind training course; a course that trains your mind to a different way of thinking about, perceiving, and responding to everyone and everything in the world; a course that teaches you how to give forgiveness, and receive it too; a course that guarantees escape from all pain, suffering, and fear of death, and leads you directly to the love and happiness which is our natural inheritance as God's Son. And which everyone in the world yearns to find, but knows not where to seek.

And finally, you will come to experience a deep understanding, appreciation, and gratitude for the truth found in these words used by the author as a brief and simple summary of his course:

Nothing real can be threatened.
Nothing unreal exists.
Herein lies the peace of God.

Appendix A

A SUMMARY OF THE TEACHINGS
IN *A COURSE IN MIRACLES*

The following summary of the Course's teachings was written by Helen Schucman in 1977 in response to many requests for a brief introduction to *A Course in Miracles*. It was scribed by the same process of "inner dictation" by which the Course was scribed. This process of scribing is itself described in the Preface to the Second Edition where this wonderful summary also appears. The paragraphs as they appear in the Preface are not numbered. I have numbered them here for easy reference.

WHAT IT SAYS

Nothing real can be threatened.
Nothing unreal exists.
Herein lies the peace of God.

1. This is how *A Course in Miracles* begins. It makes a fundamental distinction between the real and the unreal; between knowledge and perception. Knowledge is truth, under one law, the law of love or God. Truth is unalterable, eternal and unambiguous. It can be unrecognized, but it cannot be changed. It applies to everything that God created, and only what He created is real. It is beyond learning because it is beyond time and process. It has no opposite; no beginning and no end. It merely is.

2. The world of perception, on the other hand, is the world of time, of change, of beginnings and endings. It is based on interpretation, not on facts. It is the world of birth and death, founded on the belief in scarcity, loss, separation

and death. It is learned rather than given, selective in its perceptual emphases, unstable in its functioning, and inaccurate in its interpretations.

3. From knowledge and perception respectively, two distinct thought systems arise which are opposite in every respect. In the realm of knowledge no thoughts exist apart from God, because God and His Creation share one Will. The world of perception, however, is made by the belief in opposites and separate wills, in perpetual conflict with each other and with God. What perception sees and hears appears to be real because it permits into awareness only what conforms to the wishes of the perceiver. This leads to a world of illusions, a world which needs constant defense precisely *because* it is not real.

4. When you have been caught in the world of perception you are caught in a dream. You cannot escape without help, because everything your senses show merely witnesses to the reality of the dream. God has provided the Answer, the only Way out, the true Helper. It is the function of His Voice, His Holy Spirit, to mediate between the two worlds. He can do this because, while on the one hand He knows the truth, on the other He also recognizes our illusions, but without believing in them. It is the Holy Spirit's goal to help us escape from the dream world by teaching us how to reverse our thinking, and unlearn our mistakes. Forgiveness is the Holy Spirit's great learning aid in bringing this thought reversal about. However, the Course has its own definition of what forgiveness really is just as it defines the world in its own way.

5. The world we see merely reflects our own internal frame of reference - the dominant ideas, wishes and emotions in our minds. "Projection makes perception" (21.1,1:1). We look inside first, decide the kind of world we want to see and then project that world outside, making it the truth *as we see it*. We make it true by our interpretations of

what it is we are seeing. If we are using perception to justify our own mistakes - our anger, our impulses to attack, our lack of love in whatever form it may take - we will see a world of evil, destruction, malice, envy and despair. All this we must learn to forgive, not because we are being "good" and "charitable," but because what we are seeing is not true. We have distorted the world by our twisted defenses, and are therefore seeing what is not there. As we learn to recognize our perceptual errors, we also learn to look past them or "forgive." At the same time we are forgiving ourselves, looking past our distorted self-concepts to the Self That God created in us and as us.

6. Sin is defined as "lack of love" (1.4,3:1). Since love is all there is, sin in the sight of the Holy Spirit is a mistake to be corrected, rather than an evil to be punished. Our sense of inadequacy, weakness and incompletion comes from the strong investment in the "scarcity principle" that governs the whole world of illusions. From that point of view, we seek in others what we feel is wanting in ourselves. We "love" another in order to get something ourselves. That in fact, is what passes for love in the dream world. There can be no greater mistake than that, for love is incapable of asking for anything.

7. Only minds can really join, and whom God has joined no man can put asunder (17.3,7:3). It is, however, only at the level of Christ Mind that true union is possible, and has, in fact, never been lost. The "little I" seeks to enhance itself by external approval, external possessions and external "love." The Self That God created needs nothing. It is forever complete, safe, loved and loving. It seeks to share rather than to get; to extend rather than project. It has no needs and wants to join with others out of their mutual awareness of abundance.

8. The special relationships of the world are destructive, selfish and childishly egocentric. Yet, if given to

the Holy Spirits, these relationships can become the holiest things on earth - the miracles that point the way to the return to Heaven. The world uses its special relationships as a final weapon of exclusion and a demonstration of separateness. The Holy Spirit transforms them into perfect lessons in forgiveness and in awakening from the dream. Each one is an opportunity to let perceptions be healed and errors corrected. Each one is another chance to forgive oneself by forgiving the other. And each one becomes still another invitation to the Holy Spirit and to the remembrance of God.

9. Perception is a function of the body, and therefore represents a limit on awareness. Perception sees through the body's eyes and hears through the body's ears. It evokes the limited responses which the body makes. The body appears to be largely self-motivated and independent, yet it actually responds only to the intentions of the mind. If the mind wants to use it for attack in any form, it becomes prey to sickness, age and decay. If the mind accepts the Holy Spirit's purpose for it instead, it becomes a useful way of communicating with others, invulnerable as long as it is needed, and to be gently laid by when its use is over. Of itself it is neutral, as is everything in the world of perception. Whether it is used for the goals of the ego or the Holy Spirit depends entirely on what the mind wants.

10. The opposite of seeing through the body's eyes is the vision of Christ, which reflects strength rather than weakness, unity rather than separation, and love rather than fear. The opposite of hearing through the body's ears is communication through the Voice for God, the Holy Spirit, which abides in each of us. His Voice seems distant and difficult to hear because the ego, which speaks for the little, separated self, seems to be much louder. This is actually reversed. The Holy Spirit speaks with unmistakable clarity and overwhelming appeal. No one who does not choose to identify with the body could possibly be deaf to His

messages of release and hope, nor could he fail to accept joyously the vision of Christ in glad exchange for his miserable picture of himself.

11. Christ's vision is the Holy Spirit's gift, God's alternative to the illusion of separation and to the belief in the reality of sin, guilt and death. It is the one correction for all errors of perception; the reconciliation of the seeming opposites on which this world is based. Its kindly light shows all things from another point of view, reflecting the thought system that arises from knowledge and making return to God not only possible but inevitable. What was regarded as injustices done to one by someone else, now becomes a call for help and for union. Sin, sickness and attack are seen as misperceptions calling for remedy through gentleness and love. Defenses are laid down because where there is no attack there is no need for them. Our brothers' needs become our own, because they are taking the journey with us as we go to God. Without us they would lose their way. Without them we could never find our own.

12. Forgiveness is unknown in Heaven, where the need for it would be inconceivable. However, in this world, forgiveness is a necessary correction for all the mistakes that we have made. To offer forgiveness is the only way for us to have it, for it reflects the law of Heaven that giving and receiving are the same. Heaven is the natural state of all the Sons of God as He created them. Such is their reality forever. It has not changed because it has been forgotten.

13. Forgiveness is the means by which we will remember. Through forgiveness the thinking of the world is reversed. The forgiven world becomes the gate of Heaven, because by its mercy we can at last forgive ourselves. Holding no one prisoner to guilt, we become free. Acknowledging Christ in all our brothers, we recognize His Presence in ourselves. Forgetting all our misperceptions, and with nothing from the past to hold us back, we can

remember God. Beyond this, learning cannot go. When we are ready, God Himself will take the final step in our return to Him.

Appendix B

REFERENCING *A COURSE IN MIRACLES*

A Quick Glance at primary references to *A Course in Miracles*:

29.6,4:2   Read: "Chapter 29. Section 6, paragraph 4: sentence 2"

Citations that do not contain a letter refer to the **Text**. Citations that refer to any other part of the Course will contain a letter.

L121,6   "Lesson 121, paragraph 6"   **Workbook**
R4,2   "Review 4, paragraph 2"   **Workbook**
Th8,4   "Theme 8, paragraph 4"   **Workbook**

Q20,5   "Question 20, paragraph 5"   **Manual**

C6   "Clarification Term 6"   **Clarification of Terms**

P2.1,4   **"Psychotherapy** Chapter 2. Section 1, paragraph 4"

S3.2,1:8 **"Song** Chapter 3. Section 2, paragraph 1: sentence 8"

For the sake of convenience for both reader and writer, I have used a style of referencing which is an abbreviated version of the computer referencing style. It is a style I have used in my personal notes and newsletter long before the computer search program was available.

One convenience for the reader, especially one familiar with the Course, is that he can recognize a reference immediately, without the need for much deciphering. For example, all Lessons in the Workbook are referenced with an "L". Thus L14 means Lesson 14. Paragraphs and sentences are indicated in a manner similar to the computer version. Thus L14,1:4 is read: "Lesson 14, paragraph 1: sentence 4." When the reader sees this reference he quickly recognizes it as a Lesson in the Workbook. If he is a student well familiar with the Course he may even recall the Lesson's title: "God did not create a meaningless world" (L14). This may be helpful in numerous ways, including reinforcing his memory of the Course's teachings.

On the other hand, when the reader sees W-PI-14.1:4, which is the computer version of this same reference, he does not as quickly recognize it as a lesson number; especially in light of the fact that he may encounter another reference W-PII-14.1:4 which looks very similar but does not refer to Lesson 14 at all, but to the 14th "What is" section in Part II of the Workbook.

These "What is" sections - for example, "What is forgiveness?" "What is the Real World?" "What am I?" - are described in the Course itself as "instructions on a theme of special relevance". The student is assigned to read the instructions on the theme each day for 10 consecutive days after which instructions on the next theme are given.

As will be seen in the list below, I reference these "Themes" in Part II of the Workbook as "Th". The computer version of this reference, W-PII-14.1:4, is replaced with Th14,1:4 (read "Theme 14, paragraph 1: sentence 4"). Thus when one encounters this reference at the end of a sentence he quickly recognizes it as one of the Themes without the need to decipher a lengthy reference symbol. Again, some students may immediately recall that Theme 14 is "What am I?" This gives the reader a quicker sense of the context from which the passage is quoted.

For readers not at all familiar with the Course neither reference style is very informative until instructions are given. But once instructions are given, this abbreviated style provides ample information for the reader, whether student or not, to find the cited passage.

This reference style also saves considerable print space, since it requires less printed characters (4 to 5 less in many cases, and up to 9 in some cases). It also avoids the large and distracting gaps between sentences made by more lengthy citations.

You will notice that I list "primary references" and "secondary references". The primary reference is the typical and most frequently used reference to the volume in question. For example, since the *Workbook* consists primarily of lessons the primary reference to the Workbook will be to a Lesson number. Since the *Text* consists primarily of Chapters and Sections the primary reference will be to a Chapter and Section number. Secondary references include things like Introductions and Epilogues. I have replaced all Roman numerals with Arabic numerals. This also cuts back on the number of characters, not only saving print space but also providing a more quickly recognized reference.

Text: Primary References:

2.8,3 Read: "Chapter 2. Section 8, Paragraph 3"

2.8,3:4 Read: "Chapter 2. Section 8, Paragraph 3:
Sentence 4"

2.8,3:4-8   Read: "Chapter 2. Section 8, Paragraph 3:
Sentences 4 through 8".

This is the primary reference to the *Text*. The *Text* is divided into 31 Chapters. Each Chapter is divided into

Sections, each numbered and titled. The average number of sections per chapter is eight. Any reference not preceded by a letter is immediately recognized as a reference to the *Text*. References to volumes other the *Text* are preceded by a letter.

4.IN,2:1   Read: "Chapter 4. Introduction, Paragraph 2: Sentence 1"

Of the 31 chapters in the *Text*, 13 have an Introductory section consisting of a few paragraphs. These Introductions are referenced like any other section, that is, with a dot between the chapter number and the section number. It is as if the "IN" is the section number.

Text: Secondary References:

T-IN,2:4 Read: "Text-Introduction, Paragraph 2: Sentence 4"

This is a reference to the Introduction to the *Text*. The "T-" is necessary because the Workbook, Manual, and Clarification of Terms also have their own general Introduction.

Pf.3,9:2 Read: "Preface. Section 3, Paragraph 9: Sentence 2"

The Preface was added to the Text on the publication of the Second Edition in 1992. It has three sections. The third section of the Preface is reprinted as Appendix A of this book.

Workbook: Primary References:

L121 Read: "Lesson 121"

Without paragraph or sentence numbers this refers to the Lesson title. In this case, "Forgiveness is the key to happiness" (L121).

L121,6:1   Read: "Lesson 121, Paragraph 6: Sentence 1"

L325,1:4-6   Read: "Lesson 325, Paragraph 1: Sentences 4 through 6"

The reader does not need the information that Lesson 325 is in Part II of the Workbook rather than in Part I. This information serves no purpose as far as referencing a quoted passage is concerned. The Lessons are in numerical order and thus easy to locate. Furthermore, those familiar with the Course already know that Lessons numbered 221 and higher are in Part II.

R1,4   Read: "Review 1, Paragraph 4

R6,3:1 Read: "Review 6, Paragraph 3: Sentence 1"

No need to put "PI" to indicate Part I of the Workbook, because Part II of the Workbook has no "Reviews". Nor is there a need to put "IN" after R1 to indicate it is the "Introduction" to the Review. The "R" is all that is needed to inform the reader that it is the Introduction, because the Introduction is the only thing to which the "R" refers. Everything else in the Review is a Lesson itself, which has its own unique number and reference. These Review Lessons, like any other Lesson, are referenced with an "L" followed by the number of the Lesson, e.g., L51,3:7. This is all that is needed to locate the sentence in the Course.

Th8,3:1   Read: "Theme 8, Paragraph 3: Sentence 1"

As mentioned above, "Th" refers to one of the 14 Themes in Part II of the Workbook. I have called these sections "Themes" based on the following passage from the Introduction to Part II of the Workbook: "From time to time, instructions on a *theme* of special relevance will intersperse our daily lessons".

I have chosen to use the small "h" in "Th", rather than the capital "H", because it provides more space between the letter and number in the reference. This makes it easier to read these particular references. For example, instead of TH1 we write Th1; instead of TH2, we write Th2.

Workbook: Secondary References:

W-IN,9 Read: "Workbook-Introduction, Paragraph 9"

W-IN2,4:6 Read: "Workbook-Introduction to Part 2, Paragraph 4: Sentence 6"

Besides the general Introduction to the Workbook, the Workbook also contains an Introduction to Part 2.

L181-IN,2:6 Read "Lesson 181-Introduction, Paragraph 2: Sentence 6"

Lessons 181 through 200 are the only set of regular Lessons (as opposed to Review Lessons) which have their own Introduction. These 3 paragraphs are entitled, "Introduction to Lessons 181-200".

FL-IN,1:3 Read: "Final Lessons-Introduction, paragraph 1: sentence 3"

These "Final Lessons", Lessons 361-365, are actually one Lesson repeated for the last 5 days of the year. There is a 6 paragraph Introduction to these Final Lessons.

W-Ep,3:2   Read: "Workbook-Epilogue, Paragraph 3: Sentence 2"

Manual: Primary Reference

Q7,2 Read: "Question 7, Paragraph 2

All the title headings in the Manual for Teachers are stated in the form of a Question. So a "Q" followed by the Question number seems to be an appropriate way to reference them.

Q29,8:3 Read: "Question 29, Paragraph 8: Sentences 3"

This refers to the last section of the Manual entitled "As For the Rest". Its title is not written in the form of a Question, but the section is numbered in consecutive order after Q28, as if it were the question: "What about the rest of the questions?" So it is referred to as Q29 for convenience sake.

Manual: Secondary Reference

M-IN,2:1   Read: "Manual-Introduction, Paragraph 2: Sentence 1"

Clarification of Terms: Primary Reference

C1,7:1 Read: "Clarification Term 1, Paragraph 7: Sentence 1"

The *Clarifications of Terms* was actually scribed by Helen three years after the *Text, Workbook, and Manual* had been completed, but before the Course was published in book form as a three volume set. When the Course was published in 1976, the *Clarification of Terms* was placed at the end of the third volume entitled *Manual For Teachers.* However, *Clarification Of Terms* is usually referenced as a separate work, rather than as part of the Manual. All four, *Text, Workbook for Students, Manual for Teachers, and Clarification of Terms,* are now published in a one volume set.

Clarification of Terms: Secondary References

C-IN,3   Read: "Clarification of Terms-Introduction, Paragraph 3"

C-Ep,4:3   Read: "Clarification of Terms-Epilogue, Paragraph 4: Sentence 3"

Psychotherapy: Primary Reference:

P3.2,5:1   Read: "Psychotherapy Chapter 3. Section 2, Paragraph 5: Sentence 1"

The references to the *Psychotherapy* pamphlet, as well as to the *Song of Prayer* pamphlet, are like those to the *Text,* since they have Chapter and Section numbers. The only difference is that the pamphlet references are preceded by the appropriate letter.

Psychotherapy: Secondary Reference:

P-IN,1:5 Read: "Psychotherapy-Introduction, Paragraph 1: Sentence 5"

Song of Prayer: Primary References:

S1.3,5   Read: "Song of Prayer Chapter 1. Section 3, Paragraph 5"

S3.IN,1:9 Read: "Song of Prayer Chapter 3. Introduction, Paragraph 1: Sentence 9"

This pamphlet does not have a general Introduction. Each of its three chapters, however, does have an Introductory section. The Introduction to each chapter, then, is referenced like any other section, that is, with a dot between the chapter number and the section number, just as we did with the Introductions found in 13 of the 31 chapters of the *Text*. This pamphlet has no Secondary References.

Referencing Lengthy or Combined Passages:

13.3,10-12   Read: "Chapter 13. Section 3, Paragraphs 10 through 12"

13.3,10,12 Read: "Chapter 13. Section 3, Paragraph 10, and Paragraph 12"

L122,1-4:2   Read: "Lesson 122, Paragraph 1 through Paragraph 4: Sentence 2"

C6,1:4-3:1   Read: "Clarification of Terms 6, Paragraph 1: Sentence 4 through Paragraph 3: Sentence 1"

Bibliography

Books on the Problem of Evil
Written by Professional Theodicists

Davis, Stephen, ed. *Encountering Evil: Live Options in Theodicy*. Atlanta, GA: John Knox Press, 1981.

Geivett, R.D. *Evil & the Evidence for God: The Challenge of John Hick's Theodicy*. Philadelphia: Temple University Press, 1993.

Griffin, David Ray. *God, Power, and Evil: A Process Theodicy*. Philadelphia: Westminster Press, 1976.

Griffin, David Ray. *Evil Revisited: Responses & Reconsiderations*. Albany, New York: State University of New York Press, 1991.

Hick, John. *Evil and the God of Love*. San Francisco: Harper and Row, 1966. Revised Edition, 1977.

Howard-Synder, Daniel, ed. *The Evidential Argument From Evil*. Bloomington & Indianapolis: Indiana University Press, 1996.

Mesle, C. Robert. *John Hick's Theodicy: A Process Humanist Critique*. New York: St. Martin's Press, 1991.

Musson, John. *Evil -- Is It Real? A Theological Analysis*. Lewiston: The Edwin Mellen Press, 1991.

Trau, Jane M. *The Co-Existence of God & Evil*. New York: Peter Lang, 1991.

Trau, Jane M. *The Co-Existence of God & Evil*. New York: Peter Lang, 1991.

Whitney, Barry L. *Theodicy: An Annotated Bibliography on the Problem of Evil 1960-1990*. New York & London: Garland Publishing, Inc., 1993.

Books Presenting the Teachings
in *A Course in Miracles*

Perry, Robert. *The Elder Brother: Jesus in "A Course in Miracles"*. West Sedona, AZ: Circle of Atonement, 1990.

Perry, Robert. *Reality and Illusion: An Overview of Course Metaphysics* (2 pamphlets, Part I and Part II). West Sedona, AZ: Circle of Atonement, 1993.

Perry, Robert. *A Course Glossary*. West Sedona, AZ: Circle of Atonement, 1996.

Perry, Robert. *Relationships as a Spiritual Journey: From Specialness to Holiness*. West Sedona, AZ: Circle of Atonement, 1997.

Wapnick, Kenneth. *Glossary-Index for A "Course in Miracles"*. Roscoe, NY: Foundation for ACIM, 1982. Revised, presently in Fourth Edition.

Wapnick, Kenneth. *Forgiveness and Jesus: The Meeting Place of "A Course in Miracles" and Christianity*. Roscoe, NY: Foundation for ACIM, 1982. Revised, presently in Fourth Edition.

Wapnick, Kenneth and Gloria. *Awaken From The Dream*. Roscoe, NY: Foundation for ACIM, 1987.

Wapnick, Kenneth. *Love Does Not Condemn: The World, the Flesh, and the Devil According to Platonism, Christianity, Gnosticism, and "A Course in Miracles".* Roscoe, NY: Foundation for ACIM, 1989.

Wapnick, Kenneth. *A Vast Illusion: Time According to "A Course in Miracles".* Roscoe, NY: Foundation for ACIM, 1990.

Wapnick, Kenneth. *"A Course in Miracles" and Christianity: A Dialogue.* Roscoe, NY: Foundation for ACIM, 1995. (This is a later publication of a dialogue that took place in 1989 between Kenneth and W. Norris Clark, a Jesuit priest and philosopher.)

Wapnick, Kenneth. *The Message of "A Course in Miracles": Volume One, All are Called; Volume Two, Few Choose to Listen.* Roscoe, NY: Foundation for ACIM, 1997.

Watson, Allen. *Seeing the Bible Differently: How "A Course in Miracles" Views the Bible.* West Sedona, AZ: Circle of Atonement, 1997.

Books Relating the Story of the Scribing of *A Course in Miracles* and its Impact in the World.

Miller, D. Patrick. *The Complete Story of The Course: The History, The People, and the Controversies Behind "A Course in Miracles".* Berkeley: Fearless Books, 1997.

Skutch, Robert. *Journey Without Distance: The Story Behind "A Course in Miracles".* Berkeley: Celestial Arts, 1984.

Wapnick, Kenneth. *Absence From Felicity: The Story of Helen Schucman and Her Scribing of "A Course in Miracles"*. Roscoe, NY: Foundation for ACIM, 1991.

DETAILED TABLE OF CONTENTS

GOD, SELF, AND EVIL:
A Miracle Theodicy

ORDERING INFORMATION

To order additional copies of this book use the form below (or copy it on a separate sheet of paper). Make check or money order payable to *Enlightenment Publications*, and send to the following address:

> For updated information, go to
> **www.acim-book. com**
> or call *757-793-8006*
> and leave a voicemail.

The price of the book is $28.00. Add $3.85 for shipping and handling.

For each additional book add $2.00 for shipping.
Virginia residents add 4.5% sales tax.
Thank you for your order.

For additional information please call:
1-757-461-3262 or write to the above address.

****

Please send me _____ copy(s) of the book entitled *God, Self, and Evil: A Miracle Theodicy.* I have enclosed the proper payment.

Name_____

Address_____

City_____State_____Zip____

Phone (Optional)_____

ORDERING INFORMATION

To order additional copies of this book use the form below (Or copy it on a separate sheet of paper). Make check or money order payable to *Enlightenment Publications,* and send to the following address:

> For updated information, go to
> www.acim-book. com
> or call *757-793-8006*
> and leave a voicemail.

The price of the book is $28.00 Add $3.85 for shipping and handling.

For each additional book add $2.00 for shipping.
Virginia residents add 4.5% sales tax.
Thank you for your order.

For additional information please call:
1-757-461-3262 or write to the above address.

****

Please send me _____ copy(s) of the book entitled *God, Self, and Evil: A Miracle Theodicy.* I have enclosed the proper payment.

Name_____

Address_____

City_____State_____Zip____

Phone (Optional)_____